My Dearest Colin,
Always remember to taste
the flavors of life! You have
made my life so happy! Making
our dinner was so fun - I
will never forget!

Love Always
♡ Mom :)

Cooking Light
GLOBAL KITCHEN

Cooking Light.

GLOBAL KITCHEN

The World's Most Delicious
Food Made Easy

DAVID JOACHIM

Oxmoor
House®

Contents

*W*elcome to a world of flavor. It's an exciting time to be in the kitchen. So many incredible ingredients from around the globe are available in today's markets. We can thank globalization for stimulating our taste buds—and for making it easier to eat healthy food.

When you start watching your diet, eating healthy often means eating "ethnic." That's where the flavor is, after all. Traditional cuisines like Indian, Mexican, Thai, and Moroccan get vibrant flavors from unique spices, herbs, fruits, and vegetables. Just think of cardamom's haunting perfume of citrus and pine; the front- and back-of-the-tongue heat in smoky chipotle chiles; the clean, fresh scent of lemongrass; the savory depth of fermented miso paste; and the tropical aroma and rich taste of coconut milk. It's a godsend for American home cooks that these ingredients are now stocked in mainstream supermarkets. Suddenly, international dishes don't seem so intimidating to prepare. With everything you need at your supermarket, these high-flavor foods can easily become part of your busy weeknight routine.

When *Cooking Light* invited me to work on this book, I jumped at the chance. Help Americans bring these amazing flavors to their everyday meals? Absolutely! For over 25 years, the magazine has been publishing recipes from leading experts in the world's cuisines. It's high time to put the best of the best into a single book. With *Cooking Light*'s team of editors, I sifted through the magazine's vast archive and chose 120 of the most authentic, best-tasting, and highest reader-rated recipes from almost every continent on earth. To fill in some gaps, I developed another 30 recipes. All in all, the book includes 150 culinary greatest hits from around the globe. And it's packed with colorful photos and helpful tips. With everything here, it's a breeze to enjoy a world of flavor in your very own kitchen.

—David Joachim

Introduction

The food world in America has changed dramatically since 1967, the year I was born. Back then, *New York Times* food editor Craig Claiborne published an Israeli recipe for "Mediterranean Fish" with a note about two small stores in the city, then and still America's largest city, where you could buy tahini (sesame paste). Today, tahini is widely available in supermarket chains across the United States.

The options on our market shelves have expanded exponentially. Changing demographics and trade treaties have made a wide variety of international ingredients readily available. By the time I was 8 in 1975, I had tasted fish sauce for the first time in the home of my mother's best friend, who is Vietnamese. And by the 1980s, companies like Frieda's and Melissa's World Variety Produce were stocking once-exotic produce such as kiwi, mangos, and jicama all over America. These and other companies now bring us thousands of specialty produce items, from banana leaves and coconuts to yuca and Kaffir limes.

Think about how our population has changed, too. In 1967, 88 percent of the U.S. population was of European descent, and only 12 percent were minorities, mostly African American. Today, more than 50 percent of all American children are born to minority parents, and Latinos have become the country's largest minority group. Salsa now outsells ketchup as the country's most popular condiment.

HOW COLUMBUS CHANGED WHAT THE WORLD EATS

The United States and its food have become incredibly diverse over the past 50 years. But if you go back even further, you can see the beginnings of these changes in the Americas and all around the world. In the 1500s, after the New World was colonized, Spanish and Portuguese traders initiated an exchange of foods that forever altered how people eat all over the globe. Traders brought the potato from Peru to Europe, where it became a key ingredient throughout the continent. Just think of now-classic dishes like Italy's Potato Gnocchi with Browned Butter (page 198), England's Cottage Pie (page 181), and Spain's Patatas Bravas (page 169). Chile peppers went from the Americas not only to Europe, but also to the Middle East, Africa, and Asia. Consider the fact that 500 years ago, chile peppers did not exist in Indian cooking. But today, traditional dishes like *chana masala* (chickpeas in spicy tomato sauce) and countless other Indian curries would be unthinkable without hot peppers.

The Pacific coast in Santa Cruz, California is a dining and beach lover's paradise.

David selects fresh produce at a market in Bologna, Italy.

Chicken Tikka Masala, page 52

Historians call this massive period of trade the Columbian Exchange. And it went the other way, too. Pigs, chickens, goats, and cattle all came from the Old World to the Americas. Bananas and plantains came from Southeast Asia to South America, where plantains are now essential in dishes like Puerto Rican Mofongo (page 297) and Cuban Maduros (page 304).

THE QUEST FOR FLAVOR

It's true that people cook with local foods. But historical events change what foods are available locally. A nation's cuisine evolves over time in a complex blend of geography, history, economy, immigration, industrialization, and taste preferences, among other factors. This ongoing evolution means that no continent or country has a single, unchanging "cuisine." There is no single African cuisine or Italian cuisine. No homogenous Thai cuisine or Caribbean cuisine exists.

But there are distinctive ingredients and dishes that define every country's cooking. And Americans are hungry to taste them. Television cooking shows, the Internet, and increased international food trade have all ramped up our quest for exotic flavors. In fact, 9 out of 10 young Americans say they prepared "ethnic" food at home in the past month, according to the Mintel research group.

David dined at this local spot with a view and authentic, fresh pasta while traveling in Siena, Italy.

Udon Noodle Bowl, page 55

The Jumbo Floating Restaurant is located in Aberdeen Harbor in Hong Kong.

And American supermarkets are teeming with more and more ingredients to feed our hunger. The best news? These high-flavor cuisines, such as Indian, North African, and Japanese, are often touted as the healthiest cuisines on the planet.

TASTE THE WORLD IN YOUR KITCHEN

It's impossible to completely capture the staggering variety of dishes that people enjoy around the world. But *Cooking Light Global Kitchen* presents a fair slice. To help bring you the key flavors and dishes of each continent, I called on the expertise of professional chefs, culinary historians, and food writers. Thank you especially to Rick Bayless, Naomi Duguid, Jose Garces, Darra Goldstein, Marc Vetri, Maricel Presilla, Jessica B. Harris, Michael Solomonov, Andrea Nguyen, Steven Raichlen, Cecilia Hae-Jin Lee, Judith Finlayson, Hiroko Shimbo, Raghavan Iyer, and Grace Young. Their invaluable insights, advice, and recipes are at the heart of this book.

Cooking Light Global Kitchen brings you freedom of choice in the kitchen. It lets you choose from a wide range of the world's most delicious dishes, including everything from African Chicken Yassa (page 146) to Haitian Picadillo Puffs (page 266); Indian Fall Vegetable Curry (page 26) to Thai Masaman Curry (page 80); Spicy Korean Pork Barbecue (page 38) to North Carolina Pulled Pork Barbecue Sandwiches (page 291); and Australian Lamingtons (page 110) to Nicaraguan Tres Leches Cake (page 272).

Most of the recipes use authentic ingredients and cooking methods to create a dish that's close to what you might eat in the country where it originated. Fortunately, these ingredients are now widely available. For any ingredient that isn't universally stocked in supermarkets, I include an easy-to-find substitute. Some recipes take judicious shortcuts so the dish is approachable in a North American kitchen, and most dishes come together quickly enough that you can make them a regular part of your busy weeknight repertoire. A handful of "melting pot" recipes take some liberties by blending cuisines from various countries. But this is not a book of culinary mash-ups like Kimchi Hash Browns with Pesto and Melted Brie. Oddly compelling as that combination may sound, it doesn't fit the aesthetic of *Cooking Light Global Kitchen.* This book is focused on bringing the world's signature dishes to American cooks.

Every recipe was tested in the *Cooking Light* Test Kitchen and meets the magazine's guidelines for speed, ease, and nutrition. Not a single ingredient is off limits. Balance, variety, and moderation are the mantra. You'll find tips on buying and using dozens of international ingredients like miso and plantains. You'll see 11 techniques demonstrated in step-by-step color photographs so you know exactly how to shape Chinese dumplings and stuff grape leaves. And you'll come across helpful insights into the customary food ways of various cultures around the world. Nearly 150 gorgeous photographs bring it all to life.

Cooking another country's food can expand your sense of taste and may even improve your health. It can also broaden your horizons by giving you a deeper understanding of your own culture. With this book and the mosaic of ingredients available at your local market, it's easier than ever to savor the many delicious flavors of the world.

East Asia & India

The Flavors of East Asia and India

Ever wonder why Asian food tastes so different from the food in Western countries? Food scientists from Cambridge and Harvard compared signature ingredients from both regions and found that Western dishes tend to combine ingredients with similar flavor compounds, such as butter and vanilla. But Asian dishes do just the opposite—they combine contrasting flavors like soy sauce and rice vinegar or honey and hot red chiles, creating more excitement on the palate.

You can also chalk it up to geography. Naturally, people eat what grows and thrives in their part of the world. While dairy products are staples in European and American cuisine, they are uncommon in Japan, India, China, and Korea. Here are some other signature ingredients that help to create the culinary identity of East Asian and Indian cuisines.

SESAME OIL AND SEEDS:
Use toasted sesame oil sparingly for nutty, roasted aroma.

WASABI:
Pungency from a root in the horseradish family.

SOY SAUCE:
Provides salty and umami (savory) flavors; look for low-sodium varieties.

GINGER:
Rhizome (underground stem) with sharp flavor and spicy aroma; may help alleviate ailments such as nausea.

RICE VINEGAR:
Provides gentle acidity; look for types without added sugar and salt.

CORIANDER SEED:
Tan, round seeds from same plant that bears cilantro leaves; provides lemony flavor; often toasted and ground.

DRIED CHILES (CAYENNE TYPE):
Spicy-hot pepper pods with various capsaicin (heat) levels; used dried (whole and ground) and fresh (ground into chile paste).

CARDAMOM:
Seed pod in ginger family; round, black seeds have intense, resinous aroma; seeds and green pods often used whole.

CUMIN SEED:
Crescent-shaped light brown seeds in the caraway family with warm, earthy aromas; often toasted and used whole or ground.

BROWN MUSTARD SEED:
Small, round seeds with hot, pungent flavor; often toasted whole until they pop.

From fried and mild to fresh and spicy, spring rolls appear all over East Asia and Southeast Asia. The dipping sauce provides sweet, sour, salty, and spicy flavors. Traditionally, this appetizer is very high in sodium, but this recipe is significantly lower than the classic rendition.

FRESH SPRING ROLLS

HANDS-ON TIME: 36 MIN. TOTAL TIME: 36 MIN.

Rolls:
8 (8-inch) round sheets rice paper
2 cups thinly sliced Bibb lettuce leaves (about 4 large)
2 cups cooked bean threads (cellophane noodles)
1 cup fresh bean sprouts
1 cup shredded carrot (about 1 large)
½ cup coarsely chopped fresh mint
½ cup fresh cilantro leaves
¼ cup thinly sliced green onions

Sauce:
1 tablespoon sugar
3 tablespoons fresh lime juice (about 1 lime)
3 tablespoons water
2 tablespoons fish sauce
1 garlic clove, minced
1 Thai chile, thinly sliced

1. To prepare rolls, add hot water to a large, shallow dish to a depth of 1 inch. Place 1 rice paper sheet in dish, and let stand 30 seconds or just until soft. Place sheet on a flat surface. Arrange ¼ cup lettuce over half of sheet, leaving a ½-inch border. Top with ¼ cup bean threads, 2 tablespoons sprouts, 2 tablespoons carrot, 1 tablespoon mint, 1 tablespoon cilantro leaves, and 1½ teaspoons green onions. Fold sides of sheet over filling and, starting with filled side, roll up jelly-roll fashion. Gently press seam to seal. Place roll, seam side down, on a serving platter (cover to keep from drying). Repeat procedure with remaining roll ingredients.

2. To prepare sauce, combine sugar and remaining ingredients in a small bowl, stirring with a whisk until sugar dissolves. Serve sauce with rolls. Serves 8 (serving size: 1 roll and about 2 teaspoons sauce)

CALORIES 83; FAT 0.3g (sat 0g, mono 0g, poly 0.1g); PROTEIN 2.3g; CARB 18.5g; FIBER 1.1g; CHOL 0mg; IRON 0.7mg; SODIUM 371mg; CALC 22mg

Traditional Cantonese dumplings feature pork and mushrooms, but this version is completely vegetarian. Cabbage, apples, and tofu get spiked with hot sesame oil, soy sauce, rice wine, and a few other seasonings and aromatics. If you've never made Chinese dumplings before, this is an easy place to start.

VEGETABLE SUI MAI

HANDS-ON TIME: 60 MIN. TOTAL TIME: 1 HR. 18 MIN.

2 tablespoons chopped fresh cilantro
2 green onions, cut into 2-inch pieces
1 garlic clove, peeled
1 (1/2-inch) piece peeled fresh ginger
1 cup sliced napa (Chinese) cabbage
1/2 cup chopped peeled Granny Smith apple
1 tablespoon lower-sodium soy sauce
2 teaspoons mirin (sweet rice wine)
1/4 teaspoon Sriracha (hot chile sauce, such as Huy Fong)
1/4 teaspoon kosher salt
1 large egg white
6 ounces firm water-packed tofu, drained and finely chopped
20 gyoza skins
Cabbage leaves or parchment paper
2 teaspoons sesame oil
1/2 teaspoon Asian chili sesame oil or other chili oil

1. Place first 4 ingredients in a food processor; process until finely chopped. Add 1 cup cabbage and next 5 ingredients (through kosher salt); pulse 10 times or until finely chopped. Add egg white; pulse until combined. Place cabbage mixture in a medium bowl, and stir in tofu.

2. Working with 1 gyoza skin at a time (cover remaining skins to keep them from drying), moisten edge of skin with water. Spoon about 1 tablespoon tofu mixture into center of circle. Gather up edges of skin around filling; lightly squeeze skin to adhere to filling, gently pleating around filling but leaving top of dumpling open. (If skins do not open enough to see tofu mixture, use the tip of a knife to separate.) Repeat procedure with remaining skins and filling.

3. Working in batches, place dumplings in a large bamboo steamer lined with cabbage leaves or parchment paper. Steam 9 minutes or until filling and wrappers are lightly firm. Combine oils, and drizzle over tops of dumplings. Serves 4 (serving size: 5 dumplings)

CALORIES 185; FAT 6.4g (sat 1g, mono 1.6g, poly 1.6g); PROTEIN 9.3g; CARB 21.7g; FIBER 1.6g; CHOL 50mg; IRON 2mg; SODIUM 460mg; CALC 125mg

how to: SHAPE SUI MAI

Pleating the top of sui mai dumplings gives them a decorative look, but it's just as important to leave the tops of the dumplings open to reveal some of the filling.

1 Moisten gyoza skin with water so the pleats will seal.

2 Spoon 1 tablespoon filling into center. It's important not to overfill so the dumpling will seal and cook properly.

3 Gather up edges of skin around filling. Squeeze skin to adhere to filling, gently pleating skin around filling.

VEGETABLE SAMOSAS
with Mint Chutney
HANDS-ON TIME: 55 MIN. TOTAL TIME: 1 HR. 18 MIN.

Chutney:
1 cup fresh mint leaves
1 cup fresh cilantro leaves
1 tablespoon fresh lime juice
1 tablespoon water
1 teaspoon finely chopped seeded jalapeño pepper
1 teaspoon chopped fresh garlic
1/2 teaspoon minced peeled fresh ginger
1/8 teaspoon salt
Samosas:
2 tablespoons olive oil, divided
1/4 cup finely chopped onion
2/3 cup shredded carrot
2/3 cup frozen green peas, thawed
2 teaspoons mustard seeds
1 1/2 teaspoons garam masala
1/2 teaspoon salt
1 cup leftover mashed potatoes
8 (14 x 9–inch) sheets frozen phyllo dough, thawed
Cooking spray

1. Preheat oven to 350°.

2. To prepare chutney, place first 8 ingredients in a food processor; process 1 minute or until smooth. Spoon mixture into a bowl; cover and refrigerate.

3. To prepare samosas, heat a large nonstick skillet over medium heat. Add 1 tablespoon olive oil to pan; swirl to coat. Add onion to pan, and cook 2 minutes, stirring occasionally. Add carrot, and cook 2 minutes, stirring occasionally. Add peas, mustard seeds, garam masala, and salt; cover and cook 2 minutes. Stir in potatoes; remove from heat.

4. Working with 1 phyllo sheet at a time, cut each sheet lengthwise into 3 (3 x 14–inch) strips, and coat with cooking spray. (Cover remaining phyllo dough to keep from drying.) Spoon 1 tablespoon potato mixture onto 1 end of each strip. Fold 1 corner of phyllo dough over mixture, forming a triangle; keep folding back and forth into a triangle to end of strip. Repeat procedure with remaining phyllo strips and filling.

5. Place triangles, seam sides down, on a baking sheet. Brush triangles with remaining 1 tablespoon oil. Bake at 350° for 23 minutes or until lightly browned. Serve warm or at room temperature with chutney. Serves 12 (serving size: 2 samosas and 1½ teaspoons chutney)

CALORIES 89; FAT 3.6g (sat 0.7g, mono 2.3g, poly 0.5g); PROTEIN 2.2g; CARB 13g; FIBER 1.6g; CHOL 1mg; IRON 0.9mg; SODIUM 217mg; CALC 21mg

how to: SHAPE SAMOSAS

Traditional samosas are formed into a cone shape. Here's how to create a triangular shape.

1 Spoon filling onto bottom end of rectangular strip, leaving a 1-inch border.

2 Fold bottom corner over mixture, forming a triangle.

3 Keep folding back and forth to end of phyllo strip, forming a triangular packet.

In China, they're a grab-and-go street food. In the U.S., pork buns have achieved cult status, particularly among dim sum fanatics. To cook all the buns at once, use a multi-tray bamboo steamer.

STEAMED PORK BUNS

HANDS-ON TIME: 1 HR. 9 MIN. TOTAL TIME: 2 HR. 34 MIN.

Filling:
1/2 teaspoon five-spice powder
1 (1-pound) pork tenderloin, trimmed
Cooking spray
1 cup thinly sliced green onions
3 tablespoons hoisin sauce
2 tablespoons rice vinegar
1 tablespoon lower-sodium soy sauce
1 1/2 teaspoons honey
1 teaspoon minced peeled fresh ginger
1 teaspoon minced fresh garlic
1/4 teaspoon salt
Dough:
1 cup warm water (100° to 110°)
3 tablespoons sugar
1 package dry yeast (about 2 1/4 teaspoons)
14.6 ounces all-purpose flour (about 3 1/4 cups)
3 tablespoons canola oil
1/4 teaspoon salt
Cooking spray
1 1/2 teaspoons baking powder

1. To prepare filling, rub five-spice powder evenly over pork. Heat a grill pan over medium-high heat. Coat pan with cooking spray. Add pork to pan; cook 14 minutes or until a thermometer registers 145°, turning pork occasionally. Remove pork from pan, and let stand 15 minutes.

2. Cut pork crosswise into thin slices; cut slices into thin strips. Place pork in a medium bowl. Add onions and next 7 ingredients (through 1/4 teaspoon salt); stir well to combine. Cover and refrigerate.

3. To prepare dough, combine 1 cup warm water, sugar, and yeast in a large bowl; let stand 5 minutes.

4. Weigh or lightly spoon flour into dry measuring cups; level with a knife. Add flour, oil, and 1/4 teaspoon salt to yeast mixture; stir until a soft dough forms. Turn dough out onto a lightly floured surface. Knead until smooth and elastic (about 10 minutes). Place dough in a large bowl coated with cooking spray, turning to coat top. Cover and let rise in a warm place (85°), free from drafts, 1 hour or until doubled in size. (Gently press two fingers into dough. If indentation remains, dough has risen enough.)

5. Punch dough down; let rest 5 minutes. Turn dough out onto a clean surface; knead in baking powder. Let dough rest 5 minutes.

6. Divide dough into 10 equal portions, forming each into a ball. Working with 1 dough ball at a time (cover remaining dough balls to keep from drying), roll ball into a 5-inch circle. Place 1/4 cup filling in center of dough circle. Bring up sides to cover filling and meet on top. Pinch and seal closed with a twist. Repeat procedure with remaining dough balls and filling.

7. Arrange 5 buns, seam sides down, 1 inch apart, in each tier of a 2-tiered bamboo steamer. Stack tiers; cover with lid.

8. Add water to a large skillet to a depth of 1 inch; bring to a boil over medium-high heat. Place steamer in pan; steam 15 minutes or until puffed and set. Cool 10 minutes before serving. Serves 10 (serving size: 1 bun)

CALORIES 259; FAT 6.1g (sat 0.9g, mono 3.2g, poly 1.5g); PROTEIN 14.3g; CARB 35.7g; FIBER 1.6g; CHOL 27mg; IRON 2.9mg; SODIUM 343mg; CALC 54mg

RESPECT THE RICE

*f*rom Mexico to Minnesota, rice is often served as a side dish, with meat as the main course. But in Chinese cuisine, rice is considered a meal's main event. "In Chinese, the term *soong fan* means 'rice sending dishes,'" explains Chinese cooking expert Grace Young, author of *Stir-Frying to the Sky's Edge.* "The other dishes are just meant to send the rice."

The Chinese respect this ingredient so much that it's considered rude to sit down to a home-cooked Chinese meal and eat the other dishes on the table without including the rice. Another bit of rice etiquette from Korean food writer Cecilia Hae-Jin Lee: "Don't leave your chopsticks sticking up in your rice," she advises. "That is only done during funeral ceremonies to symbolize allowing the dead person to eat."

There's a lesson in this, but it's not to eat more rice. It's about paying more attention to the sides that accompany your meal, and less to the main event. Whole grains and well-seasoned vegetables add fiber and other nutrients, not to mention flavor and texture, and help you control your intake of saturated fat from meats.

In his Indian cookbook 660 Curries, author Raghavan Iyer says that chana masala is "as pervasive in northern Indian home kitchens as is macaroni and cheese" in U.S. kitchens. Here's a riff on chana masala that includes sweet potatoes and cauliflower along with the chickpeas.

FALL VEGETABLE CURRY

HANDS-ON TIME: 15 MIN. TOTAL TIME: 25 MIN.

1½ teaspoons olive oil
1 cup diced peeled sweet
   potato
1 cup small cauliflower florets
¼ cup thinly sliced yellow
   onion
2 teaspoons Madras curry
   powder
½ cup organic vegetable
   broth
¼ teaspoon salt
1 (15-ounce) can chickpeas
   (garbanzo beans), rinsed
   and drained
1 (14.5-ounce) can no-salt-
   added diced tomatoes,
   undrained
2 cups hot cooked
   basmati rice
½ cup plain 2% reduced-fat
   Greek yogurt
2 tablespoons chopped fresh
   cilantro

1. Heat a large nonstick skillet over medium-high heat. Add olive oil to pan; swirl to coat. Add sweet potato to pan; sauté 3 minutes. Decrease heat to medium. Add cauliflower, onion, and curry powder; cook 1 minute, stirring mixture constantly. Add broth and next 3 ingredients (through tomatoes); bring to a boil. Cover, reduce heat, and simmer 10 minutes or until vegetables are tender, stirring occasionally. Serve over rice and with yogurt. Sprinkle with cilantro. Serves 4 (serving size: 1 cup curry and 2 tablespoons yogurt)

CALORIES 231; FAT 3.9g (sat 0.9g, mono 1.6g, poly 0.9g); PROTEIN 10.4g; CARB 40.8g; FIBER 8.6g; CHOL 2mg; IRON 2.5mg; SODIUM 626mg; CALC 106mg

Japan has its savory ramen noodle bowls, and Korea has bold-flavored rice bowls like bibimbap. "There's nothing subtle about it," says Korean food expert Cecilia Hae-Jin Lee. "It's all about bold, strong flavor." From the chile paste to the fried eggs, each element elevates the dish.

BIBIMBAP

HANDS-ON TIME: 50 MIN. TOTAL TIME: 66 MIN.

8 ounces extra-firm tofu, drained
⅓ cup water
¼ cup apple cider vinegar
2 teaspoons sugar, divided
2 teaspoons minced fresh garlic, divided
1 teaspoon minced peeled fresh ginger, divided
¼ teaspoon crushed red pepper
1 cup julienne-cut carrot
2 tablespoons lower-sodium soy sauce
3 tablespoons plus 2 teaspoons dark sesame oil, divided
3 cups hot cooked short-grain rice
1 cup fresh bean sprouts
1 (5-ounce) package sliced shiitake mushroom caps
1 (9-ounce) package fresh baby spinach
1 teaspoon unsalted butter
4 large eggs
4 teaspoons gochujang (Korean chile paste)
¼ teaspoon kosher salt
Cracked black pepper

1. Cut tofu into ¾-inch-thick slices. Place tofu in a single layer on several layers of paper towels; cover with additional paper towels. Let stand 30 minutes, pressing down occasionally.

2. Combine ⅓ cup water, vinegar, 1 teaspoon sugar, ½ teaspoon garlic, ½ teaspoon ginger, and crushed red pepper in a small saucepan. Bring to a boil. Add carrot, and remove from heat; let stand 30 minutes. Drain.

3. Remove tofu from paper towels; cut into ¾-inch cubes. Place tofu in a medium bowl. Combine remaining 1 teaspoon sugar, ½ teaspoon garlic, remaining ½ teaspoon ginger, soy sauce, and 1 tablespoon oil, stirring with a whisk. Add 1 tablespoon soy sauce mixture to tofu; toss gently. Let stand 15 minutes.

4. Heat a 10-inch cast-iron skillet over high heat 4 minutes. Add 1 tablespoon sesame oil to pan; swirl to coat. Add rice to pan in a single layer; cook 1 minute (do not stir). Remove from heat; let stand 20 minutes.

5. Heat a large nonstick skillet over medium-high heat. Add 1 teaspoon oil to pan; swirl to coat. Add 1½ teaspoons soy sauce mixture and bean sprouts to pan; sauté 1 minute. Remove sprouts from pan; keep warm. Add 1 teaspoon oil to pan; swirl to coat. Add mushrooms to pan; sauté 2 minutes. Stir in 1½ teaspoons soy sauce mixture; sauté 1 minute. Remove mushrooms from pan; keep warm. Add 2 teaspoons oil to pan; swirl to coat. Add tofu to pan; sauté 7 minutes or until golden brown. Remove tofu from pan; keep warm. Add remaining 1 teaspoon oil to pan; swirl to coat. Add remaining 1 teaspoon garlic and remaining 1 tablespoon soy sauce mixture; sauté 30 seconds. Add spinach to pan; sauté 1 minute or until spinach wilts. Remove spinach from pan; keep warm. Reduce heat to medium. Melt butter in pan. Crack eggs into pan; cook 4 minutes or until whites are set. Remove from heat.

6. Place ¾ cup rice in each of 4 shallow bowls. Top each serving evenly with carrots, sprouts, mushrooms, tofu, and spinach. Top each serving with 1 egg and 1 teaspoon chili paste. Sprinkle evenly with salt and pepper. Serves 4

CALORIES 502; FAT 23.4g (sat 4.5g, mono 9.9g, poly 7.1g); PROTEIN 20.9g; CARB 56.4g; FIBER 6.1g; CHOL 214mg; IRON 6.8mg; SODIUM 698mg; CALC 199mg

The term "dal" covers a wide range of pea, bean, and lentil dishes prepared throughout India, Pakistan, Bangladesh, Nepal, and Sri Lanka. An inexpensive and versatile protein dish, dal usually accompanies rice and vegetables. Coconut milk enriches this red lentil dal, which can be served as a side dish or as a vegetarian main dish over basmati rice.

SPICY RED LENTIL DAL
with Naan

HANDS-ON TIME: 24 MIN. TOTAL TIME: 34 MIN.

2 cups fat-free, lower-sodium chicken broth
1 cup dried small red lentils
1 tablespoon canola oil
1½ cups chopped onion
1 tablespoon minced fresh garlic
1 teaspoon yellow mustard seeds
½ teaspoon crushed red pepper
1 teaspoon ground cumin
1 teaspoon ground turmeric
½ teaspoon ground coriander
½ teaspoon freshly ground black pepper
1 tablespoon tomato paste
½ cup light coconut milk
½ teaspoon salt
2 teaspoons fresh lime juice
5 (6-inch) naan or pita breads, each cut into 8 wedges

1. Combine broth and lentils in a medium saucepan; bring to a boil. Reduce heat, partially cover, and simmer 10 minutes or until lentils are tender. Remove from heat; cover and set aside.

2. Heat a large nonstick skillet over medium heat. Add oil to pan; swirl to coat. Add onion, garlic, mustard seeds, and red pepper, and cook 5 minutes or until onions are tender and seeds begin to pop, stirring constantly. Add cumin, turmeric, coriander, and black pepper; cook 3 minutes, stirring constantly. Add tomato paste, and cook 3 minutes, stirring constantly. Add lentils, coconut milk, and salt; cook 3 minutes, stirring frequently. Remove from heat; stir in juice. Cool to room temperature. Serve dal with pita wedges. Serves 5 (serving size: ½ cup dal and 8 pita wedges)

CALORIES 375; FAT 5.5g (sat 1.4g, mono 1g, poly 2.2g); PROTEIN 18.6g; CARB 63.2g; FIBER 14.8g; CHOL 0mg; IRON 5.8mg; SODIUM 746mg; CALC 95mg

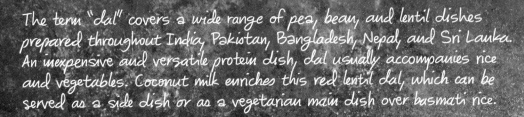

Need dinner fast? Prepared ginger preserves mixed with soy sauce and wasabi make a fabulous near-instant glaze for pan-seared tuna. Add jasmine rice and steamed asparagus for an Asian fusion meal.

TUNA STEAKS
with Wasabi-Ginger Glaze
HANDS-ON TIME: 12 MIN. TOTAL TIME: 15 MIN.

2 tablespoons lower-sodium soy sauce, divided
4 (6-ounce) tuna steaks (1 inch thick)
2 tablespoons ginger marmalade
2 teaspoons wasabi paste
Cooking spray
2 tablespoons chopped fresh cilantro

1. Spoon 1 tablespoon soy sauce over fish; let stand 5 minutes.
2. Combine remaining 1 tablespoon soy sauce, ginger marmalade, and wasabi paste in a small bowl, stirring with a whisk.
3. Heat a grill pan over medium-high heat. Coat pan with cooking spray. Add fish to pan; cook 2 minutes on each side. Spoon marmalade mixture over tuna; cook 1 minute or until medium-rare or until desired degree of doneness. Remove tuna from pan; sprinkle with cilantro. Serves 4 (serving size: 1 steak and 1½ teaspoons cilantro)

CALORIES 281; FAT 2.3g (sat 0.5g, mono 0.3g, poly 0.6g); PROTEIN 51.4g; CARB 7.7g; FIBER 0.1g; CHOL 98mg; IRON 1.8mg; SODIUM 397mg; CALC 37mg

The best-tasting fried rice has a toasty, crunchy edge on the grains of rice. To achieve that texture, the rice should be dry, not freshly cooked. Use day-old rice and, if you can, spread it on a baking sheet, and refrigerate overnight to evaporate excess moisture.

SHRIMP FRIED RICE

HANDS-ON TIME: 31 MIN. TOTAL TIME: 31 MIN.

1 cup broccoli florets
7 teaspoons canola oil, divided
1 medium red bell pepper, cut into thin strips
1 medium yellow bell pepper, cut into thin strips
1 cup sugar snap peas, trimmed and halved crosswise
1 tablespoon grated peeled fresh ginger
1 cup cooked long-grain white rice, chilled
1 tablespoon dark sesame oil
12 ounces peeled and deveined medium shrimp
1½ cups frozen edamame, thawed
¼ cup lower-sodium soy sauce
1½ tablespoons rice vinegar
1 teaspoon Sriracha (hot chile sauce, such as Huy Fong)
¼ cup thinly diagonally sliced green onions

1. Steam broccoli 4 minutes or until crisp-tender; set aside. Heat a large skillet or wok over medium-high heat. Add 1 teaspoon canola oil to pan. Add bell pepper and sugar snap peas to pan, and stir-fry 2 minutes. Transfer vegetable mixture to a large bowl. Add remaining 2 tablespoons canola oil to pan; swirl to coat. Add ginger, and stir-fry 10 seconds. Add rice, and stir-fry 5 minutes or until rice is lightly browned. Add rice mixture to vegetable mixture.
2. Wipe pan with paper towels. Return pan to medium-high heat. Add sesame oil to pan; swirl to coat. Add shrimp; stir-fry 1 minute. Add edamame; stir-fry 1 minute. Stir in soy sauce, vinegar, and Sriracha; bring to a boil. Cook 3 minutes or until liquid thickens slightly. Add steamed broccoli, vegetable mixture, and green onions; stir to combine. Cook 1 minute or until thoroughly heated, stirring frequently. Serve immediately. Serves 4 (serving size: about 2 cups)

CALORIES 368; FAT 15.7g (sat 1.5g, mono 6.9g, poly 4.5g); PROTEIN 26.6g; CARB 27.1g; FIBER 5.8g; CHOL 129mg; IRON 4.7mg; SODIUM 560mg; CALC 122mg

Among Asian chile pastes, Korea's gochujang is one of the most complex. Its sweet, spicy, salty, savory flavors come from fermented soybeans that are thickened with glutinous rice, and it is absolutely essential in Korean cooking. You can find the Annie Chun's brand in most supermarkets, or look for less-sweet varieties in Asian markets.

KOREAN-STYLE BEEF TACOS

HANDS-ON TIME: 28 MIN. TOTAL TIME: 1 HR. 28 MIN.

⅓ cup sugar
5 tablespoons lower-sodium soy sauce
1½ tablespoons gochujang (Korean chile paste)
1 tablespoon fresh lime juice
1 tablespoon dark sesame oil
4 garlic cloves, minced
12 ounces flank steak, sliced against the grain into thin strips
⅛ teaspoon salt
Cooking spray
8 (6-inch) corn tortillas
Quick Pickled Cabbage
3 tablespoons sliced green onions
8 lime wedges

1. Combine first 6 ingredients in a shallow dish. Add steak to dish; cover. Marinate in refrigerator for 1 hour, turning after 30 minutes.
2. Preheat grill to medium-high heat.
3. Remove steak from marinade, and discard marinade. Thread steak onto 8 (8-inch) skewers; sprinkle with salt. Place skewers on grill rack coated with cooking spray. Grill 2 minutes on each side or until desired degree of doneness. Grill tortillas 30 seconds on each side or until lightly charred; keep warm. Place 2 tortillas on each of 4 plates, and divide steak evenly among tortillas. Divide the Quick Pickled Cabbage evenly among tacos; sprinkle with onions. Serve with lime wedges. Serves 4 (serving size: 2 tacos)

CALORIES 270; FAT 6.3g (sat 1.6g, mono 2g, poly 1.4g); PROTEIN 18.1g; CARB 37.1g; FIBER 3g; CHOL 21mg; IRON 1.3mg; SODIUM 568mg; CALC 95mg

QUICK PICKLED CABBAGE

HANDS-ON TIME: 10 MIN. TOTAL TIME: 40 MIN.

3 cups chopped napa cabbage
2 garlic cloves, crushed
½ cup rice vinegar
2 tablespoons lower-sodium soy sauce
1 tablespoon sugar
2 teaspoons gochujang (Korean chile paste)

1. Place cabbage in a medium bowl with garlic. Bring vinegar, soy sauce, sugar, and chile paste to a boil in a small saucepan. Pour hot vinegar mixture over cabbage; toss. Let stand at least 30 minutes. Serves 4 (serving size: ½ cup)

CALORIES 33; FAT 0g; PROTEIN 1.4g; CARB 7.4g; FIBER 0.8g; CHOL 0mg; IRON 0.2mg; SODIUM 204mg; CALC 48mg

There must be a thousand ways to make this hearty dish from Kashmir—a region of the northwestern Indian subcontinent. I marinate the lamb in yogurt to tenderize it, and add flavor with saffron since the dish is really about aroma. I also add tomato paste, which is not traditional but thickens like fresh pureed Kashmiri chiles would.

HEARTY LAMB CURRY
(Roghan Josh)
HANDS-ON: 65 MIN. TOTAL: 10 HR. 5 MIN.

4 garlic cloves, minced
1 tablespoon minced peeled fresh ginger
1 teaspoon salt
1/2 cup plain 2% reduced-fat Greek yogurt
2 1/4 teaspoons garam masala, divided
1 1/2 pounds boneless leg of lamb, trimmed and cut into 1-inch pieces
1 1/2 cups water
1 tablespoon canola oil
1 teaspoon cumin seeds
1 (3-inch) cinnamon stick
6 cardamom pods
6 whole cloves
2 bay leaves
1/2 cup finely chopped red onion
2 tablespoons paprika
1/4 teaspoon ground red pepper
1/4 teaspoon crushed saffron threads
1 tablespoon tomato paste
1 tablespoon chopped fresh cilantro
1/8 teaspoon freshly ground black pepper
3 cups hot cooked basmati or jasmine rice

1. Combine garlic and ginger on a cutting board. Sprinkle with salt, and mash to a paste by dragging and pressing broad side of knife over mixture several times. Combine garlic mixture, yogurt, and 2 teaspoons garam masala in a large zip-top plastic bag. Add lamb; seal and marinate in refrigerator 8 to 24 hours, turning bag occasionally.

2. Add 1 1/2 cups water to bag; seal and shake to rinse lamb. Remove lamb from bag with a slotted spoon, reserving marinade in bag. Pat lamb dry with paper towels.

3. Heat a Dutch oven over medium-high heat. Add oil to pan; swirl to coat. Add half of lamb; cook 5 minutes or until browned, stirring occasionally. Remove lamb and juices from pan. Repeat procedure with remaining half of lamb.

4. Reduce heat to medium. Add cumin, cinnamon, cardamom, cloves, and bay leaves to pan; sauté 30 seconds. Add onion; sauté 4 minutes or until browned. Return lamb and juices to pan. Add paprika, ground red pepper, and saffron; cook 15 seconds. Add reserved marinade and tomato paste, scraping pan to loosen browned bits. Reduce heat to low; cover and simmer 1 hour or until lamb is tender. Remove from heat; stir in remaining 1/4 teaspoon garam masala, cilantro, and black pepper. Serve over rice. Serves 6 (serving size: 2/3 cup curry and 1/2 cup rice)

CALORIES 200; FAT 8.3g (sat 2.3g, mono 3.6g, poly 1.3g); PROTEIN 25.7g; CARB 5.2g; FIBER 1.3g; CHOL 74mg; IRON 3.2mg; SODIUM 496mg; CALC 36mg

To serve this dish as it would be served in a Korean barbecue restaurant, put a small hibachi (charcoal grill) in the center of an outdoor table, and allow guests to grill their own slices of marinated meat at the table. Serve with Raw Summer Kimchi (page 39) and pickled vegetables.

SPICY KOREAN PORK BARBECUE *(Daeji Bulgogi)*

HANDS-ON TIME: 22 MIN. TOTAL TIME: 2 HR. 52 MIN.

1 pound pork tenderloin, trimmed
2 tablespoons brown sugar
2 tablespoons lower-sodium soy sauce
1½ tablespoons gochujang (Korean chile paste)
1 teaspoon minced peeled fresh ginger
1 teaspoon dark sesame oil
½ teaspoon crushed red pepper
3 garlic cloves, minced
Cooking spray
½ cup cooked rice
8 lettuce leaves
¼ cup sliced green onions
Toasted sesame seeds (optional)

1. Wrap pork in plastic wrap; freeze 1½ hours or until firm. Remove plastic wrap; cut pork diagonally across the grain into ⅛-inch-thick slices.

2. Combine pork, sugar, and next 6 ingredients (through garlic) in a large zip-top plastic bag. Seal and marinate in refrigerator 1 hour, turning bag occasionally.

3. Prepare grill to medium-high heat.

4. Place a wire grilling basket on grill rack. Remove pork from bag; discard marinade. Place pork on grilling basket coated with cooking spray; grill 5 minutes or until desired degree of doneness, turning frequently.

5. Top each lettuce leaf with 1 tablespoon rice. Divide pork among lettuce leaves, and sprinkle with green onions. Garnish with sesame seeds, if desired. Serves 4 (serving size: 2 lettuce leaves, 3 ounces pork, 2 tablespoons rice, and 1 tablespoon green onions)

CALORIES 205; FAT 6.6g (sat 2.1g, mono 2.7g, poly 1g); PROTEIN 26.5g; CARB 8.9g; FIBER 0.3g; CHOL 80mg; IRON 1.6mg; SODIUM 471mg; CALC 16mg

From pleasantly fizzy to deeply funky, kimchi takes on many styles. Here's a quick one you can prepare and serve in less than a day, but it tastes even better if you let it ferment in the fridge for a few weeks. Koreans often keep kimchi in a very cold refrigerator that holds the mixture just above the freezing point so it will ferment more slowly and improve in flavor for months.

RAW SUMMER KIMCHI
(Shang Kimchi)
HANDS-ON TIME: 21 MIN. TOTAL TIME: 7 HR. 21 MIN.

14 cups coarsely chopped napa cabbage (about 2 pounds)
3 tablespoons kosher salt
1 tablespoon sesame seeds, toasted
2¹/₂ tablespoons gochujang (Korean chile paste)
2 tablespoons minced fresh garlic
2 teaspoons dark sesame oil

1. Place cabbage and salt in a large bowl, tossing gently to combine. Weigh down cabbage with another bowl. Let stand at room temperature 3 hours, tossing occasionally. Drain and rinse with cold water. Drain and squeeze dry.
2. Combine cabbage, sesame seeds, and remaining ingredients. Cover and refrigerate at least 4 hours before serving. Serves 16 (serving size: ¼ cup)

CALORIES 19; FAT 1g (sat 0.2g, mono 0.4g, poly 0.4g); PROTEIN 0.9g; CARB 2.5g; FIBER 19g; CHOL 0mg; IRON 0.3mg; SODIUM 302mg; CALC 51mg

GO GRAZING

*t*rue to European traditions of eating, meals in the United States tend to be viewed as a progression of individual courses: The appetizer is followed by a soup or a salad, and then a main course. No wonder Americans tend to feel overstuffed! My grandfather, who worked for many years in Japan, taught me that the Japanese serve an entire meal at once. "We move from one dish to the other until everything is finished," explains Japanese food writer Hiroko Shimbo, author of *Hiroko's American Kitchen.*

It's similar throughout many parts of Asia. "We like to graze," says Bombay native Raghavan Iyer, author of *Indian Cooking Unfolded* and *660 Curries.* In India, a meal consisting of rice, a wide variety of dal (lentil or bean dishes), various curries, chutney, pickles, and sometimes dessert is often presented on a single round platter called a *thali.* And in Korea, *banchan*—little dishes of pickles, kimchi, chili sauces, and vegetable dishes—are included with every meal. The thali and banchan provide an abundance of textures and flavors that proves enormously satisfying.

If it isn't grilled, Korean food is typically cooked in a single pot over a fire. Here's a classic Korean stew of chicken in a spicy sauce that can accommodate all manner of vegetables. If you don't have spinach to stir in at the end, add some potatoes, carrots, or other vegetables at the beginning of the cooking.

KOREAN STEWED CHICKEN WITH SPINACH
(Dak Bokkeum with Spinach)
HANDS-ON TIME: 35 MIN. TOTAL TIME: 1 HR. 25 MIN.

1/3 cup gochujang (Korean chile paste)
1/4 cup (1/2-inch) slices green onion bottoms
2 1/2 tablespoons lower-sodium soy sauce
2 tablespoons minced fresh garlic
2 tablespoons minced peeled fresh ginger
2 tablespoons dark sesame oil
1 tablespoon brown sugar
3/4 teaspoon crushed red pepper
2 pounds skinless, boneless chicken thighs, cut into 1/2-inch strips
1 1/2 cups uncooked short-grain white rice
1 1/2 cups water
1/3 cup water
3/4 cup (1 1/2-inch) slices green onion tops
1 (5-ounce) bag fresh baby spinach
1 tablespoon toasted sesame seeds

1. Combine first 8 ingredients in a large bowl. Stir in chicken. Cover and marinate 30 minutes.

2. Place rice in a medium saucepan; cover with water to 2 inches above rice. Stir rice; drain. Repeat procedure twice. Add 1½ cups water to drained rice in pan. Bring to a boil over medium-high heat. Cover, reduce heat, and simmer 20 minutes. Remove from heat; let stand 10 minutes.

3. While rice cooks, bring ⅓ cup water to a boil in a Dutch oven. Add chicken mixture; bring to a simmer. Cover, reduce heat, and simmer 20 minutes. Uncover and simmer 10 minutes or until mixture thickens, stirring occasionally. Remove from heat; stir in green onion tops and spinach. Sprinkle with sesame seeds. Serve with rice. Serves 6 (serving size: 1 cup chicken mixture and ¾ cup rice)

CALORIES 433; **FAT** 12g (sat 2.2g, mono 3.9g, poly 3.6g); **PROTEIN** 33.5g; **CARB** 45.2g; **FIBER** 2.9g; **CHOL** 125mg; **IRON** 6.3mg; **SODIUM** 649mg; **CALC** 54mg

In Japan, miso sometimes glazes fish, but here it's used as a marinade and a glaze for chicken. Along with sour rice vinegar, salty soy sauce, sweet honey, and spicy chile paste, the umami taste of white miso completely transforms plain pan-roasted chicken breasts into a dish of well-balanced flavors and aromas.

MISO CHICKEN

HANDS-ON TIME: 22 MIN. TOTAL TIME: 1 HR. 22 MIN.

¼ cup rice vinegar

3 tablespoons lower-sodium soy sauce

2½ tablespoons honey

1½ tablespoons white miso (soybean paste)

1½ teaspoons sambal oelek (ground fresh chile paste)

2 tablespoons minced fresh garlic

2 tablespoons dark sesame oil, divided

4 (6-ounce) skinless, boneless chicken breast halves

Cilantro leaves (optional)

1. Combine first 6 ingredients, stirring well with a whisk. Stir in 1 tablespoon oil. Place chicken in a zip-top plastic bag. Add vinegar mixture; seal. Marinate in refrigerator 1 hour, turning once.

2. Preheat oven to 400°.

3. Remove chicken from bag; reserve marinade. Place marinade in a small, heavy saucepan over medium heat; bring to a boil. Boil 2 minutes or until syrupy, stirring frequently. Remove from heat; divide mixture in half.

4. Heat a large ovenproof skillet over medium-high heat. Add remaining 1 tablespoon oil to pan; swirl to coat. Add chicken; cook 4 minutes. Turn chicken over; brush chicken with half of marinade mixture. Place pan in oven; bake at 400° for 6 minutes or until done. Remove chicken from oven; brush with remaining half of marinade mixture, turning to coat. Garnish with cilantro leaves, if desired. Serves 4 (serving size: 1 breast half)

CALORIES 314; FAT 9.1g (sat 1.6g, mono 3.5g, poly 3.5g); PROTEIN 41.5g; CARB 15.7g; FIBER 1.3g; CHOL 99mg; IRON 1.9mg; SODIUM 608mg; CALC 29mg

Miso

Made from fermented soybeans and rice, miso amplifies the umami (savory) flavor in Japanese dishes. According to Hiroko Shimbo, author of the award-winning *Hiroko's American Kitchen*, you can think of miso like cheese: "There is young, medium, and aged miso," she explains. "Aged (dark) miso is fermented longer and has more umami, a more complex flavor, and a darker color." For a sweeter taste and lighter color, use young (light or white) miso.

These days, it seems like anything can be wrapped in a tortilla. Why not spicy, sweet, salty Kung Pao chicken? If you can get a hold of some Sichuan peppercorns, toss a tablespoon or two into the wok along with the chicken for a tongue-numbing flavor buzz. That will give the tacos the flavor of the original dish made in China's Sichuan province.

KUNG PAO CHICKEN TACOS

HANDS-ON TIME: 30 MIN. TOTAL TIME: 60 MIN.

6 skinless, boneless chicken thighs, cut into bite-sized pieces
3 tablespoons lower-sodium soy sauce, divided
1/4 cup plus 1 1/2 teaspoons cornstarch, divided
1/4 teaspoon kosher salt
2 tablespoons canola oil, divided
1 1/2 tablespoons honey
1 tablespoon dark sesame oil
2 teaspoons rice vinegar
1 teaspoon sambal oelek (ground fresh chile paste)
1 large garlic clove, minced
3 tablespoons coarsely chopped dry-roasted peanuts
3/4 cup diagonally sliced celery (about 2 stalks)
8 (6-inch) corn tortillas
1/3 cup sliced green onions
1/2 medium red bell pepper, thinly sliced
4 lime wedges

1. Place chicken in a large zip-top plastic bag. Add 1 tablespoon soy sauce to bag; seal. Marinate at room temperature 30 minutes. Remove chicken from bag; discard marinade. Place 1/4 cup cornstarch in a shallow dish. Sprinkle chicken evenly with salt. Add chicken to cornstarch in dish, and toss chicken to thoroughly coat. Shake off excess cornstarch.

2. Heat a wok or large skillet over medium-high heat. Add 1 tablespoon canola oil to pan; swirl to coat. Add half of coated chicken; sauté 6 minutes or until done, turning to brown. Remove chicken from pan using a slotted spoon; drain on paper towels. Repeat procedure with remaining 1 tablespoon canola oil and coated chicken.

3. Combine remaining 1 1/2 teaspoons cornstarch, remaining 2 tablespoons soy sauce, honey, and next 3 ingredients (through sambal oelek) in a microwave-safe bowl, stirring with a whisk until smooth. Microwave at HIGH 1 1/2 minutes or until slightly thick, stirring twice. Stir in garlic. Combine soy sauce mixture, chicken, peanuts, and celery; toss to coat chicken.

4. Toast tortillas under broiler or on a griddle until lightly blistered, turning frequently. Place 2 tortillas on each of 4 plates; divide chicken mixture evenly among tortillas. Top each taco with green onions and bell pepper strips; serve with lime wedges. Serves 4 (serving size: 2 tacos)

CALORIES 418; FAT 19.1g (sat 2.5g, mono 8.9g, poly 6.1g); PROTEIN 25.2g; CARB 39.3g; FIBER 4g; CHOL 86mg; IRON 1.6mg; SODIUM 531mg; CALC 53mg

The tandoor, India's wood-fired clay oven, turns out fantastic barbecued chicken. An ordinary outdoor grill with a tight-fitting lid and prepared for indirect heat (see below) mimics the gentle heat of the authentic clay ovens. Tandoori chicken originated in the Punjab region of northern India and Pakistan and gets its traditional red color from ground chiles.

TANDOORI GRILLED CHICKEN
with Mint Raita
HANDS-ON TIME: 1 HR. 50 MIN. TOTAL TIME: 9 HR. 50 MIN.

Marinade:
¾ cup fat-free Greek yogurt
2 tablespoons chopped peeled
    fresh ginger
1 tablespoon paprika
1 tablespoon fresh lime juice
1 teaspoon chili powder
¾ teaspoon salt
½ teaspoon ground turmeric
½ teaspoon ground cumin
⅛ teaspoon ground red pepper
3 garlic cloves, chopped
4 (12-ounce) bone-in chicken
    leg-thigh quarters, skinned
Raita:
¾ cup fat-free Greek yogurt
¾ cup chopped seeded cucumber
2 tablespoons chopped fresh mint
½ teaspoon ground cumin
¼ teaspoon salt
Cooking spray

1. To prepare marinade, place first 10 ingredients in a blender; process until smooth. Pour into a large zip-top plastic bag. Add chicken; turn to coat. Marinate chicken in refrigerator at least 4 hours or overnight.
2. To prepare raita, combine ¾ cup yogurt and next 4 ingredients (through ¼ teaspoon salt) in a small bowl; cover and refrigerate.
3. Remove chicken from refrigerator, and let stand at room temperature 45 minutes.
4. Prepare grill for indirect grilling. If using a gas grill, heat one side to medium-high and leave one side with no heat. If using a charcoal grill, arrange hot coals on on one side of charcoal grate, leaving other side empty.
5. Remove chicken from marinade, and discard remaining marinade. Place chicken on unheated part of grill rack coated with cooking spray. Close lid, and grill 90 minutes or until a thermometer inserted into meaty part of thigh registers 165°, turning chicken every 20 minutes. Serve with raita. Serves 4 (serving size: 1 chicken quarter and about ⅓ cup raita)

CALORIES 284; FAT 7.9g (sat 2g, mono 2.4g, poly 2g); PROTEIN 45.7g; CARB 4.9g; FIBER 0.7g; CHOL 161mg; IRON 2.5mg; SODIUM 502mg; CALC 76mg

how to:
USE INDIRECT HEAT
Compared to cooking over direct heat,
this method cooks foods more gently, like the heat in an oven.
It's perfect for thicker foods or bone-in cuts.

1 Bank hot coals on one side of the kettle grill.

2 Radiant heat from indirect coals cooks the chicken slowly and without burning.

Also known as butter chicken, this Punjabi dish gets its richness from cashew butter, half-and-half, and yogurt. A host of spices from coriander and ginger to cardamom and cinnamon give it head-swirling aromas. Serve over brown basmati rice or with naan bread to soak up the creamy sauce.

INDIAN CASHEW CHICKEN
(Murgh Makhani)
HANDS-ON TIME: 30 MIN. TOTAL TIME: 4 HR. 30 MIN.

²/₃ cup cashews, toasted
²/₃ cup fat-free Greek yogurt
¼ cup tomato paste
2 tablespoons white vinegar
1¼ teaspoons garam masala
1 teaspoon ground coriander
1 teaspoon grated peeled fresh ginger
¼ teaspoon ground red pepper
2 garlic cloves, chopped
4 skinless, boneless chicken thighs, cut into bite-sized pieces (about 14 ounces)
2 (8-ounce) skinless, boneless chicken breasts, cut into bite-sized pieces
Cooking spray
2³/₄ cups finely chopped onion (2 large)
2 green cardamom pods, lightly crushed
1 (2-inch) cinnamon stick
2 cups fat-free, lower-sodium chicken broth
1 cup organic tomato puree
1 teaspoon sweet paprika
¼ teaspoon salt
3 tablespoons half-and-half
Chopped fresh cilantro (optional)

1. Place first 9 ingredients in a blender or food processor; process until smooth. Combine nut mixture and chicken in a large bowl; cover and refrigerate 3 hours or overnight.
2. Heat a large Dutch oven over medium-low heat. Coat pan with cooking spray. Add onion, cardamom, and cinnamon stick to pan; cover and cook 10 minutes or until onion is golden, stirring often.
3. Add chicken mixture to pan; cook 10 minutes, stirring frequently. Stir in broth, tomato puree, paprika, and salt, scraping pan to loosen browned bits. Cook 1 hour or until thick. Stir in half-and-half; cook 1 minute, stirring occasionally. Remove from heat. Discard cinnamon stick. Garnish with fresh cilantro, if desired. Serves 6 (serving size: about 1 cup)

CALORIES 340; FAT 13.6g (sat 3.4g, mono 5.8g, poly 2.6g); PROTEIN 36.7g; CARB 18.7g; FIBER 3.8g; CHOL 91mg; IRON 3.2mg; SODIUM 435mg; CALC 83mg

Chicken tikka—chicken marinated in spicy yogurt and charred in a tandoor—has origins in India. So do the spices in the masala sauce. But chicken tikka masala as it stands today is not traditional in Indian cuisine. Most food historians point to the U.K. to explain how the two parts of the dish (tikka and masala) came together.

CHICKEN TIKKA MASALA

HANDS-ON TIME: 56 MIN. TOTAL TIME: 9 HR. 28 MIN.

4 large garlic cloves, coarsely chopped (2 tablespoons)
1 tablespoon minced peeled fresh ginger
¼ teaspoon salt
½ cup 2% reduced-fat Greek yogurt
¼ cup fresh lemon juice
1½ teaspoons paprika
1 teaspoon garam masala
1 teaspoon ground cumin
¼ teaspoon ground red pepper
1½ pounds skinless, boneless chicken thighs, cut into 1-inch pieces
1¼ pounds ripe tomatoes, cored and quartered
2 tablespoons canola oil
½ cup finely chopped red onion
1 tablespoon minced peeled fresh ginger
4 garlic cloves, minced
2 teaspoons ground coriander
2 teaspoons paprika
½ teaspoon ground turmeric
⅛ teaspoon ground red pepper
½ teaspoon salt
½ teaspoon garam masala
¼ cup 2% reduced-fat Greek yogurt
2 tablespoons chopped fresh cilantro
2½ cups hot cooked basmati rice

1. Combine garlic and ginger on a cutting board. Sprinkle with salt, and mash to a paste by dragging and pressing broad side of knife over mixture several times. Combine garlic mixture, yogurt, and next 5 ingredients (through ground red pepper) in a large zip-top plastic bag. Add chicken; seal and marinate in refrigerator 8 to 24 hours, turning bag occasionally.
2. Place tomatoes in a food processor; process until pureed to measure 2 cups. Heat a Dutch oven over medium heat. Add oil to pan; swirl to coat. Add onion; sauté 4 minutes or until browned. Add ginger and garlic; sauté 1 minute. Add coriander, paprika, turmeric, and ground red pepper; cook 1 minute. Stir in tomato puree, and bring to boil. Cover, reduce heat to low, and simmer 20 minutes or until thick.
3. Preheat grill or broiler.
4. While masala sauce simmers, remove chicken from marinade; discard marinade. Thread chicken onto 4 (12-inch) metal skewers. Place skewers on grill rack or broiler pan; cook 3 minutes. Turn skewers over; cook 3 minutes or until browned on all sides but still undercooked in center (chicken will finish cooking in sauce).
5. Remove chicken from skewers; add to masala sauce. Stir in salt and garam masala; cover and simmer an additional 6 minutes or until chicken is done. Remove from heat; stir in yogurt and cilantro. Serve over rice. Serves 5 (serving size: ¾ cup chicken mixture and ½ cup rice)

CALORIES 285; FAT 12.4g (sat 2.3g, mono 5.3g, poly 3.2g); PROTEIN 31.6g; CARB 12.1g; FIBER 3.0g; CHOL 115mg; IRON 2.7mg; SODIUM 493mg; CALC 75mg

Move over chicken noodle soup—udon is the new bowl of comfort. Here's a twist on Japanese-style chicken soup featuring miso, soy sauce, chile paste, porcini mushrooms, and, of course, udon noodles. It's the perfect soother on a chilly or rainy day.

UDON NOODLE BOWL

HANDS-ON TIME: 68 MIN. TOTAL TIME: 68 MIN.

4 cups boiling water
½ ounce dried porcini mushrooms
1 bacon slice
½ cup chopped onion
1 carrot, coarsely chopped
2 tablespoons yellow miso (soybean paste)
2 tablespoons lower-sodium soy sauce
2 cups no-salt-added chicken stock
3 garlic cloves, crushed
1 (½-inch) piece fresh ginger, thinly sliced
8 ounces fresh udon noodles or ramen noodles
2 tablespoons dark sesame oil, divided
1 (8-ounce) package presliced exotic mushroom blend (such as shiitake, cremini, and oyster)
6 (3-ounce) skin-on, boneless chicken thighs
3 large eggs
1 cup thinly sliced green onion strips, divided
2 tablespoons sambal oelek (ground fresh chile paste)

1. Combine 4 cups boiling water and porcini; let stand 15 minutes. Drain through a sieve over a bowl; reserve porcini and soaking liquid. Slice porcini; set aside.
2. Heat a Dutch oven over medium heat. Add bacon; cook until almost crisp. Increase heat to medium-high. Add onion and carrot; sauté 2 minutes. Combine miso and soy sauce. Add miso mixture, porcini liquid, stock, garlic, and ginger to pan; bring to a boil. Reduce heat, and simmer 20 minutes. Strain mixture through a sieve over a bowl; discard solids. Wipe pan clean. Return broth to pan; bring to a boil. Add noodles; cook 8 minutes or until tender. Remove from heat.
3. Heat a large skillet over medium-high heat. Add 1 tablespoon oil to pan; swirl to coat. Add fresh mushrooms; sauté 8 minutes. Remove from pan; combine porcini and fresh mushrooms. Add remaining 1 tablespoon oil to pan; swirl to coat. Add chicken, skin side down; sauté 7 minutes or until skin is very crisp and golden brown. Turn chicken over; sauté 2 minutes or until done.
4. Place eggs in a small saucepan; add water to cover. Bring to a boil; cook 1 minute. Remove from heat; let stand 3 minutes. Drain; rinse under cold water. Drain and peel.
5. Divide noodle mixture among 6 bowls; top each serving with 3 tablespoons mushroom mixture, 2 tablespoons green onions, 1 chicken thigh, ½ egg, and 1 teaspoon sambal oelek. Garnish with remaining ¼ cup green onion strips. Serves 6

CALORIES 449; FAT 23.9g (sat 6.3g, mono 9.8g, poly 6g); PROTEIN 30g; CARB 28.1g; FIBER 2.6g; CHOL 186mg; IRON 2.7mg; SODIUM 654mg; CALC 56mg

Wok hay or "wok aroma" can make the difference between a so-so stir-fry and an incredible one, says Chinese cooking expert Grace Young. "When fresh ingredients cook quickly in a hot wok, the constant tossing infuses the ingredients with the aroma of the wok and the flavor of the last meal." Wok hay deepens over time as you use an iron wok, similar to how a cast-iron skillet is seasoned.

LO MEIN *with Tofu*
HANDS-ON TIME: 39 MIN. TOTAL TIME: 68 MIN.

1 (14-ounce) package firm water-packed tofu, drained and cut crosswise into 4 (1-inch-thick) pieces
8 ounces whole-wheat linguine or fresh Chinese egg noodles
1 teaspoon dark sesame oil
1/2 teaspoon salt, divided
1/4 teaspoon freshly ground black pepper, divided
2 tablespoons canola oil, divided
3 tablespoons oyster sauce
1 1/2 tablespoons mirin (sweet rice wine)
1 1/2 tablespoons lower-sodium soy sauce
1 teaspoon rice vinegar
3/4 cup vertically sliced onion
2 cups shredded cabbage
2 cups peeled, thinly diagonally sliced carrot
2 large garlic cloves, thinly sliced
1 1/2 cups fresh bean sprouts
1/4 cup thickly sliced green onion tops

1. Place tofu in a single layer on several layers of paper towels. Cover tofu with several more layers of paper towels, and top with a cast-iron skillet or other heavy pan. Let stand 30 minutes. Discard paper towels.
2. Cook noodles in boiling water until al dente; drain. Combine noodles, sesame oil, 1/4 teaspoon salt, and 1/8 teaspoon pepper; toss. Set aside.
3. Sprinkle remaining 1/4 teaspoon salt and remaining 1/8 teaspoon pepper evenly over tofu. Heat a large cast-iron skillet over medium-high heat. Add 1 tablespoon canola oil to pan; swirl to coat. Add tofu to pan; cook 4 minutes on each side or until golden. Remove from pan; cut into bite-sized pieces. Combine oyster sauce and next 3 ingredients (through vinegar) in a small bowl, stirring well.
4. Heat a wok or cast-iron skillet over medium-high heat. Add remaining 1 tablespoon canola oil to pan; swirl to coat. Add onion; stir-fry 2 minutes or until lightly browned. Add cabbage, carrot, and garlic; stir-fry 2 minutes or until cabbage wilts. Reduce heat to medium; stir in tofu and vinegar mixture, tossing to coat. Add noodles and bean sprouts; toss. Cook 2 minutes or until thoroughly heated. Sprinkle with green onions. Serves 4 (serving size: 1 3/4 cups)

CALORIES 397; **FAT** 15.4g (sat 1.3g, mono 8.8g, poly 4.1g); **PROTEIN** 18.2g; **CARB** 55.1g; **FIBER** 9g; **CHOL** 0mg; **IRON** 4mg; **SODIUM** 736mg; **CALC** 248mg

Tofu

Made from soy milk that is curdled, drained, and pressed, tofu comes in two basic styles: regular and silken. Both styles can be made soft, firm, or extra-firm, but silken tofu usually comes in an aseptic box and has a custard-like texture that can be pureed to make creamy soups, dips, sauces, and dressings. Think of it as firm sour cream or yogurt without the acidic tang. More often you'll see recipes calling for the style of tofu sold in a tub of water. To give tofu a firmer texture, freeze it in plastic wrap, and then thaw it before using. Freezing also makes tofu more sponge-like so that it soaks up more flavorful marinade or sauce.

This recipe comes from chef Suvir Saran, who earned a Michelin star for his brilliant cooking at New York's Dévi. Author of the best-selling Indian Home Cooking, Saran knows how to simplify Indian cooking for Westerners. North Indian cuisine isn't as fiery hot as the food in the South, so if you want more heat here, add a ¼ teaspoon of ground cayenne pepper.

ROASTED POTATOES
with North Indian Spices
HANDS-ON TIME: 20 MIN. TOTAL TIME: 60 MIN.

3½ tablespoons canola oil, divided
3 pounds small red potatoes, halved (about 8 cups)
1¾ teaspoons black mustard seeds
6 dried red chiles
2 teaspoons minced peeled fresh ginger
3 garlic cloves, minced
½ jalapeño, seeded and minced
1½ teaspoons kosher salt
1 teaspoon ground turmeric
½ teaspoon garam masala
Cooking spray
½ cup chopped fresh cilantro
½ cup chopped fresh mint
1 tablespoon fresh lime juice
8 lime wedges

1. Preheat oven to 400°.
2. Combine 1 tablespoon oil and potatoes, tossing to coat. Set aside.
3. Heat remaining 2½ tablespoons oil, mustard seeds, and chiles in a large skillet over medium-high heat; cook 1½ minutes or until seeds begin to pop. Reduce heat to medium-low. Add ginger, garlic, and jalapeño to pan; cook 1 minute, stirring constantly. Stir in salt, turmeric, and garam masala; cook 1 minute, stirring constantly. Add spice mixture to potatoes, tossing to coat. Arrange potato mixture in a single layer in a 13 x 9–inch baking dish coated with cooking spray.
4. Bake at 400° for 40 minutes or until potatoes are tender and browned, stirring every 10 minutes. Stir in cilantro, mint, and juice. Serve with lime wedges. Serves 8 (serving size: about ¾ cup potato mixture and 1 lime wedge)

CALORIES 241; **FAT** 7.4g (sat 0.6g, mono 3.7g, poly 2.4g); **PROTEIN** 5.9g; **CARB** 38.9g; **FIBER** 5.5g; **CHOL** 0mg; **IRON** 3.2mg; **SODIUM** 370mg; **CALC** 19mg

The Japanese often begin their day with a warm bowl of miso soup. But it's good anytime—especially if you're feeling sick. If you have the Japanese pantry staples miso, kombu (kelp), and katsuobushi (dried bonito flakes or tuna flakes) on hand, the soup is ready in less than 15 minutes. The original is full of savory, umami flavor but also high in sodium, so I've cut back a bit on the miso and bonito flakes.

MISO SOUP *with Tofu*
HANDS-ON TIME: 10 MIN. TOTAL TIME: 15 MIN.

¼ cup dried katsuobushi (bonito flakes)

1 (3½-ounce) package shiitake mushrooms

4 cups water

1 (3 x 4-inch) piece kombu (edible kelp)

3 tablespoons white or red miso (soybean paste)

1½ cups cubed soft or firm tofu (about 8 ounces)

⅓ cup thinly sliced green onion tops

1. Place bonito flakes on a double layer of cheesecloth. Gather edges of cheesecloth together; tie securely. Remove and discard stems from mushrooms; thinly slice mushroom caps.

2. Combine 4 cups water and kombu in a medium saucepan; bring almost to a boil. Remove from heat; add cheesecloth bag to water. Let stand 5 minutes. Remove and discard kombu and cheesecloth bag.

3. Combine miso and 3 tablespoons soup broth in a small bowl; stir with a whisk until miso dissolves.

4. Add mushrooms and tofu to soup; cook over low heat 3 minutes or until tofu is warm. Remove from heat; stir in miso mixture and green onions. Let stand 1 minute. Serves 5 (serving size: 1 cup)

CALORIES 73; **FAT** 2.7g (sat 0.3g, mono 0.7g, poly 1.6g); **PROTEIN** 6.1g; **CARB** 6.3g; **FIBER** 2.0g; **CHOL** 0mg;

SICHUAN BEEF SOUP

HANDS-ON TIME: 30 MIN. TOTAL TIME: 11 HR. 30 MIN.

3 quarts water

2 pounds (2-inch-thick) bone-in beef shanks

2 teaspoons peanut oil or canola oil

1 cup chopped white onion

2 teaspoons minced peeled fresh ginger

2 garlic cloves, chopped

6 cups water

1 tablespoon chile garlic sauce

1½ teaspoons black bean garlic sauce (such as Lee Kum Kee)

1 teaspoon Sichuan peppercorns

3 star anise

1 cup sliced green onions, divided

1 tablespoon brown sugar

2 tablespoons lower-sodium soy sauce

2 plum tomatoes, chopped

2 baby bok choy, cut in half lengthwise

½ pound fresh Chinese-style wheat noodles

¼ cup chopped fresh cilantro

1. Bring 3 quarts water to a boil in a large Dutch oven. Add beef shanks; boil until surface of meat is no longer red (about 6 minutes). Drain shanks; cool slightly. Remove meat from bones; reserve bones. Cut meat into cubes.

2. Rinse pan; wipe clean with paper towels. Heat pan over high heat. Add oil; swirl to coat. Add white onion, ginger, and garlic; stir-fry 4 minutes or until browned. Stir in 6 cups water, chile garlic sauce, and black bean sauce. Place peppercorns and star anise on a double layer of cheesecloth. Gather edges of cheesecloth together; tie securely. Add cheesecloth bag, ½ cup green onions, sugar, and soy sauce to pan. Return meat and bones to pan. Bring to a simmer. Partially cover, and simmer gently for 2 hours or until meat is tender. Uncover and simmer 1 hour or until reduced to about 5 cups. Cool to room temperature; cover and chill overnight.

3. Skim fat from soup; discard fat. Discard bones and cheesecloth bag. Bring soup to a simmer. Add tomatoes and bok choy; cook 5 minutes or until bok choy is tender.

4. Cook noodles according to package directions. Place about ½ cup noodles in each of 4 bowls. Ladle 1 cup soup into each bowl, dividing bok choy evenly. Sprinkle each serving with 2 tablespoons green onions and 1 tablespoon cilantro. Serves 4

CALORIES 408; **FAT** 8.6g (sat 2.4g, mono 3.5g, poly 1.1g); **PROTEIN** 40.3g; **CARB** 4.1g; **FIBER** 2.9g; **CHOL** 53mg; **IRON** 4.5mg; **SODIUM** 635mg; **CALC** 97mg

Sichuan Peppercorns

Also known as flower peppers, Sichuan peppercorns are the dried red berries of the prickly ash tree. They bring a peppery zing, citrus aroma, and unique fizzy sensation that lingers on the tongue. They also turn up in Chinese five-spice powder and the Japanese spice blend *shichimi togarashi*. When ground to a powder, the berries are known as *sansho* in Japanese cooking, which makes a fine substitute for whole Sichuan peppercorns.

Situated on the East China Sea, Shanghai incorporates plenty of seafood into its cooking. This comfort-food stew usually includes flash-fried and then long-simmered fish heads. If you have them, add some fish heads here along with the broth (remove before serving). But if you don't, this streamlined version uses tilapia fillets to keep things simple.

SHANGHAI-INSPIRED FISH STEW

HANDS-ON TIME: 13 MIN. TOTAL TIME: 66 MIN.

3 ounces uncooked bean threads (cellophane noodles)
2 cups boiling water
1 ounce dried wood ear mushrooms
4 cups fat-free, lower-sodium chicken broth
2 tablespoons julienne-cut peeled fresh ginger
1 tablespoon rice vinegar
1 tablespoon lower-sodium soy sauce
1 tablespoon Chinese black vinegar or Worcestershire sauce
1/2 teaspoon ground white pepper
1/2 teaspoon dark sesame oil
1/4 teaspoon salt
1 pound tilapia fillets, cut into bite-sized pieces
8 ounces firm silken tofu, drained and cubed
1/4 cup thinly sliced green onions

1. Prepare noodles according to package directions. Drain and rinse with cold water. Drain. Snip noodles several times with kitchen shears.

2. Combine 2 cups boiling water and mushrooms in a medium bowl; let stand 20 minutes. Drain mushrooms in a sieve over a bowl; discard mushrooms. Combine mushroom soaking liquid, broth, and next 7 ingredients (through salt) in a Dutch oven. Bring to a boil. Cover, reduce heat, and simmer 20 minutes. Add tilapia; cover and simmer 10 minutes. Stir in noodles and tofu; simmer, uncovered, 5 minutes. Ladle 1 cup soup into each of 8 bowls; sprinkle each serving with 1½ teaspoons green onions. Serves 8

CALORIES 121; FAT 2g (sat 0.5g, mono 0.6g, poly 0.8g); PROTEIN 14g; CARB 11.1g; FIBER 0.5g; CHOL 28mg; IRON 0.8mg; SODIUM 407mg; CALC 19mg

how to: PREPARE CELLOPHANE NOODLES

Unlike firm wheat noodles, cellophane noodles (made from mung bean starch) are so delicate that they're ready to eat with only a brief soak in hot water.

1 Soak noodles in hot water for 15 minutes.

2 Drain and rinse in cold water. Drain once again.

3 Snip with kitchen shears into manageable lengths.

During Diwali, the Festival of Lights, Indians often share this dessert with friends. It's so easy and delicious that you could riff on the idea with all manner of nuts and spices, like peanuts and cinnamon, pine nuts and allspice, or pistachios and clove.

CASHEW FUDGE *(Kaju Katli)*

HANDS-ON TIME: 15 MIN. TOTAL TIME: 1 HR. 15 MIN.

Cooking spray
1 cup unsalted raw cashews
1 cup plus 2 tablespoons sugar, divided
1⅓ cups water
¼ teaspoon saffron threads
4 tablespoons butter
½ teaspoon ground cardamom

1. Line bottom of an 11 x 17–inch jelly-roll pan with parchment paper or wax paper; coat paper with cooking spray.

2. Place cashews and 6 tablespoons sugar in a food processor; process 30 seconds or until cashews are very finely chopped (do not form a nut butter).

3. Combine remaining ¾ cup sugar, 1⅛ cups water, and saffron in a 3-quart saucepan. Bring to a boil over medium heat, and cook, stirring constantly, until a candy thermometer registers 230° and syrup falls in double-threads from spoon, about 8 to 10 minutes. Gradually stir in cashew mixture. Add butter and cardamom; cook 2 to 3 minutes or until mixture thickens and resembles loose dough, stirring constantly.

4. Turn out into prepared pan; quickly spread with a lightly greased offset spatula to ¼-inch thickness, forming a 9 x 7½-inch rectangle. Cool completely. Cut fudge into 56 (1-inch) diamond-shaped pieces. Serves 56 (serving size: 1 piece)

CALORIES 37; **FAT** 1.9g (sat 0.7g, mono 0.8g, poly 0.2g); **PROTEIN** 0.5g; **CARB** 5g; **FIBER** 0.1g; **CHOL** 2mg; **IRON** 0.2mg; **SODIUM** 8mg, **CALC** 1mg

Cashews

Indian cooks use nuts like cashews for flavor, richness, and sometimes for their sauce-thickening quality. Ground cashews can be used anywhere you would use ground peanuts (as in the recipe for Cashew Fudge). When taken a step further and finely ground into cashew butter, the nuts thicken and flavor classic Indian curries like *murgh makhani*. Look for raw (unroasted and unsalted) cashews. It's rare to find cashews sold in the shell because the shell contains a toxic substance. But when the shell is removed, the nut inside is perfectly safe and absolutely delicious.

Southeast Asia & Australia

CILANTRO:
Leaves of the coriander plant; used mostly fresh and whole. Note that Vietnamese coriander/mint comes from a different botanical family and is more commonly known as *rau ram or laksa leaf.*

KECAP MANIS:
Thick, sweet soy sauce that provides salty and umami flavors.

FISH SAUCE:
Primary seasoning and source of umami (savory) flavor; made from salted, fermented fish; see page 78 for more details.

The Flavors of Southeast Asia & Australia

Imagine fiery chile peppers sprinkled with sweet palm sugar. Sour limes alongside salty, savory fish sauce. Southeast Asian food is all about contrasting tastes. From Thailand and Vietnam to Malaysia and Indonesia, you find vibrant ingredients paired in dynamic ways. "It is a dance of flavor," muses Naomi Duguid, co-author of six award-winning cookbooks including, *Hot Sour Salty Sweet* and her latest, *Burma: Rivers of Flavor.* "Think of meals as a deconstruction of flavors that might be simmered together in France, for instance," says Duguid. The host or hostess sets the stage by putting various dishes on the table, then it's up to you to choreograph the dance. Fresh herbs play an aromatic role along with lemongrass, ginger, and other intensely perfumed ingredients.

Some of these ingredients make their way into modern Australian cuisine as well. But most Australian cooking stems from colonial British dishes like roast beef, lamb, meat pies, and fish and chips. Australian cooks also use aboriginal "bush tucker" like kangaroo, emu, and quandongs (native peaches). Here's a quick look at the most distinctive flavors in this part of the world.

CHILE PASTE:
A heat source; includes Indonesia's sambal oelek, Thailand's *nam prik,* and Vietnam's *tuong ot toi,* among others. (Note that Sriracha is not a traditional Vietnamese chile paste but a modern Chinese-Vietnamese hybrid.)

MINT:
Fresh, whole leaves provide clean, bracing taste and aroma. Sometimes combined with Thai basil to add anise and citrus aromas.

COCONUT:
Provides richness and tropical aromas. May be freshly grated, simmered to make coconut "milk," pressed for its rich oil, made into vinegar, or sipped as nutrient-dense coconut "water."

GINGER:
Rhizome (underground stem) with pungent, floral aroma; used fresh and cooked.

LEMONGRASS:
Lends refreshing citrus scents; used whole and chopped.

LIME:
Provides sourness along with citron—the oldest form of citrus fruit; kaffir lime is used mostly for its bitter leaves.

SHALLOTS:
More common than onions; often fried, caramelized, ground to a paste, sliced fresh for salads, or infused into shallot oil for drizzling.

Think of this Vietnamese noodle salad as a deconstructed spring roll. Cucumber, carrots, and mung bean sprouts lend crunch. Grilled shrimp is the crowning touch. The sauce, called nuoc cham, shows up at almost every Vietnamese meal for drizzling over rice, noodles, and grilled meats. Ditto for the fried shallots and shallot oil.

LEMONGRASS SHRIMP
over Rice Vermicelli and Vegetables
HANDS-ON TIME: 37 MIN. TOTAL TIME: 1 HR. 35 MIN.

1/3 cup Thai fish sauce (such as Three Crabs)

1/4 cup sugar

2 tablespoons finely chopped peeled fresh lemongrass

1 tablespoon canola oil

2 garlic cloves, minced

32 large shrimp, peeled and deveined (about 1½ pounds)

1 cup fresh lime juice (about 9 limes)

3/4 cup shredded carrot

1/2 cup sugar

1/4 cup Thai fish sauce (such as Three Crabs)

2 garlic cloves, minced

2 red Thai chiles, seeded and minced

1/4 cup canola oil

3/4 cup thinly sliced shallots

8 ounces rice vermicelli (banh hoi or bun giang tay)

3½ cups shredded Boston lettuce, divided

2 cups fresh bean sprouts, divided

1¾ cups shredded carrot, divided

1 medium cucumber, halved lengthwise, seeded, and thinly sliced (about 1½ cups), divided

Cooking spray

1/2 cup chopped fresh mint

1/2 cup unsalted dry-roasted peanuts, finely chopped

1. Combine first 6 ingredients in a large zip-top plastic bag; seal. Marinate in refrigerator 1 hour, turning occasionally. Remove shrimp from bag; discard marinade.

2. Combine lime juice and next 5 ingredients (through chiles), stirring with a whisk until sugar dissolves. Set aside.

3. Heat a small saucepan over medium heat. Add ¼ cup oil; swirl to coat. Add shallots; cook 5 minutes or until golden brown. Strain shallot mixture through a sieve over a bowl. Reserve oil. Set fried shallots aside.

4. Place rice vermicelli in a large bowl; cover with boiling water. Let stand 20 minutes. Drain. Combine noodles, shallot oil, 1¾ cups lettuce, 1 cup sprouts, 1 cup carrot, and ¾ cup cucumber, tossing well.

5. To cook shrimp, prepare grill to medium-high heat.

6. Place shrimp on grill rack coated with cooking spray; grill 2½ minutes on each side or until done. Place ¾ cup noodle mixture in each of 8 bowls; top each serving with 4 shrimp, about 3 tablespoons of sauce, and about 1 tablespoon fried shallots. Serve with remaining lettuce, bean sprouts, carrot, cucumber, mint, and peanuts. Serves 8

CALORIES 423; FAT 13.5g (sat 2.1g, mono 4.1g, poly 6g); PROTEIN 26.6g; CARB 51.9g; FIBER 4.3g; CHOL 29mg; IRON 4.2mg; SODIUM 960mg; CALC 102mg

Rice Vermicelli

Asian noodles are made from a staggering variety of starches and vegetables, from wheat and arrowroot to mung beans and sweet potatoes. But most Southeast Asian noodles consist of rice. The thin, delicate strands of white or off-white rice noodles known as rice vermicelli are popular in soups and noodle bowls. They are usually packaged in brick-like nests and may be labeled *banh hoi, bee hoon, sen mee,* or *mai fun.* Similar noodles labeled rice sticks may be thinner or thicker and packaged in longer, narrower nests or as straight, individual sticks like linguine. Either way, rice noodles are typically soaked in hot water for 15 to 30 minutes (depending on thickness), and then quickly stir-fried or simmered in the dish.

Chefs Jane and Jeremy Strode wouldn't even consider hosting an Australian barbecue without whole fish—preferably small, freshly caught snapper—on the grill. Spoon anchovy-spiked herb sauce over the grilled fish to serve as an appetizer.

WHOLE BABY SNAPPER
with Green Sauce

HANDS-ON TIME: 7 MIN. TOTAL TIME: 27 MIN.

3 whole baby snapper (about 12
   ounces each), cleaned
1/2 teaspoon black pepper, divided
1/4 teaspoon kosher salt
1 lemon, cut into 1/8-inch-thick slices
Cooking spray
1 cup loosely packed fresh flat-leaf
   parsley leaves
2/3 cup loosely packed fresh mint
   leaves
1/4 cup loosely packed fresh dill
1/4 cup loosely packed fresh basil
   leaves
3 tablespoons extra-virgin olive oil
2 tablespoons capers
4 anchovy fillets
3 garlic cloves, peeled

1. Preheat grill to medium-high heat.
2. Score snapper by making 4 (1-inch) crosswise cuts on each side of skin with a sharp knife. Sprinkle 1/4 teaspoon pepper and salt evenly inside cavities; arrange lemon slices evenly in cavities. Wrap fish tightly in foil coated with cooking spray. Place fish on grill rack; grill 15 minutes or until fish flakes easily when tested with a fork, turning once. Let stand 5 minutes before unwrapping.
3. Place parsley and remaining ingredients in a food processor; process until finely chopped. Stir in remaining 1/4 teaspoon pepper. Serve sauce with fish. Serves 6 (serving size: 1/2 fish and about 2 tablespoons sauce)

CALORIES 146; **FAT** 8.1g (sat 1.2g, mono 5.2g, poly 1.2g); **PROTEIN** 16.1g; **CARB** 1.9g; **FIBER** 0.8g; **CHOL** 29mg; **IRON** 1.3mg; **SODIUM** 300mg; **CALC** 57mg

how to: CLEAN WHOLE FISH

When cooked whole, fish skin and bones release gelatin when heated, giving the flesh a moister, richer mouthfeel.

1 Carefully snip off fins, lifting dorsal fin to avoid sharp points.

2 Lift up collar, snip red gills at top, and remove. Repeat on other side.

3 Remove scales by scraping from tail to head with spoon or dull edge of knife.

4 Gut fish by slitting from rear fin to collar. Remove innards, and then rinse well.

From Indonesia, satay spread like wildfire all over Southeast Asia. Singapore, Malaysia, and Thailand all have different versions of the grilled skewers, routinely sold at street carts with peanut sauce for dipping. Don't feel beholden to beef: Chicken, pork, lamb, and rabbit all work well on sticks.

BEEF SATAY
with Peanut Dipping Sauce
HANDS-ON TIME: 42 MIN. TOTAL TIME: 9 HR. 57 MIN.

3 tablespoons (about 1½ ounces) palm sugar or brown sugar
¼ cup water, divided
1 teaspoon tamarind paste
1 tablespoon coriander seeds
½ teaspoon cumin seeds
¼ teaspoon fennel seeds
2 tablespoons chopped peeled fresh galangal or 4 teaspoons chopped peeled fresh ginger
4 teaspoons chopped peeled fresh lemongrass
4 shallots, coarsely chopped
3 candlenuts or macadamia nuts
1 garlic clove, chopped
1 fresh red chile, chopped
½ teaspoon ground turmeric
½ teaspoon salt
2 pounds rib-eye steak, trimmed and cut into (¼ x 1–inch) strips
1 tablespoon canola oil
Cooking spray
Peanut dipping sauce or satay sauce

1. Place sugar and 2 tablespoons water in a small saucepan over low heat; cook 8 minutes or until sugar dissolves. Strain through a fine sieve over a bowl; discard solids. Cool completely. Combine tamarind paste with remaining 2 tablespoons water, stirring until smooth. Combine sugar mixture and tamarind mixture in a large zip-top plastic bag; seal. Set aside.
2. Heat a small skillet over medium-high heat. Add coriander, cumin, and fennel seeds; cook 2 minutes, shaking pan occasionally. Cool. Place mixture in a spice or coffee grinder, and process until finely ground. Place galangal, lemongrass, shallots, candlenuts, garlic, and red chile in a food processor; process until finely chopped.
3. Add galangal mixture, coriander mixture, turmeric, and salt to sugar mixture in bag; seal. Knead to combine. Add beef to bag, turning to coat; seal. Marinate in refrigerator 1 hour, turning twice. Add oil to bag, turning to coat; seal. Marinate in refrigerator overnight, turning occasionally.
4. Preheat grill to medium-high heat.
5. Remove beef from bag; discard marinade. Thread beef evenly onto each of 32 (8-inch) skewers. Place skewers on grill rack coated with cooking spray. Cook 1 minute on each side or until desired degree of doneness. Serve with peanut dipping sauce. Serves 8 (serving size: 4 skewers and about 2 tablespoons sauce)

CALORIES 339; FAT 22.8g (sat 6.4g, mono 9.3g, poly 3.5g); PROTEIN 25g; CARB 8.5g; FIBER 19g; CHOL 139mg; IRON 2.4mg; SODIUM 312mg; CALC 42mg

Thailand's Chiang Mai province is home to sai ua, the country's most popular grilled sausage. In the hands of Naomi Duguid, America's Southeast Asian food guru, the mixture of ground pork, lemongrass, cilantro, and kaffir lime makes a satisfying burger. She pan-fries the herb-flecked patties, but you could grill them. Serve with Thai Sticky Rice.

CHIANG MAI PORK PATTIES

HANDS-ON TIME: 15 MIN. TOTAL TIME: 25 MIN.

1¼ pounds ground pork
¾ teaspoon salt
½ cup coarsely chopped shallots
¼ cup finely chopped fresh cilantro
2 tablespoons minced peeled fresh lemongrass
2 tablespoons thinly sliced kaffir lime leaves or 1 tablespoon minced lime rind
1 tablespoon minced peeled fresh galangal or 2 teaspoons minced peeled fresh ginger
3 garlic cloves, minced
3 fresh Thai red bird chiles, minced
15 Bibb or Boston lettuce leaves
⅔ cup fresh cilantro leaves
⅔ cup fresh mint leaves
10 lime wedges

1. Combine pork and salt in a medium bowl; toss to combine.
2. Place shallots in a food processor; pulse until finely chopped. Add chopped cilantro and next 5 ingredients (through chiles); process until mixture is finely chopped. Add pork mixture; pulse 5 times or until mixture is well combined.
3. Using wet hands, shape mixture into 15 (1-inch-thick) patties (about 2 tablespoons per patty). Heat a large grill pan over high heat. Add half of pork patties. Cook 5 minutes on each side or until done. Repeat procedure with remaining patties. Arrange 3 lettuce leaves and 3 pork patties on each of 5 plates, and serve each serving with about ¼ cup herbs and 2 lime wedges. Serves 5

CALORIES 291; FAT 17.9g (sat 6.6g, mono 7.9g, poly 1.7g); PROTEIN 23.4g; CARB 8.8g; FIBER 1.4g; CHOL 80mg; IRON 2.2mg; SODIUM 424mg; CALC 50mg

THAI STICKY RICE

HANDS-ON TIME: 2 MIN. TOTAL TIME: 8 HR. 30 MIN.

2 cups uncooked long-grain sweet or glutinous rice

1. Place rice in a large bowl. Cover rice with cool water to 2 inches above rice; cover and let stand 8 hours or overnight. Drain rice.
2. Line a bamboo steamer with a double layer of cheesecloth; pour rice over cheesecloth. Cover with lid. Add water to a large skillet to a depth of 1 inch; bring to a boil. Place steamer in pan, making sure water doesn't touch rice; steam 25 minutes or until rice is shiny and cooked through. Serves 8 (serving size: ½ cup)

CALORIES 171; FAT 0.3g (sat 0.1g, mono 0.1g, poly 0.1g); PROTEIN 3.2g; CARB 37.8g; FIBER 1.3g; CHOL 0mg; IRON 0.7mg; SODIUM 3mg; CALC 5mg

Steven Raichlen traveled to 60 countries for his book Planet Barbecue! and discovered something thousands of miles from his Miami home: Asians love to grill. And they love to wrap grilled meat in lettuce leaves. Don't be scared off by all the ingredients here; most of them come together quickly to marinate the pork.

VIETNAMESE PORK TENDERLOIN

HANDS-ON TIME: 1 HR. TOTAL TIME: 1 HR. 23 MIN.

4 tablespoons sugar, divided
1 teaspoon black pepper
2 garlic cloves, peeled
1 shallot, halved
1 (4-inch) piece fresh lemongrass
1 (1-inch) piece peeled ginger
1 tablespoon lower-sodium soy sauce
2 1/2 tablespoons fish sauce, divided
1 tablespoon canola oil
1 (1-pound) pork tenderloin, trimmed and cut crosswise into 1/4-inch-thick slices
1/3 cup grated carrot
1/4 cup fresh lemon juice
1/4 cup rice vinegar
1 teaspoon minced fresh garlic
1 Thai or serrano chile, thinly sliced
2 ounces rice vermicelli
Cooking spray
16 Bibb lettuce leaves
1 cup fresh cilantro leaves
1 cup sliced English cucumber
1 cup fresh bean sprouts
1/3 cup finely chopped unsalted, dry-roasted peanuts
16 fresh basil leaves
16 fresh mint leaves
2 Thai or serrano chiles, thinly sliced

1. Place 2 tablespoons sugar and next 5 ingredients in a mini food processor; pulse until coarsely ground. With processor on, add soy sauce, 1 tablespoon fish sauce, and oil; process until blended. Combine mixture and pork in a zip-top plastic bag; seal and marinate in refrigerator 1 hour, turning occasionally.

2. Combine carrot and remaining 2 tablespoons sugar in a medium bowl; let stand 10 minutes. Add juice, vinegar, remaining 1½ tablespoons fish sauce, garlic, and 1 sliced chile; stir until sugar dissolves.

3. Cook noodles according to package directions, omitting salt and fat. Drain and rinse with cold water; drain well.

4. Preheat grill to high heat.

5. Remove pork from marinade; discard marinade. Thread pork evenly onto 6 (12-inch) skewers. Place skewers on grill rack coated with cooking spray; grill 2 minutes on each side or until lightly charred.

6. Top each lettuce leaf evenly with pork, noodles, and remaining ingredients. Serve with dipping sauce. Serves 4 (serving size: 4 wraps and 3 tablespoons sauce)

CALORIES 343; FAT 9.9g (sat 1.8g, mono 4.7g, poly 2.8g); PROTEIN 29.7g; CARB 36.1g; FIBER 3.3g; CHOL 74mg; IRON 2.8mg; SODIUM 620mg; CALC 53mg

Fish Sauce

"Fear not the fish sauce," says Andrea Nguyen, author of Into the Vietnamese Kitchen and her forthcoming Banh Mi Handbook. Even though it's made from salted, fermented fish (typically anchovies), "Fish sauce should never smell stinky," she notes, "It should have a clean aroma." It's the essential source of umami (savory flavor) in Southeast Asian cuisines, particularly those with long coastlines. Nguyen recommends tasting three or four brands, such as Three Crabs or Red Boat, to find your favorite. The best come from Vietnam and Thailand, preferably from the first pressing, sometimes labeled nuoc mam nhi. Look for a reddish hue. "Strictly amber-colored fish sauce may not be all that great," says Nguyen.

This fragrant curry took shape when medieval Muslim spice traders carried coriander, cumin, and other spices to Thailand. Most renditions include lemongrass and coconut milk for their signature flavor and aroma. Due to its Muslim origins, Masaman curry is usually made with beef, but duck, chicken, and tofu taste great, too.

MASAMAN CURRY

HANDS-ON TIME: 21 MIN. TOTAL TIME: 1 HR. 26 MIN.

1 teaspoon cumin seeds
1 teaspoon coriander seeds
½ teaspoon ground cinnamon
½ teaspoon ground nutmeg
3 large dried New Mexico chiles, halved lengthwise, seeded, and torn into large pieces
2 cardamom pods
2 tablespoons chopped peeled fresh lemongrass
1 tablespoon chopped peeled fresh ginger
3 garlic cloves, halved
1 (14-ounce) can lower-sodium beef broth, divided
2 teaspoons peanut oil
3 cups thinly vertically sliced onion
1 pound boneless sirloin steak, trimmed and cut into 1-inch cubes
1 cup water
1 tablespoon tamarind paste
³/₄ teaspoon salt
1 pound small white potatoes, halved
⅓ cup light coconut milk
Chopped fresh cilantro (optional)

1. Heat a large nonstick skillet over medium heat. Add first 6 ingredients; cook 2 minutes or until fragrant, stirring frequently. Remove from heat; cool 5 minutes. Place spice mixture in a food processor; add lemongrass, ginger, garlic, and ¼ cup broth. Process 1 minute, scraping sides occasionally; set aside.

2. Heat a Dutch oven over medium heat. Add oil to pan; swirl to coat. Add onion; cook 3 minutes or until tender, stirring occasionally. Stir in spice mixture; cook 1 minute, stirring constantly. Add beef, and cook 3 minutes, stirring frequently. Stir in remaining broth and 1 cup water, scraping pan to loosen browned bits. Stir in tamarind paste, salt, and potatoes; bring to a simmer. Cover, reduce heat, and simmer 1 hour or until beef is very tender. Remove from heat; stir in coconut milk. Sprinkle with cilantro, if desired. Serves 6 (serving size: about ¾ cup)

CALORIES 239; FAT 7.2g (sat 2.7g, mono 2.8g, poly 0.8g); PROTEIN 19.3g; CARB 23.5g; FIBER 3.1g; CHOL 49mg; IRON 2.8mg; SODIUM 347mg; CALC 45mg

On the streets of Cambodia's capital, aromas of grilled pork signal breakfast time. The dish usually comes with rice, pickles, and a bowl of warm chicken broth. You dip a bite of pork and rice into the broth, and then clean your palate with pickles. If the pickles aren't enough of a wake-up call, serve the dish with a bowl of chili sauce.

COCONUT-MARINATED PORK
with Rice (Bai Sach Chrouk)
HANDS-ON: 56 MIN. TOTAL: 24 HR. 56 MIN.

2 small pickling cucumbers, diagonally cut into 1/4-inch-thick slices

1 small carrot, diagonally cut into 1/8-inch-thick slices (about 1/2 cup)

2 ounces daikon or other radish, diagonally cut into 1/8-inch-thick slices

1 (1-inch) piece peeled fresh ginger, diagonally cut into 1/8-inch-thick slices

1 cup water

1/4 cup sugar

1 teaspoon salt

1/2 cup rice vinegar

1/4 cup light coconut milk

3 tablespoons lower-sodium soy sauce

1 tablespoon oyster sauce or hoisin sauce

1 tablespoon honey

1 tablespoon fresh lime juice

1/2 teaspoon five-spice powder

1/4 teaspoon freshly ground black pepper

3 garlic cloves, crushed

1 pound boneless pork shoulder (Boston butt), trimmed and cut crosswise into 1-inch-thick steaks

1 tablespoon peanut oil or canola oil

1 cup chopped green onion tops, divided

2 cups fat-free, lower-sodium chicken broth

2 cups hot cooked white rice

1. Combine first 4 ingredients in a shallow baking dish. Combine 1 cup water, sugar, and salt in a saucepan; bring to boil over high heat, and cook until sugar and salt dissolve, stirring occasionally. Remove from heat; stir in vinegar. Pour vinegar mixture over vegetables to cover; stir well. Cover and chill at least 24 hours or up to 48 hours, keeping vegetables submerged and stirring occasionally.

2. Combine coconut milk and next 7 ingredients (through garlic) in a large zip-top plastic bag. Add pork slices, massaging to coat; seal and marinate in refrigerator 8 hours or overnight.

3. Preheat grill to high heat.

4. Remove pork from bag, reserving marinade. Place pork slices on grill rack; grill 10 to 12 minutes on each side or until a thermometer registers 160° (slightly pink), basting occasionally with reserved marinade. Let stand 5 minutes.

5. Heat a small skillet over medium heat. Add oil to pan; swirl to coat. Add 3/4 cup onion; sauté 1 minute. Remove from heat.

6. Heat broth in small saucepan over medium heat. Pour broth into small dipping bowls; sprinkle evenly with remaining 1/4 cup onion. Cut pork steaks into thin slices. Serve pork over rice; drizzle with onion-oil mixture. Serve with pickles and broth. Serves 4 (serving size: 3 ounces pork, 1/2 cup rice, 2 1/4 teaspoons onion-oil mixture, and 1/2 cup broth)

CALORIES 434; FAT 15.2g (sat 4.5g, mono 6g, poly 2.1g); PROTEIN 25.9g; CARB 36g; FIBER 1.3g; CHOL 72mg; IRON 2.3mg; SODIUM 754mg; CALC 81mg

Similar to Chinese congee and Italian risotto, arroz caldo (rice soup) is Filipino comfort food—perfect for a rainy day. You slowly simmer chicken and rice until the rice breaks apart and gets creamy, and then flavor it with ginger, garlic, saffron, and fish sauce. Hard-cooked eggs go on top. For a shot of heat, dot the dish with Sriracha sauce.

RICE PORRIDGE
with Chicken and Eggs

HANDS-ON TIME: 55 MIN. TOTAL TIME: 1 HR. 13 MIN.

Broth and chicken:

4 cups fat-free, lower-sodium chicken broth

2 cups water

1 cup cilantro stems (from 1 bunch)

2 pounds bone-in chicken breast halves

1 (1½-ounce) piece peeled fresh ginger, cut into ¼-inch slices

3 (1½-inch) lime rind strips

1 small white onion, coarsely chopped

1 small carrot, coarsely chopped

2 garlic cloves, crushed

Porridge:

1 tablespoon dark sesame oil

1 medium white onion, vertically sliced

1 cup uncooked long-grain white rice

1½ tablespoons minced peeled fresh ginger

⅛ teaspoon crushed saffron threads

6 garlic cloves, minced

2 tablespoons cream sherry

1 tablespoon fish sauce

1 tablespoon distilled white vinegar

¾ cup fresh cilantro leaves

¾ cup sliced green onions

6 hard-cooked large eggs, each cut in half

1. To prepare broth and chicken, combine first 9 ingredients in a large Dutch oven. Bring to a boil. Reduce heat to low; simmer 20 to 25 minutes or until chicken is done, skimming off and discarding foam as needed. Strain broth through a sieve into a large bowl, reserving chicken and 5 cups broth (add additional water as needed to measure 5 cups). Discard remaining solids. Remove chicken from bones; shred meat. Discard skin and bones.

2. To prepare porridge, heat a large saucepan over medium heat. Add sesame oil to pan; swirl to coat. Add sliced white onion; cook 5 minutes or until tender, stirring occasionally. Add rice and next 3 ingredients (through minced garlic); cook 30 seconds, stirring constantly. Add reserved 5 cups broth and sherry; bring to a boil. Cover; reduce heat to medium-low, and simmer 30 to 35 minutes or until mixture thickens and rice begins to break down, stirring occasionally. (Mixture should be consistency of rice pudding.) Stir in shredded chicken, fish sauce, and vinegar; cook 2 minutes or until chicken is thoroughly heated. Spoon porridge into bowls; top with cilantro, green onions, and eggs. Serves 6 (serving size: about 1 cup porridge, 2 tablespoons cilantro, 2 tablespoons green onions, and 2 egg halves)

CALORIES 367; FAT 9.9g (sat 2.7g, mono 3.7g, poly 2.5g); PROTEIN 33.6g; CARB 33.5g; FIBER 2g; CHOL 246mg; IRON 3.4mg; SODIUM 672mg; CALC 81mg

Also known as lap and lahb, this minced-meat salad is the national dish of Laos. Some Lao and Thai versions include fish sauce and some favor mint over cilantro, but the core of the dish remains a chopped salad of lightly spiced pork, beef, chicken, or duck brightened with fresh herbs.

CHICKEN LARB

HANDS-ON TIME: 27 MIN. TOTAL TIME: 27 MIN.

2 tablespoons red curry paste
1 pound skinless, boneless chicken breast halves
1/2 teaspoon salt
1 tablespoon canola oil
1/3 cup chopped English cucumber
1/4 cup finely chopped shallots
3 tablespoons chopped fresh cilantro
2 tablespoons fresh lime juice
8 cabbage leaves
Thai chile paste (optional)

1. Place curry paste, chicken, and salt in a food processor; process until smooth. Heat a large skillet over medium-high heat. Add oil to pan; swirl to coat. Add chicken to pan; sauté 6 minutes or until done, stirring to crumble. Remove pan from heat; stir in cucumber and next 3 ingredients (through juice). Place 2 cabbage leaves on each of 4 plates; divide chicken mixture evenly among leaves. Serve with chile paste, if desired. Serves 4 (serving size: 2 filled cabbage leaves)

CALORIES 174; FAT 4.9g (sat 0.6g, mono 2.6g, poly 1.3g); PROTEIN 26.7g; CARB 4.1g; FIBER 0.3g; CHOL 66mg; IRON 1mg; SODIUM 507mg; CALC 29mg

Cucumber

Southeast Asian cucumbers tend to grow shorter and thicker than Western varieties. They're also slightly sweeter from cross-breeding with various Asian melons. But any cucumber will do. The recipes here call for small Kirby (pickling) cucumbers as well as longer English (hothouse) cucumbers. The latter often come wrapped in plastic in American supermarkets and tend to have fewer seeds and softer, less bitter-tasting skins. Both varieties bring crunch, freshness, and a burst of juicy liquid to everything from satay and salads to noodle bowls and bánh mì.

THE MIDDAY MEAL

*a*s a teenager, I traveled to Greece and Italy with my parents. It stuck with me that lunch was a leisurely family affair. It was so different from lunchtime in America, where people eat quickly, alone, or even skip the midday meal.

More travel taught me that lunch is the day's big meal in much of the world. "In Burma, the main meal is at noontime," concurs *Cooking Light* contributor Naomi Duguid. "That's when you'll find the best rice meal with a variety of grilled meats or seafood, and vegetables or salad."

What's the benefit of eating big at noon? It can give you more energy for the rest of the workday. Plus, recent research suggests that it may help you maintain a healthy weight. Studies at Vanderbilt University in Nashville indicate that we may metabolize food more efficiently during the day when we're active rather than at night when we're inclined to relax. To beat the midday slump, try eating a bigger lunch and a smaller dinner, and work in some exercise before nighttime.

In Spain and Mexico, adobo is a seasoning, but in the Philippines, it's an ancient method of stewing meat slowly in vinegar. Use coconut vinegar, if you can find it, or distilled white vinegar. Soy sauce and honey round out the stew's sweet-and-sour flavors. For a quick go-with, slice a few calamondin (calamansi), tangy tangerines native to the Philippines, or some navel orange.

ADOBO CHICKEN

HANDS-ON TIME: 24 MIN. TOTAL TIME: 56 MIN.

1 tablespoon canola oil

8 bone-in chicken thighs, skinned

2 cups chopped onion

5 garlic cloves, minced

6 tablespoons lower-sodium soy sauce

3 tablespoons water

3 tablespoons white vinegar

2 tablespoons honey

½ teaspoon black pepper

1 bay leaf

3 cups hot cooked long-grain rice

Fresh cilantro leaves

Freshly ground black pepper

1. Heat a large nonstick skillet over medium-high heat. Add oil to pan; swirl to coat. Add chicken; sauté 4 minutes on each side or until browned. Remove chicken from pan. Add onion to pan; sauté 3 minutes. Add garlic; sauté 1 minute.

2. Return chicken to pan. Add soy sauce and next 5 ingredients (through bay leaf); bring to a boil. Reduce heat to medium; cover and cook 12 minutes. Uncover and cook 20 minutes or until chicken is done and sauce thickens. Discard bay leaf.

3. Spoon rice into a serving bowl; top with cilantro, and sprinkle with pepper. Serve chicken mixture with rice. Serves 4 (serving size: 2 thighs, ¾ cup rice, and about 6 tablespoons sauce)

CALORIES 483; FAT 14.7g (sat 3.4g, mono 6.3g, poly 3.6g); PROTEIN 33.1g; CARB 53g; FIBER 2.2g; CHOL 99mg; IRON 3.8mg; SODIUM 888mg; CALC 55mg

I asked my Filipino friends for an authentic recipe for chicken inasal, which basically means, "chicken grilled." The variations are endless, but lemongrass, citrus, and annatto oil are standard for bright flavor and color. Don't skip the vinegar dipping sauce—tartness is a defining flavor of Filipino cuisine. After it's grilled, the chicken needs that acidic spark.

CHICKEN INASAL

HANDS-ON: 37 MIN. TOTAL: 2 HR. 37 MIN.

2 tablespoons canola oil
1½ teaspoons annatto seeds
⅔ cup chopped peeled fresh
   lemongrass
½ cup fresh orange juice
¼ cup fresh lemon juice
3 tablespoons cider vinegar
2 tablespoons lower-sodium
   soy sauce
1 tablespoon chopped peeled
   fresh ginger
1 teaspoon brown sugar
½ teaspoon salt
½ teaspoon black pepper
4 garlic cloves
4 chicken drumsticks
   (about 1¼ pounds), skinned
4 chicken thighs (about 1¼
   pounds), skinned
Cooking spray
2 tablespoons honey
1 tablespoon butter
½ cup cider vinegar
¼ cup finely chopped red onion
2 teaspoons sugar
½ teaspoon crushed red pepper
⅛ teaspoon salt
3 garlic cloves, chopped

1. Heat a small skillet over medium-high heat. Add oil to pan; swirl to coat. Stir in annatto seeds, and remove from heat. Let stand 15 minutes. Discard annatto seeds, reserving oil in pan.
2. Place lemongrass and next 9 ingredients (through garlic) in a blender; process until finely chopped. Pour mixture into large zip-top plastic bag; add annatto oil and chicken pieces. Seal bag, and marinate in refrigerator at least 2 hours or up to 8 hours.
3. Preheat grill to high. Remove chicken from bag; discard marinade. Place chicken on grill rack coated with cooking spray; grill 19 to 20 minutes, turning occasionally.
4. While chicken cooks, place a small skillet over medium-low heat; add honey and butter, and cook 5 minutes or until butter melts. Baste chicken with honey-butter mixture. Cook chicken 5 minutes or until done, turning and basting frequently with honey-butter mixture.
5. Combine cider vinegar and remaining ingredients in small bowl, stirring until sugar and salt dissolve. Serve chicken with sauce. Serves 4 (serving size: 1 chicken thigh, 1 chicken drumstick, and about 2½ tablespoons vinegar dipping sauce)

CALORIES 458; **FAT** 21.0g (sat 5.0g, mono 8.4g, poly 4.7g); **PROTEIN** 46.2g; **CARB** 18g; **FIBER** 0.4g; **CHOL** 189mg; **IRON** 3.2mg; **SODIUM** 531mg; **CALC** 47mg

Thailand's famous, ubiquitous, and endlessly adaptable stir-fried noodle dish is like a warm salad. For a vegetarian version, replace the fish sauce with soy sauce, leave out the dried shrimp, and double the amount of tofu instead of using chicken. In that case, consider adding mushrooms for more umami (savory) flavor.

CLASSIC PAD THAI

HANDS-ON TIME: 35 MIN. TOTAL TIME: 35 MIN.

6 ounces uncooked flat rice noodles (pad Thai noodles)
1/4 cup rice vinegar
1 tablespoon plus 1 teaspoon sugar, divided
2 tablespoons very thinly sliced banana pepper
3 ounces extra-firm tofu, cut into thin strips
1 tablespoon fresh lime juice
1 tablespoon water
1 tablespoon lower-sodium soy sauce
1 tablespoon fish sauce
2 large eggs, lightly beaten
1/8 teaspoon salt
3 tablespoons peanut oil, divided
3 garlic cloves, minced
1 (2-ounce) skinless, boneless chicken thigh, cut into thin strips
4 cups fresh bean sprouts, divided
3 green onions, trimmed, crushed with flat side of a knife, and cut into 1½-inch pieces
1 tablespoon small dried shrimp
1/4 cup unsalted, dry-roasted peanuts, chopped
1/4 cup fresh cilantro leaves

1. Prepare noodles according to package directions; drain.
2. Combine vinegar and 1 tablespoon sugar, stirring until sugar dissolves. Add banana pepper; set aside.
3. Place tofu on several layers of heavy-duty paper towels; cover with additional paper towels. Let stand 20 minutes, pressing down occasionally.
4. Combine remaining 1 teaspoon sugar, lime juice, and next 3 ingredients (through fish sauce). Combine eggs and salt, stirring well.
5. Heat a large wok over high heat. Add 1½ tablespoons oil; swirl to coat. Add garlic; stir-fry 15 seconds. Add chicken; stir-fry 2 minutes or until browned. Add pressed tofu; cook 1 minute on each side or until browned. Pour in egg mixture; cook 45 seconds or until egg begins to set around chicken and tofu. Remove from pan; cut into large pieces.
6. Add remaining 1½ tablespoons oil to wok; swirl to coat. Add 2 cups bean sprouts, green onions, and dried shrimp; stir-fry 1 minute. Add noodles and soy sauce mixture; stir-fry 2 minutes, tossing until noodles are lightly browned. Add reserved egg mixture; toss to combine. Arrange remaining 2 cups bean sprouts on a platter; top with noodle mixture. Sprinkle with peanuts and cilantro. Serve with vinegar mixture. Serves 4 (serving size: 1½ cups noodle mixture and 1½ tablespoons vinegar sauce)

CALORIES 432; FAT 19.1g (sat 3.6g, mono 8.3g, poly 6.1g); PROTEIN 14.3g; CARB 52.7g; FIBER 3.6g; CHOL 110mg; IRON 3.3mg; SODIUM 640mg; CALC 80mg

Dried Shrimp

Also known as *kung haeng* (Thailand), *bazun-chauk* (Burma), and *ebi* (Indonesia), sun-dried small shrimp provide a layer of umami (savory) flavor in Southeast Asian cooking. They're often tossed into simmering dishes to rehydrate the shrimp and release the flavors, but sometimes the dried shrimp are just added whole. They can even be ground to a powder and sprinkled like salt as a seasoning. Don't confuse dried shrimp with shrimp paste, a more pungent fermented paste known as *kapi* (Thailand), *terasi* (Indonesia), and *belacan* (Malaysia).

Kecap manis (KEH-chup MAH-nees) is the flavor key to this classic noodle bowl. It's Indonesia's version of ketchup, like a sweet soy sauce but as thick as molasses. If you can't find it, make a homemade version by mixing 1 part molasses, 2 parts brown sugar, and 3 parts soy sauce with crushed garlic and ground star anise. Heat the mixture until the sugar dissolves.

INDONESIAN STIR-FRIED NOODLES
(Bakmi Goreng)

HANDS-ON TIME: 28 MIN. TOTAL TIME: 35 MIN.

3 tablespoons peanut oil, divided
2 large eggs, lightly beaten
6 ounces dried Chinese egg noodles or spaghetti
6 ounces skinless, boneless chicken breast, thinly sliced
4 ounces boneless pork loin chop, sliced
2 garlic cloves, minced
2 cups thinly sliced napa cabbage
3/4 cup sliced green onions
1 celery stalk, thinly sliced
3 tablespoons fat-free, lower-sodium chicken broth
1 tablespoon kecap manis (sweet soy sauce)
1 tablespoon lower-sodium soy sauce
1/2 cup packaged fried onions

1. Heat a large nonstick skillet over medium-high heat. Add 1 tablespoon oil; swirl to coat. Pour eggs into pan; swirl to form a thin omelet. Cook 1 minute or until cooked on bottom. Carefully turn omelet over; cook 30 seconds. Remove from pan. Roll up omelet; cut roll crosswise into thin strips. Keep warm.

2. Cook noodles according to package directions. Drain and rinse with cold water; drain and set aside.

3. Heat a wok over high heat. Add remaining 2 tablespoons oil to pan; swirl to coat. Add chicken, pork, and garlic; stir-fry 1½ minutes. Add cabbage, green onions, and celery; stir-fry 1 minute. Stir in broth, kecap manis, and soy sauce. Add noodles; stir-fry 3 minutes or until thoroughly heated and noodles begin to lightly brown. Add egg; toss gently. Top with fried onions. Serve immediately. Serves 4 (serving size: 1½ cups)

CALORIES 419; FAT 20.6g (sat 4.7g, mono 9.2g, poly 4.4g); PROTEIN 23.8g; CARB 33g; FIBER 2.3g; CHOL 147mg; IRON 2.7mg; SODIUM 543mg; CALC 86mg

"We're scrappy, clever cooks," says Vietnamese cookbook author Andrea Nguyen. The proof is in this complete meal that stretches the main protein (shrimp) with lettuce, cucumbers, herbs, and nuts. The bold taste comes from nuoc cham, Vietnam's go-to sauce for dipping and drizzling sweet, sour, salty, hot, and savory flavor all at once.

VIETNAMESE SHRIMP NOODLE BOWL *(Bun Tom Xao)*

HANDS-ON TIME: 45 MIN. TOTAL TIME: 45 MIN.

5 ounces uncooked rice vermicelli noodles
½ cup lukewarm water
3 tablespoons granulated sugar
¼ cup fresh lime juice
1 tablespoon rice vinegar
5 teaspoons fish sauce (such as Three Crabs)
2 serrano chiles, thinly sliced
4 cups (¼-inch) slices green leaf lettuce
3 cups diagonally cut slices seeded Kirby (pickling) cucumber (about 2)
¼ cup fresh cilantro leaves
¼ cup torn fresh Thai basil leaves
¼ cup torn fresh mint leaves
2 teaspoons cornstarch
1 teaspoon dark brown sugar
¼ teaspoon salt
¾ teaspoon white pepper
1 pound large shrimp, peeled and deveined
2 tablespoons canola oil, divided
⅓ cup (¼-inch) slices green onions
3 garlic cloves, finely chopped
½ cup unsalted, dry-roasted peanuts, coarsely chopped

1. Cook noodles according to package directions. Drain and rinse with cold water; drain.

2. Combine ½ cup lukewarm water and granulated sugar in a medium bowl, stirring until sugar dissolves. Add lime juice, vinegar, fish sauce, and chiles; set aside. Combine lettuce, cucumber, and herbs; set aside.

3. Combine cornstarch, brown sugar, salt, and pepper in a large bowl; stir until well combined. Add shrimp; toss to coat. Heat a wok or large skillet over high heat. Add 1½ teaspoons oil to pan; swirl to coat. Add half of shrimp; cook 1½ minutes on each side or until shrimp are seared. Remove from pan. Add 1½ teaspoons oil to wok; swirl to coat. Repeat procedure with remaining shrimp. Reduce heat to medium-high. Add remaining 1 table-spoon oil to wok; swirl to coat. Add onions and garlic; stir-fry 30 seconds. Return shrimp to pan; stir-fry 1 minute.

4. Arrange about 1 cup lettuce mixture in each of 4 large bowls, and top each serving with about 1 cup noodles and 2 tablespoons chopped peanuts. Divide the shrimp evenly among servings, and serve each with ¼ cup sauce. Serves 4

CALORIES 462; FAT 17.6g (sat 1.9g, mono 9g, poly 5.1g); PROTEIN 24.6g; CARB 52.9g; FIBER 4.4g; CHOL 143mg; IRON 3.2mg; SODIUM 802mg; CALC 146mg

Along with satay, this hodge-podge salad ranks as the national dish of Indonesia. The vegetarian version here gets extra protein from hard-cooked eggs and stir-fried tofu. It also uses shortcut ingredients like peanut butter and curry paste. For a spicier dressing, stir in sambal oelek or Sriracha sauce.

INDONESIAN VEGETABLE SALAD
with Peanut Dressing (Shortcut Gado Gado)
HANDS-ON TIME: 56 MIN. TOTAL TIME: 68 MIN.

4 large eggs
1½ cups julienne-cut carrot
1½ cups green beans, trimmed
1½ cups fresh bean sprouts
1 red bell pepper, seeded and cut into thin strips
½ English cucumber, halved lengthwise and cut crosswise into ¼-inch-thick slices (about 2 cups)
1 (14-ounce) package water-packed extra-firm tofu, drained
1 tablespoon cornstarch
2 teaspoons red curry powder or Madras curry powder
¼ teaspoon salt
2 tablespoons canola oil
⅓ cup creamy peanut butter
3 tablespoons hot water
3 tablespoons fresh lime juice
1 tablespoon lower-sodium soy sauce
2 teaspoons brown sugar
2 teaspoons Thai red curry paste
¼ teaspoon salt

1. Place eggs in a large saucepan; cover with water. Bring to a rolling boil; cover, remove from heat, and let stand 12 minutes. Remove eggs from pan with a slotted spoon; rinse with cold water. Peel eggs; cut in half.
2. Return water to a boil. Add carrot, and cook 1 minute. Remove carrot with a slotted spoon; drain and rinse with cold water. Drain and place in a bowl. Add green beans to boiling water, and cook 4 minutes or until crisp-tender. Remove green beans with a slotted spoon; drain and rinse with cold water. Drain and place in a separate bowl. Arrange 2 egg halves, about ⅓ cup carrot, ⅓ cup green beans, ⅓ cup bean sprouts, ¼ cup red bell pepper, and ½ cup cucumber on each of 4 plates.
3. Cut tofu lengthwise into 4 (½-inch-thick) slices. Place tofu slices on several layers of paper towels. Cover tofu with additional paper towels; let stand 5 minutes. Cut each tofu slice crosswise into ½-inch-thick strips. Combine cornstarch, curry powder, and ¼ teaspoon salt; gently toss with tofu to coat.
4. Heat a large nonstick skillet over medium-high heat. Add oil to pan; swirl to coat. Add tofu to pan; cook 10 minutes or until crisp and browned, turning to brown on all sides. Divide tofu evenly among plates.
5. Combine peanut butter and next 6 ingredients in a bowl; stir with a whisk until smooth. Serve each salad with about 3 tablespoons dressing. Serves 4

CALORIES 449; FAT 29.1g (sat 5.6g; mono 12.7g, poly 9.3g); PROTEIN 24.3g; CARB 27.1g; FIBER 5.9g; CHOL 212mg; IRON 4.1mg; SODIUM 645mg; CALC 158mg

Peanuts

A favorite nut in the Americas, peanuts arrived in Asia by way of Spanish traders traveling from Mexico. Indonesian cooks ground the nuts into a dipping sauce for skewered grilled meat (satay) and for dressing salads like *gado gado*. Chopped peanuts made their way into other Southeast Asian dishes, such as Thailand's pad Thai and Vietnam's *goi mit* (jackfruit salad).

French colonists made baguettes, pâté, mayonnaise, and beef bones permanent fixtures in Vietnam's culinary landscape. Vietnamese cooks turned the beef bones into pho and the baguettes into bánh mì, a sandwich that's typically spread with mayo and pâté, and then filled with pork and vegetables like cucumbers and carrots.

LEMONGRASS TOFU BÁNH MÌ

HANDS-ON TIME: 26 MIN. TOTAL TIME: 1 HR. 26 MIN.

1/4 cup rice vinegar
1/4 cup water
1 tablespoon sugar
1/4 teaspoon salt
1 1/4 cups matchstick-cut carrot
1 1/4 cups matchstick-cut peeled daikon radish
1 1/2 tablespoons chopped fresh cilantro
1 (14-ounce) package water-packed extra-firm tofu, drained
2 tablespoons finely chopped peeled fresh lemongrass
2 tablespoons water
1 tablespoon lower-sodium soy sauce
2 teaspoons sesame oil, divided
3 tablespoons canola mayonnaise
1 1/2 teaspoons Sriracha
1 (12-ounce) French bread baguette, halved lengthwise and toasted
Cooking spray
1 cup thinly sliced English cucumber

1. Combine first 4 ingredients (through salt) in a medium bowl, stirring until sugar and salt dissolve. Add carrot and radish; toss well. Let stand 30 minutes, stirring occasionally. Drain; stir in cilantro.

2. Cut tofu crosswise into 6 (⅔-inch-thick) slices. Arrange tofu on several layers of paper towels. Cover with additional paper towels; top with a cast-iron skillet or other heavy pan. Let stand 15 minutes. Remove tofu from paper towels.

3. Combine lemongrass, 2 tablespoons water, soy sauce, and 1 teaspoon sesame oil in a 13 x 9–inch glass or ceramic baking dish. Arrange tofu slices in a single layer in soy mixture, turning to coat. Let stand 15 minutes.

4. Combine remaining 1 teaspoon sesame oil, mayonnaise, and Sriracha in a small bowl, stirring with a whisk. Spread mayonnaise mixture evenly on cut sides of bread.

5. Heat a large nonstick skillet over medium-high heat. Coat pan with cooking spray. Remove tofu from marinade, and discard marinade. Pat tofu slices dry with paper towels. Add tofu slices to pan, and cook 4 minutes on each side or until crisp and golden. Arrange tofu slices on bottom half of bread; top tofu slices with carrot mixture and cucumber slices. Cut loaf crosswise into 6 equal pieces. Serves 6 (serving size: 1 sandwich)

CALORIES 297; **FAT** 12g (sat 1.1g, mono 4.3g, poly 4g); **PROTEIN** 12g; **CARB** 34.9g; **FIBER** 3.1g; **CHOL** 3mg; **IRON** 2.8mg; **SODIUM** 499mg; **CALC** 91mg

PERSONALIZE YOUR PLATE

When I was young, my mother's best friend was a Vietnamese woman named Hanh. The first time I ate with her, small bowls were set out on the table. Some held pickled vegetables, others grilled meat, lettuce, and kimchi. I was puzzled; I didn't know how to eat Vietnamese. Hanh said, "You just take what looks good to you."

"There are no hard and fast rules," says Andrea Nguyen, author of *Into the Vietnamese Kitchen.* "It's a highly personalized cuisine. The chiles may be on the table, but it's OK if you don't want them." The point is to make each dish your own by adding flavor with a variety of condiments. And recent studies suggest that personalizing your plate may be more satisfying. Researchers at Harvard University found that rituals that engage us with our food ultimately enhance our enjoyment of consuming the food itself.

For the most complex flavor, look to the basic tastes. Include something sweet (fruit), salty (lean bacon), sour (citrus), bitter (cabbage), and umami—the fifth savory taste that comes from foods like soy sauce and mushrooms. A little bit of each flavor in every bite will send your taste buds soaring.

In this simplified tom kha gai, coconut milk tames the heat of the Thai chile paste and gives the soup a velvety texture. Lao versions of this dish replace the cilantro with a type of dill that grows in Laos.

CHICKEN COCONUT SOUP
(Tom Kha Gai)
HANDS-ON TIME: 25 MIN. TOTAL TIME: 32 MIN.

2 teaspoons canola oil
1 cup sliced mushrooms
½ cup chopped red bell pepper
4 teaspoons minced peeled fresh ginger
4 garlic cloves, minced
1 (3-inch) stalk lemongrass, halved lengthwise
2 teaspoons sambal oelek (ground fresh chile paste)
3 cups Chicken Stock or fat-free, lower-sodium chicken broth
1¼ cups light coconut milk
4 teaspoons fish sauce
1 tablespoon sugar
2 cups shredded cooked chicken breast (about 8 ounces)
½ cup green onion strips
3 tablespoons chopped fresh cilantro
2 tablespoons fresh lime juice

1. Heat a Dutch oven over medium heat. Add oil to pan; swirl to coat. Add mushrooms and next 4 ingredients (through lemongrass); cook 3 minutes, stirring occasionally. Add sambal oelek; cook 1 minute. Add Chicken Stock, coconut milk, fish sauce, and sugar; bring to a simmer. Reduce heat to low; simmer 10 minutes. Add chicken to pan; cook 1 minute or until thoroughly heated. Discard lemongrass. Top with onions, cilantro, and juice. Serves 4 (serving size: about 1⅓ cups)

CALORIES 224; FAT 9g (sat 4.5g, mono 2.4g, poly 1.3g); PROTEIN 22.7g; CARB 15g; FIBER 1g; CHOL 58mg; IRON 1.1mg; SODIUM 463mg; CALC 35mg

CHICKEN STOCK
HANDS-ON TIME: 30 MIN. TOTAL TIME: 12 HR.

4 pounds chicken backs, necks, or wings
2 carrots, chopped
2 celery stalks, chopped
2 onions, chopped
8 black peppercorns
6 fresh parsley sprigs
5 fresh thyme sprigs
2 bay leaves
3 quarts cold water

1. Preheat oven to 425°.
2. Roast chicken pieces, carrot, celery, and onion on a jelly-roll pan 35 minutes, stirring once. Scrape pan contents into a large stockpot. Add remaining ingredients, and bring to a boil. Reduce heat, and simmer 4 hours, skimming and discarding foam. Strain through a sieve over a large bowl; discard solids. Cool stock to room temperature. Cover and refrigerate 6 hours or overnight. Skim fat from surface; discard fat. Serves 10 (serving size: 1 cup)

CALORIES 28; FAT 1.1g (sat 0.3g, mono 0.3g, poly 0.3g); PROTEIN 3.6g; CARB 0.7g; FIBER 0.1g; CHOL 15mg; IRON 0.2mg; SODIUM 23mg; CALC 12mg

Barbara Kafka, recipient of the James Beard Foundation's Lifetime Achievement Award, gets authentic Thai flavors in this soup with galangal, kaffir lime leaves, lemongrass, and fish sauce. If you can't find the galangal and kaffir lime, substitute ⅓ cup ginger for the galangal and 3 (2-inch) lime rind strips for the kaffir lime leaves.

THAI SHRIMP SOUP
(Tom Yum Goong)
HANDS-ON TIME: 25 MIN. TOTAL TIME: 1 HR. 25 MIN.

1½ pounds medium shrimp
9½ cups water, divided
½ cup chopped peeled fresh galangal (about 2 ounces)
½ cup (2-inch) pieces peeled fresh lemongrass (about 4 stalks)
6 fresh or frozen kaffir lime leaves
½ cup canned straw mushrooms, quartered
2 tablespoons roasted red chile paste
1 tablespoon fish sauce
2 Thai chiles
½ cup chopped green onions
½ cup chopped fresh cilantro
2 cups uncooked rice noodles (about 4 ounces)
1 tablespoon fresh lime juice
6 tablespoons chopped dry-roasted unsalted peanuts
4 lime wedges

1. Peel and devein shrimp, reserving shells. Combine shrimp shells and 6 cups water in a Dutch oven; bring to a simmer. Cook 1 hour. Strain broth through a sieve into a bowl; discard solids.
2. Combine broth and remaining 3½ cups water in a large saucepan; bring to a boil. Add galangal, lemongrass, and kaffir lime leaves to pan; simmer 10 minutes. Strain broth mixture through a sieve into a bowl; discard solids. Return broth mixture to pan. Add mushrooms, chili paste, fish sauce, and chiles; bring to a boil. Stir in shrimp, green onions, and cilantro; cook 3 minutes or until shrimp are done. Discard chiles. Stir in rice noodles and fresh lime juice. Ladle 2 cups soup into each of 4 bowls; top each serving with 1½ tablespoons peanuts. Serve with lime wedges. Serves 6

CALORIES 188; FAT 6.7g (sat 1g, mono 2.5g, poly 2.3g); PROTEIN 26.1g; CARB 5.8g; FIBER 1.7g; CHOL 173mg; IRON 3.5mg; SODIUM 664mg; CALC 77mg

A rich broth forms the backbone of Vietnam's most famous noodle soup. This version gives you a good excuse to use up those Thanksgiving leftovers. Just follow the Chicken Stock recipe on page 102 and replace the chicken with turkey. Roasting vegetables along with the turkey carcass deepens the flavor of the stock.

TURKEY PHO

HANDS-ON TIME: 29 MIN. TOTAL TIME: 66 MIN.

8 cups Chicken Stock (page 102) or unsalted chicken stock
3 tablespoons fish sauce
2 teaspoons brown sugar
6 whole cloves
4 star anise
1 (3-inch) cinnamon stick, broken
1 (3-inch) piece peeled fresh ginger, halved
4 ounces uncooked wide rice stick noodles (banh pho)
Cooking spray
1 medium onion, peeled and halved
3 cups shredded cooked dark-meat turkey
2 cups fresh bean sprouts
1/3 cup thinly sliced green onions (about 2)
1/4 cup thinly sliced fresh Thai basil
1/4 cup chopped fresh cilantro
1/4 teaspoon salt
1/2 cup fresh cilantro sprigs
1/2 cup fresh mint sprigs
6 lime wedges
1 jalapeño pepper, seeded and thinly sliced
Hoisin sauce (optional)
Sriracha (hot chile sauce; optional)

1. Combine first 7 ingredients in a large stockpot over medium-high heat; bring to a boil. Reduce heat, and simmer 30 minutes. Strain broth through a sieve into a large bowl; discard solids. Return broth to pan; keep warm.
2. Cook noodles according to package directions, omitting salt and fat.
3. Heat a grill pan over medium-high heat. Coat pan with cooking spray. Add onion; cook 8 minutes or until charred on each side. Remove from heat; cool slightly. Slice onion thinly; add to broth.
4. Add turkey and next 5 ingredients (through salt) to pan; bring to a boil. Cook 2 minutes or until thoroughly heated. Place about 1/2 cup noodles in each of 6 bowls. Ladle about 1 1/3 cups broth mixture over each serving. Serve with cilantro, mint, lime wedges, and jalapeño. Serve with hoisin and Sriracha, if desired. Serves 8

CALORIES 187; FAT 4.3g (sat 1.4g, mono 0.1g, poly 1.3g); PROTEIN 18.4g; CARB 18.3g; FIBER 1.9g; CHOL 49mg; IRON 2.6mg; SODIUM 679mg; CALC 62mg

Probably the most well-known Malaysian dish, rendang is a curried stew that cooks down to concentrate the flavors. You'll know it's done when the pan goes nearly dry. That's what distinguishes a rendang dish from a saucy curry, according to Corinne Trang, author of Authentic Vietnamese Cooking.

TEMPEH RENDANG

HANDS-ON TIME: 24 MIN. TOTAL TIME: 44 MIN.

6 red Thai chiles
Cooking spray
1 cup minced shallots (about 6)
1½ tablespoons grated peeled fresh galangal
1 tablespoon grated peeled fresh ginger
1 tablespoon finely chopped peeled fresh lemongrass (about 1 stalk)
¼ teaspoon ground turmeric
1 cup light coconut milk
½ cup water
⅓ cup shredded unsweetened coconut, toasted and divided
1 teaspoon kosher salt
2 kaffir lime leaves
1½ pounds tempeh, cut into ½-inch cubes
2 tablespoons chopped fresh cilantro

1. Seed 5 chiles; leave seeds in 1 chile. Thinly slice chiles.
2. Heat a large nonstick skillet over medium heat. Coat pan with cooking spray. Add chiles, shallots, and next 4 ingredients (through turmeric) to pan; cook 5 minutes or until fragrant, stirring frequently. Add coconut milk, ½ cup water, 3 tablespoons coconut, salt, lime leaves, and tempeh to pan. Cover, reduce heat, and simmer 20 minutes or until sauce thickens. Discard lime leaves. Sprinkle with remaining coconut and cilantro. Serves 6 (serving size: 1 cup tempeh, 1 teaspoon coconut, and 1 teaspoon cilantro)

CALORIES 353, FAT 13.9g (sat 5.8g, mono 3.1g, poly 2.2g), PROTEIN 28.4g, CARB 36.5g, FIBER 10.7g, CHOL 0mg, IRON 4.8mg, SODIUM 332mg, CALC 47mg

The Shan people of Myanmar and cooks in northern Thailand use the oop method of cooking—slowly simmering ingredients under a tight lid with a minimum of water and oil. Here, cabbage (galaam) and tomato release enough water to create a sauce yet not so much as to dilute the rich taste of the beef.

SIMMERED CABBAGE
with Beef, Shan Style (Galaam Oop)
HANDS-ON TIME: 32 MIN. TOTAL TIME: 32 MIN.

2 tablespoons peanut oil
1 cup thinly vertically sliced shallots
1 teaspoon salt
1 teaspoon turmeric
½ teaspoon ground red pepper
¼ pound ground sirloin
4 cups finely shredded cabbage (about 1 small head)
1 cup thin plum tomato wedges (about 2 medium)
⅓ cup coarsely chopped unsalted, dry-roasted peanuts
Fresh cilantro leaves

1. Heat a wok or Dutch oven over medium heat. Add peanut oil to pan, and swirl to coat. Add shallots, salt, turmeric, and red pepper; cook 3 minutes or until shallots are tender, stirring frequently. Add beef; cook 2 minutes or until beef begins to brown. Add cabbage and tomato; toss well to combine. Reduce heat to medium-low; cover and cook 10 minutes or until cabbage wilts. Stir in peanuts; cover and cook 10 minutes or until cabbage is tender. Serve with cilantro leaves. Serves 4 (serving size: 1 cup)

CALORIES 238; FAT 15.9g (sat 3.2g, mono 7.4g, poly 4.3g); PROTEIN 10.9g; CARB 15.7g; FIBER 3.4g; CHOL 180mg; IRON 2.1mg; SODIUM 629mg; CALC 59mg

Turmeric

In the ginger family, turmeric is a rhizome (underground stem) that's sometimes used fresh but most often boiled, dried, and ground to a powder. It's valued as much for its brilliant golden color as its earthy, astringent flavor. Turmeric may be used to dye fabrics, brighten prepared mustards, or lend yellow color to cheese. But cooks typically use turmeric powder for bright color and deep flavor in Indian and Nepalese curries, Vietnamese stir-fries, and Burmese hot pots.

In Burma, depending on where you go, this soup may include galangal or ginger and tamarind or lime juice. My version combines what I like best about the southern Rangoon mohinga and the Rakhine mohinga on the coast.

MOHINGA

HANDS-ON TIME: 1 HR. 30 MIN. TOTAL TIME: 1 HR. 35 MIN.

3 tablespoons peanut or canola oil, divided

1 teaspoon sugar

12 small shallots, thinly sliced lengthwise (about 2½ cups)

6 garlic cloves, peeled and divided

4 lemongrass stalks, trimmed and divided

4¾ cups water, divided

1½ teaspoons ground turmeric, divided

1½ teaspoons anchovy paste

4 (½-inch) slices peeled fresh ginger, divided

2 pounds farm-raised catfish fillets

1 teaspoon crushed red pepper

10 small shallots, halved and divided

¼ cup garbanzo bean flour

1½ tablespoons fish sauce

1 teaspoon Hungarian sweet paprika

5 ounces uncooked rice noodles

6 tablespoons chopped fresh cilantro

4 green onion tops, chopped

1 lime, cut into 6 wedges

1. Heat a large skillet over medium heat. Add 2 tablespoons oil; swirl to coat. Sprinkle sugar over oil; cook 1 minute or until sugar melts. Add shallots, stirring to coat. Cook 15 minutes or until golden brown, stirring frequently. Set caramelized shallots aside.

2. Crush 3 garlic cloves. Cut 2 lemongrass stalks in half lengthwise. Combine crushed garlic, halved lemongrass stalks, 4 cups water, 1 teaspoon turmeric, anchovy paste, and 2 ginger slices in a large Dutch oven. Add fish; bring to boil over high heat. Cover, reduce heat, and simmer 10 minutes or until fish flakes when tested with a fork. Remove fish from pan. Strain broth through a sieve into a large bowl, reserving 4 cups stock, discarding solids.

3. Coarsely chop white portion of remaining 2 lemongrass stalks; reserve green portion for another use. Place chopped lemongrass, remaining 3 garlic cloves, remaining 2 ginger slices, crushed red pepper, and 7 shallots in a food processor; process until a coarse paste forms.

4. Place garbanzo bean flour in skillet; cook over medium heat 2 minutes or until fragrant and slightly darker in color, stirring constantly with a whisk. Pour flour into a small bowl; set aside.

5. Add 1 tablespoon oil to Dutch oven; swirl to coat. Add shallot paste, and cook 2 minutes or until fragrant, stirring occasionally. Return fish to pan; cook 3 minutes, stirring gently to coat with paste. Remove fish mixture from pan; set aside.

6. Add remaining ½ teaspoon turmeric, reserved fish stock, fish sauce, and paprika to pan; bring to a boil. Gradually add remaining ¾ cup water to garbanzo bean flour, stirring with a whisk until smooth. Gradually add flour mixture to boiling stock mixture, stirring constantly with a whisk. Return to a boil. Reduce heat, and simmer 12 minutes or until slightly thick, stirring occasionally. Add remaining 3 halved shallots; simmer 10 minutes or until shallots are tender. Add fish mixture; simmer just until hot.

7. Cook noodles in boiling water 2 minutes or until tender; drain. Spoon ½ cup noodles into each of 6 bowls. Ladle 1⅓ cups soup into each bowl, ensuring each serving gets a shallot half. Top each serving with 2 tablespoons caramelized shallots, 1 tablespoon cilantro, and about 1 tablespoon green onions. Serve with lime wedges. Serves 6

CALORIES 448; FAT 16.9g (sat 3.3g, mono 7.4g, poly 4.3g); PROTEIN 28g; CARB 47g; FIBER 1.5g; CHOL 84mg; IRON 3.1mg; SODIUM 537mg; CALC 97mg

You'd find these lime iced cakes at every Australian bake sale. Some versions include a swath of berry jam in the center. Some coat the icing with fresh shaved coconut. To keep the calories down, I skip the jam and use shredded dried coconut and a slimmed-down cake based on a sponge from Flo Braker (she used it to make her famous jelly rolls).

LAMINGTONS

HANDS-ON TIME: 50 MIN. TOTAL TIME: 3 HR. 25 MIN.

Cooking spray
4 large egg whites
³/₄ cup granulated sugar, divided
4 large egg yolks
2 teaspoons vanilla extract
4 ounces cake flour (about 1 cup)
½ teaspoon baking powder
⅛ teaspoon salt
⅔ cup 2% reduced-fat milk
2½ ounces bittersweet or semisweet chocolate, chopped
3¾ cups powdered sugar
⅓ cup unsweetened cocoa
2 cups reduced-fat unsweetened finely shredded dehydrated coconut

1. Preheat oven to 350°. Coat a 9-inch square metal baking pan with cooking spray; line bottom of pan with parchment paper, allowing parchment paper to extend over edge of pan.
2. Beat egg whites with a mixer at high speed until foamy. Gradually add 6 tablespoons granulated sugar, 1 tablespoon at a time, beating until stiff peaks form.
3. Place egg yolks and remaining 6 tablespoons granulated sugar in a medium bowl; beat with a mixer at medium-high speed until thick and pale (about 3 minutes). Beat in vanilla. Gently fold egg yolk mixture into egg white mixture.
4. Weigh or lightly spoon flour into a dry measuring cup; level with a knife. Combine flour, baking powder, and salt; sift mixture over egg mixture, ⅓ cup at a time; fold in. Spoon batter into prepared pan, spreading evenly. Bake at 350° for 15 to 20 minutes or until cake springs back when lightly touched. Cool in pan 5 minutes on a wire rack; remove cake from pan, using parchment paper sides as handles. Cool completely on a wire rack (with parchment paper in place). Wrap cake and parchment paper in plastic wrap; chill 2 hours.
5. Remove plastic wrap from cake; place cake (with parchment paper in place) on a cutting board. Cut cake into 16 squares, using a serrated knife.
6. Combine milk and chopped chocolate in a small saucepan; cook over medium heat 2 minutes or until chocolate melts. Remove from heat; stir with a whisk until smooth. Add powdered sugar and cocoa, stirring with a whisk until smooth.
7. Place coconut in a medium bowl. Dip cake squares, 1 at a time, into melted chocolate mixture, using 2 forks to gently turn the cake to coat; scrape off excess chocolate on side of pan. Place chocolate-coated cake in coconut, using 2 forks to gently turn the cake to coat. Place lamingtons on wire rack; let stand 15 minutes or until chocolate is set. Serves 16 (serving size: 1 cake)

CALORIES 263; FAT 6.7g (sat 4.3g, mono 0.6g, poly 0.2g); PROTEIN 3.7g; CARB 49.1g; FIBER 1.8g; CHOL 47mg; IRON 1.1mg; SODIUM 55mg; CALC 32mg

The Middle East & Africa

TAHINI:
A paste of ground sesame seeds that adds a creamy texture and slightly bitter, nutty flavor; higher-quality brands tend to come from Lebanon.

DATES:
Sugar-rich drupe fruits cultivated in North Africa and the Middle East for more than 5,000 years; most often dried to concentrate flavor.

CHICKPEAS:
Native Middle Eastern legume used fresh, pureed, or dried and ground into chickpea (garbanzo bean) flour.

POMEGRANATE MOLASSES:
Thick, deep purple, sweet-tart syrup made from boiled pomegranate juice; often stirred into pilafs, salads, and dips for fruity acidity.

ALEPPO PEPPER:
Also known as Halaby pepper, this dried and ground chile has a dull brick color, mild heat, and fruity, raisin-like flavor; a mix of ground ancho and cayenne makes a good substitute.

EGGPLANT:
Meaty-tasting fruit of a plant in the nightshade family (which includes tomatoes and peppers); naturally bitter-tasting, but bitterness has been bred out of most American cultivars; often marinated, stuffed whole, baked in casseroles, or roasted and pureed.

The Flavors of the Middle East and Africa

Wander through a North African or Middle Eastern bazaar, and piney caraway, gingery cardamom, and citrusy coriander will engulf your senses. Red saffron and golden turmeric radiate the color of fire. The sun-baked flavors of the Middle East and Africa come alive in signature spice blends and pastes like harissa, Tunisia's fiery chile-garlic paste; dukkah, Egypt's all-purpose dip of crushed nuts, seeds, and spices; za'atar, an Arab spice blend of dried sumac, thyme, and sesame seeds; ras el hanout, the North African spice merchant's top-shelf house blend; and berbere, Ethiopia's dried mix of ground chiles, garlic, fenugreek, coriander, and allspice.

Most of these seasonings can be made ahead in bulk and enjoyed for months. Many, like za'atar and ras el hanout, are now available premade in American supermarkets. With the explosion of interest in Middle Eastern cuisines around the world, key preparations like hummus have also become widely available. Here are some other signature flavors that make Middle Eastern and African food so enchanting.

FRESH THYME: Short-leafed herb with an earthy, floral, piney aroma. Often paired with lamb.

WALNUTS: Second only to almonds in worldwide consumption; rich in heart-healthy omega-3 fatty acids and often ground into spice pastes or incorporated into desserts.

COUSCOUS: Tiny grains of pasta made from semolina; Israeli couscous is made with bulgur wheat and flour and toasted for deeper flavor.

PISTACHIOS: Native Middle Eastern nut that adds rich flavor and pale green color.

Fresh lemongrass and ginger give this drink a citrus aroma and spicy kick. African food historian Jessica B. Harris says that cooks on the Ivory Coast make the beverage as a thrifty way to use up leftover pineapple skins. If you can't find lemongrass, replace it with a tablespoon of grated lemon rind.

GINGERED PINEAPPLE JUICE

(Gnamacoudji)

HANDS-ON TIME: 18 MIN. TOTAL TIME: 1 HR. 23 MIN.

2 whole unpeeled pineapples
10 cups water, divided
1 (3-inch) piece peeled fresh ginger, coarsely chopped (about 3 ounces fresh ginger)
¼ cup coarsely chopped peeled fresh lemongrass
2 tablespoons water
1 cup powdered sugar
Fresh mint leaves (optional)

1. Remove peel from pineapples; cut peel into 3-inch pieces (reserve pulp for another use). Combine peel and 6 cups water in Dutch oven; bring to a boil. Reduce heat; simmer 30 minutes. Drain in a colander, pressing peels to release moisture; reserve 4 cups cooking liquid. Discard peels.

2. Place ginger, lemongrass, and 2 tablespoons water in a food processor; process until finely chopped. Place ginger mixture on a dampened double layer of cheesecloth. Gather edges of cheesecloth together; tie securely. Place cheesecloth bag and 4 cups water in a medium bowl; let stand 30 minutes. Strain reserved pineapple cooking liquid and ginger mixture into a large pitcher; discard cheesecloth bag. Add sugar; stir well. Chill. Serve over ice. Garnish with mint leaves, if desired. Serves 8 (serving size: 1 cup)

CALORIES 67; FAT 0.1g (sat 0g, mono 0g, poly 0.1g); PROTEIN 0.1g; CARB 17.1g; FIBER 0.2g; CHOL 0mg; IRON 0.1mg; SODIUM 1mg; CALC 2mg

Almost every one of the world's continents boasts some kind of dumpling or filled dough. In Tunisia, it's brik, a savory pastry traditionally made with super-thin warka dough and filled with tuna and egg. This vegetarian version comes from Joan Nathan, author of Jewish Cooking in America. Stuffed with potatoes instead of tuna, it's a culinary play on Jewish latkes.

POTATO-CILANTRO PASTRIES
with Harissa (Potato-Cilantro Brik)
HANDS-ON TIME: 40 MIN. TOTAL TIME: 60 MIN.

1 cup chopped peeled
  baking potato
¼ cup finely chopped onion
2 tablespoons chopped fresh
  cilantro
2 teaspoons extra-virgin
  olive oil
½ teaspoon hot paprika
¼ teaspoon salt
¼ teaspoon freshly ground
  black pepper
16 wonton wrappers
Cooking spray
½ cup harissa
Cilantro sprigs (optional)

1. Preheat oven to 375°.
2. Cook potato in boiling water 8 minutes or until tender; drain. Mash with a fork. Combine potato and next 6 ingredients (through pepper). Spoon about 2 teaspoons potato mixture into center of each wonton wrapper. Moisten edges of wrapper with water; bring 2 opposite corners together. Press edges together to seal, forming a triangle. Place brik on a large baking sheet coated with cooking spray. Lightly coat tops of brik with cooking spray. Bake at 375° for 12 minutes or until golden. Serve with harissa. Garnish with cilantro sprigs, if desired. Serves 8 (serving size: 2 brik and 1 tablespoon harissa)

CALORIES 165; FAT 3.6g (sat 0.5g, mono 2.4g, poly 0.4g); PROTEIN 5.2g; CARB 32.7g; FIBER 1.1g; CHOL 7mg; IRON 1.3mg; SODIUM 416mg; CALC 18mg

In Lebanon, some cooks replace the lemon juice in this classic eggplant dip with pomegranate molasses for a touch of sweetness. Either way, smokiness is essential to the dish. If you can broil or grill the eggplant until the skin blackens all over, you'll get a more authentic flavor.

BABA GHANOUSH

HANDS-ON TIME: 16 MIN. TOTAL TIME: 1 HR. 31 MIN.

1 large eggplant (about 1½ pounds)

Cooking spray

¼ cup pine nuts, toasted

¾ teaspoon cumin seeds, toasted and crushed

½ teaspoon minced fresh garlic

3 tablespoons fresh lemon juice

2 tablespoons low-fat mayonnaise

2 tablespoons tahini (roasted sesame seed paste)

1 teaspoon kosher salt

¼ teaspoon freshly ground black pepper

3 tablespoons chopped fresh parsley

Chopped fresh parsley (optional)

1. Preheat oven to 375°.

2. Pierce eggplant several times with a fork; place on a foil-lined baking sheet coated with cooking spray. Bake at 375° for 45 minutes or until tender. Cut eggplant in half. Scoop out pulp; discard skins. Drain eggplant pulp in a colander 30 minutes.

3. Place pine nuts, cumin seeds, and garlic in a food processor; pulse until finely chopped. Add eggplant, lemon juice, mayonnaise, tahini, salt, and pepper to food processor; process until smooth. Spoon eggplant mixture into a medium bowl; stir in chopped parsley. Garnish with chopped fresh parsley, if desired. Serves 8 (serving size: ¼ cup)

CALORIES 75; FAT 5.3g (sat 0.5g, mono 1.6g, poly 2.5g); PROTEIN 2.1g; CARB 6.7g; FIBER 2.8g; CHOL 0mg; IRON 0.8mg; SODIUM 277mg; CALC 17mg

Pita

Known as *khubz* in the Arabic world, pita is an ancient, circular flatbread that is cooked on a flat surface such as a hot pan or in an oven. It's cooked at a high temperature, causing the bread to puff and form a pocket in the center. Middle Eastern dishes like hummus, falafel, shawarma, and kebabs are often served in or on pita. For more fiber, look for whole-grain versions.

Dukkah is an incredibly versatile mix of nuts, seeds, and spices that's perfect for flavoring pita bread and cut vegetables that have been dipped in olive oil. Dip the vegetables or bread in the oil, and then the dukkah. You can also use dukkah to season grilled or roasted meat, fish, and vegetables.

DUKKAH

HANDS-ON TIME: 20 MIN. TOTAL TIME: 20 MIN.

¼ cup sesame seeds
2 tablespoons chickpea (garbanzo bean) flour (optional)
2 tablespoons blanched hazelnuts (without skins)
2 tablespoons coriander seeds
1 tablespoon cumin seeds
½ teaspoon dried thyme
½ teaspoon kosher salt
¼ teaspoon black peppercorns

1. Place first 5 ingredients in a large skillet over medium heat; cook 4 minutes or until fragrant and toasted, shaking pan frequently.
2. Pour spice mixture onto a plate; cool 5 minutes. Place mixture in a spice or coffee grinder (or in a mortar and pestle); add remaining ingredients. Process or grind until coarsely ground. Spread in a shallow bowl. Serves 8 (serving size: 2 tablespoons)

CALORIES 53; FAT 3.9g (sat 0.1g, mono 1.3g, poly 0.2g); PROTEIN 2g; CARB 3.3g; FIBER 1.6g; CHOL 0mg; IRON 1.3mg; SODIUM 131mg; CALC 37mg

During Ramadan, Muslims traditionally break the day's fast by eating dates in the evening; this follows the example of the Prophet Muhammad. Dates carry heavy religious and cultural significance among Middle Eastern cultures. The almond paste and green food coloring used here replaces the traditional pistachio paste filling.

ALGERIAN STUFFED DATES
HANDS-ON TIME: 20 MIN. TOTAL TIME: 20 MIN.

24 Medjool dates (about 1 pound)
2 drops green food coloring
   (optional)
²/₃ cup marzipan (almond paste)
2 teaspoons powdered sugar

1. Cut a lengthwise slit down the center, but not through, each date; remove seeds.

2. Sprinkle food coloring over marzipan, if desired; gently knead 4 to 5 times or until color is incorporated into marzipan. Divide marzipan mixture evenly among dates; stuff into slits. Sprinkle with powdered sugar. Serves 24 (serving size: 1 stuffed date)

CALORIES 50; FAT 0.9g (sat 0.1g, mono 0.6g, poly 0.2g); PROTEIN 0.6g; CARB 10.8g; FIBER 0.6g; CHOL 0mg; IRON 0.1mg; SODIUM 0mg; CALC 7mg

Like sourdough bread, injera batter usually ferments for days, developing the flatbread's signature sour taste. Here's a streamlined version from award-winning Ethiopian-born chef Marcus Samuelsson. Yogurt adds sourness, while club soda aerates and lightens the batter.

TEFF INJERA FLATBREAD
with Carrot-Ginger Chutney
HANDS-ON TIME: 36 MIN. TOTAL TIME: 1 HR. 31 MIN.

Chutney:
2 tablespoons olive oil
4 cups (½-inch) cubed peeled carrot (4 medium)
¾ cup finely chopped shallots (about 3 large)
4 garlic cloves, minced
2 (3 x ½-inch) julienne-cut strips peeled fresh ginger
2 tablespoons sugar
2 tablespoons honey
1 tablespoon butter
4 cardamom pods, bruised
2 fresh thyme sprigs
2 cups organic vegetable broth
½ teaspoon salt
Injera:
9 ounces whole-grain teff flour (about 2 cups)
4.5 ounces all-purpose flour (about 1 cup)
1½ teaspoons baking soda
1 teaspoon salt
2½ cups club soda
¾ cup plain yogurt
Cooking spray

1. To prepare chutney, heat a large nonstick skillet over medium-high heat. Add oil to pan; swirl to coat. Add carrot, shallots, garlic, and ginger to pan. Reduce heat to low, and cook 10 minutes, stirring occasionally. Add sugar and next 4 ingredients (through thyme); cook 1 minute, stirring constantly. Stir in broth; bring to a boil. Reduce heat, and simmer 45 minutes or until carrot is tender and liquid almost evaporates. Discard thyme sprigs and ginger. Stir in ½ teaspoon salt; cool.
2. To prepare injera, weigh or lightly spoon flours into dry measuring cups; level with a knife. Combine flours, baking soda, and 1 teaspoon salt in a large bowl; stir with a whisk. Combine club soda and yogurt in a small bowl, stirring with a whisk until smooth. Add yogurt mixture to flour mixture; stir with a whisk until smooth.
3. Heat a large skillet over medium-high heat. Coat pan with cooking spray. Pour about ⅓ cup batter per flatbread onto pan in a spiral, starting at the center; cook 20 seconds. Cover pan; cook an additional 40 seconds or just until set. Transfer to a plate, and cover with a cloth to keep warm. Repeat procedure with cooking spray and remaining batter, wiping the pan dry with a paper towel between flatbreads. Serve flatbreads with chutney. Serves 14 (serving size: 1 flatbread and 2 tablespoons chutney)

CALORIES 171; **FAT** 3.8g (sat 1.1g, mono 1.8g, poly 0.3g); **PROTEIN** 4.2g; **CARB** 30.5g; **FIBER** 3.8g; **CHOL** 4mg; **IRON** 2mg; **SODIUM** 520mg; **CALC** 70mg

Teff Flour

Teff is the seed of a North African species of lovegrass. The world's tiniest grain, teff grows in the Ethiopian highlands and forms the foundation of the local diet. Like a small version of millet, teff is high in protein, fiber, and iron, and contains all eight essential amino acids.

NO EQUIPMENT NEEDED

*t*hink you can't live without modern appliances like a microwave oven, blender, and electric mixer? Think again. "Cooking is not about the equipment," says Jessica B. Harris, African food historian and author of *High on the Hog.*

Throughout much of the world, cooking is a rudimentary affair, often done over an open fire with pans that need to last a lifetime. In poorer parts of Africa, a primitive three-rock "stove"—simply a base for a grate over an open flame—is used to prepare every meal. Despite the lack of convenience, African cooks turn out richly flavored stews, spicy curries, velvety soups, fluffy couscous and rice, smoky roasted vegetables, grilled meats, and poached fish. It's all about the technique.

If you find yourself lusting after the latest gadget, think of all the incredible food you can make with a few incredibly fresh ingredients, a good knife, a trusted skillet, and the skills to use them. That's just about all you need to make delicious dishes like Potato-Cilantro Pastries with Harissa (page 117), Dukkah (page 120), Algerian Stuffed Dates (page 121), Pan-Fried Fish Balls (page 128), and Fish in Coconut Curry (page 130).

Probably the most famous Middle Eastern sweet pastry, baklava layers phyllo dough with pistachios, walnuts, or almonds, and sugar syrup or honey. In this version, chocolate-hazelnut spread enrobes four different kinds of chopped nuts—hazelnuts, pistachios, walnuts, and almonds. Cinnamon-scented honey syrup crowns the top.

CHOCOLATE BAKLAVA

HANDS-ON TIME: 25 MIN. TOTAL TIME: 1 HR. 21 MIN.

³/₄ cup honey
½ cup water
1 (3-inch) cinnamon stick
1 cup hazelnut-chocolate spread (such as Nutella)
½ cup toasted hazelnuts, coarsely chopped
½ cup roasted pistachios, coarsely chopped
⅓ cup blanched toasted almonds, coarsely chopped
⅓ cup toasted walnuts, coarsely chopped
½ teaspoon ground cinnamon
⅛ teaspoon salt
Cooking spray
24 (14 x 9-inch) sheets frozen phyllo dough, thawed
½ cup butter, melted

1. Combine first 3 ingredients in a medium saucepan over low heat; stir until honey dissolves. Increase heat to medium; cook, without stirring, until a candy thermometer registers 230° (about 10 minutes). Remove from heat; keep warm. Discard cinnamon stick.
2. Preheat oven to 350°.
3. Place hazelnut-chocolate spread in a microwave-safe bowl; microwave at HIGH 30 seconds or until melted. Combine hazelnuts and next 5 ingredients (through salt). Lightly coat a 13 x 9–inch glass or ceramic baking dish with cooking spray. Working with 1 phyllo sheet at a time (cover remaining dough to prevent drying), place 1 phyllo sheet lengthwise in bottom of prepared pan, allowing ends of sheet to extend over edges of dish; lightly brush with butter. Repeat procedure with 5 phyllo sheets and butter. Drizzle about ⅓ cup melted hazelnut-chocolate spread over phyllo. Sprinkle evenly with one-third of nut mixture (about ½ cup). Repeat procedure twice with phyllo, butter, hazelnut-chocolate spread, and nut mixture. Top last layer of nut mixture with remaining 6 sheets phyllo, each lightly brushed with butter. Press gently into pan.
4. Make 3 lengthwise cuts and 5 crosswise cuts to form 24 portions using a sharp knife. Bake at 350° for 35 minutes or until phyllo is golden. Remove from oven. Drizzle honey mixture over baklava. Cool in pan on a wire rack. Cover; store at room temperature. Serves 24 (serving size: 1 piece)

CALORIES 238; FAT 13.4g (sat 4.3g, mono 5.6g, poly 2g); PROTEIN 4g; CARB 27.8g; FIBER 1.6g; CHOL 10mg; IRON 1.3mg; SODIUM 148mg; CALC 29mg

Phyllo

The secret to crisp pastries like baklava and tyropita is layer upon layer of paper-thin sheets of phyllo dough. Brushing each sheet with butter or oil helps them crisp up when baked and create their signature flaky-rich texture. Phyllo is extremely thin and delicate, so handle with care to avoid tearing the sheets. Only work with one sheet at a time, and keep the remaining stack of sheets covered with plastic wrap and a damp towel so they won't dry out.

When fish is plentiful in Senegal, cooks often make boulettes de poisson, according to African food historian Jessica B. Harris. The little round fish cakes are usually flavored with garlic, parsley, and chiles, browned in a pan, and served with spicy tomato sauce. This simplified sauce spikes up prepared cocktail sauce with chili powder.

PAN-FRIED FISH BALLS
(Boulettes de Poisson)
HANDS-ON TIME: 20 MIN. TOTAL TIME: 20 MIN.

2 tablespoons water
¾ teaspoon chili powder, divided
½ teaspoon salt
¼ teaspoon freshly ground black pepper
2 large eggs
1 (1-ounce) slice white bread
1 pound cod or other flaky whitefish fillets, chopped
1 tablespoon chopped fresh parsley
2 garlic cloves, minced
2 teaspoons canola oil
½ cup all-purpose flour
½ cup prepared cocktail sauce

1. Combine 2 tablespoons water, ¼ teaspoon chili powder, salt, pepper, and eggs in a small bowl, stirring well with a whisk.

2. Place bread in a food processor; pulse 5 times or until coarse crumbs measure ½ cup. Add 2 tablespoons egg mixture, fish, parsley, and garlic; process until a thick dough forms. Shape dough into 16 (1-inch) balls.

3. Heat a large nonstick skillet over medium-high heat. Add oil to pan; swirl to coat. Dredge fish balls in flour and dip in remaining egg mixture. Add fish balls to pan; sauté 10 minutes or until browned on all sides, turning frequently.

4. Combine remaining ½ teaspoon chili powder and cocktail sauce. Serve with fish balls. Serves 4 (serving size: 4 fish balls and 2 tablespoons sauce)

CALORIES 136; FAT 2.9g (sat 0.7g, mono 0.1g, poly 0.7g); PROTEIN 13.1g; CARB 13.8g; FIBER 0.3g; CHOL 74mg; IRON 0.9mg; SODIUM 452mg; CALC 16mg

This recipe comes from Claudia Roden, author of The New Book of Middle Eastern Food. The sauce, tarator (tara-TOR), is a nut-based puree that's popular in the Middle East. Here, it's ladled over poached salmon, but you could also use grouper.

POACHED FISH
with Pine Nut Sauce (Samak Tarator)

HANDS-ON TIME: 16 MIN. TOTAL TIME: 1 HR. 16 MIN.

Fish:
2 cups water
¼ teaspoon salt
6 (6-ounce) salmon fillets
  (about 1 inch thick)
Sauce:
1 cup water
2 (1-ounce) slices white
  bread, crusts removed
½ cup pine nuts
3 tablespoons fresh lemon
  juice
¼ teaspoon salt
⅛ teaspoon white pepper
1 garlic clove, crushed
3 tablespoons clam juice
Chopped fresh flat-leaf
  parsley (optional)
12 lemon wedges (optional)

1. To prepare fish, bring 2 cups water to a boil in a large skillet. Add ¼ teaspoon salt and fish. Return to a boil; reduce heat, and simmer 8 minutes or until fish flakes easily when tested with a fork. Remove fish from pan. Cover and refrigerate fish until chilled.

2. To prepare sauce, place 1 cup water in a shallow dish. Dip bread into water, and remove; squeeze bread to remove excess moisture. Place bread, pine nuts, and next 4 ingredients (through garlic) in a food processor. With the processor on, slowly pour clam juice through food chute, and process until smooth. Serve over chilled fish. Garnish with parsley, and serve with lemon wedges, if desired. Serves 6 (serving size: 1 fillet and 2 tablespoons sauce)

CALORIES 321; FAT 16.7g (sat 3.5g, mono 6.9g, poly 4.9g); PROTEIN 34.7g; CARB 7.3g; FIBER 0.7g; CHOL 80.6mg; IRON 1.9mg; SODIUM 335mg; CALC 31mg

Tanzania sits at a crossroads in the spice trade routes from India. That's why Indian spices ended up in so many Tanzanian dishes like this fish curry. The dish originated in Zanzibar but is now enjoyed all over the eastern coast of Africa. Coconut milk enriches the curry and gives it a tropical flavor. Serve over boiled yuca, potatoes, or rice.

FISH IN COCONUT CURRY
(Mtuzi wa Samaki)
HANDS-ON TIME: 20 MIN. TOTAL TIME: 47 MIN.

1 (1¼-pound) skinless halibut or other firm white fish fillet
1½ teaspoons Madras curry powder, divided
¾ teaspoon salt, divided
¼ teaspoon freshly ground black pepper, divided
1 tablespoon canola oil
1 cup finely chopped onion
1 cup finely chopped red bell pepper
2 teaspoons minced peeled fresh ginger
3 garlic cloves, minced
2¾ cups chopped tomato (2 large)
2 tablespoons fresh lemon juice
¾ cup light coconut milk
4 lemon wedges
Chopped fresh cilantro (optional)

1. Sprinkle fish with ¾ teaspoon curry powder, ⅜ teaspoon salt, and ⅛ teaspoon black pepper.

2. Heat a large nonstick skillet over medium-high heat. Add oil to pan; swirl to coat. Add fish; cook 4 minutes or until deeply browned on bottom but undercooked on top (fish will finish cooking later in sauce). Remove fish from pan.

3. Add onion and bell pepper to pan; sauté 4 minutes or until tender. Add ginger and garlic; sauté 1 minute. Add remaining ¾ teaspoon curry powder, remaining ⅜ teaspoon salt, remaining ⅛ teaspoon black pepper, tomato, and lemon juice. Reduce heat to medium-low, and cook 10 minutes or until tomato breaks down, stirring occasionally. Mash tomato with a wooden spoon.

4. Stir in coconut milk. Return fish along with accumulated juices to pan, browned side up. Reduce heat to low; cover and cook 8 minutes or until fish flakes easily when tested with a fork. Cut fish into 4 equal portions. Spoon sauce into individual, shallow bowls; top each with a piece of fish. Serve with lemon wedges and chopped fresh cilantro, if desired. Serves 4 (serving size: ½ cup sauce, 5 ounces fish, and 1 lemon wedge)

CALORIES 265; FAT 10.1g (sat 3g, mono 3g, poly 1.6g); PROTEIN 28.9g; CARB 15g; FIBER 3.3g; CHOL 70mg; IRON 1.3mg; SODIUM 549mg; CALC 51mg

A sandwich of chickpea fritters in pita bread, falafel ranks among the world's most popular Middle Eastern foods. Here's a re-imagining of the same elements—seasoned mashed chickpeas, tahini sauce, and tomato relish—stuffed into roasted eggplant instead of pita pockets. It makes a satisfying vegetarian main dish.

FALAFEL-STUFFED EGGPLANT
with Tahini Sauce and Tomato Relish

HANDS-ON TIME: 27 MIN. TOTAL TIME: 59 MIN.

3 tablespoons warm water
3 tablespoons tahini (roasted sesame seed paste), divided
4 teaspoons fresh lemon juice
1 teaspoon honey
½ teaspoon ground cumin
3 garlic cloves, minced and divided
2 eggplants
Cooking spray
¾ teaspoon kosher salt, divided
¾ cup chopped fresh flat-leaf parsley, divided
¼ cup chopped onion
¼ cup fresh breadcrumbs
2 teaspoons olive oil
1½ teaspoons ground cumin
½ teaspoon ground coriander
¼ teaspoon black pepper
¼ teaspoon ground red pepper
2 large eggs
1 (15-ounce) can no-salt-added chickpeas (garbanzo beans), rinsed and drained
1 cup chopped seeded tomato
½ cup chopped seeded peeled cucumber
½ cup sliced red onion
1 tablespoon fresh lemon juice
1 tablespoon olive oil

1. Combine 3 tablespoons warm water, 2 tablespoons tahini, 4 teaspoons fresh lemon juice, honey, ½ teaspoon ground cumin, and 1 minced garlic clove in a small bowl, and stir with a whisk. Set aside.

2. Preheat oven to 475°.

3. Slice eggplants in half lengthwise; score cut sides with a crosshatch pattern. Place eggplant halves, cut sides down, on a baking sheet coated with cooking spray. Bake at 475° for 7 minutes or until slightly tender and browned. Remove from oven; carefully scoop out pulp, leaving a ¾-inch shell. Reserve pulp for another use. Season cut sides of eggplant shells with ¼ teaspoon salt.

4. Place 1 tablespoon tahini, 2 minced garlic cloves, ½ teaspoon salt, ¼ cup parsley, onion, and next 8 ingredients (through chickpeas) in a food processor; process until smooth. Spoon ½ cup chickpea mixture into each eggplant shell. Bake at 475° for 25 minutes or until eggplant halves are tender and chickpea mixture is lightly browned.

5. Combine ½ cup parsley, tomato, and remaining ingredients in a bowl; stir to combine. Place 1 eggplant half on each of 4 plates. Top each half with ¼ cup relish and 1½ tablespoons sauce. Serves 4 (serving size: 1 stuffed eggplant half)

CALORIES 308; FAT 15.6g (sat 2.5g, mono 7.4g, poly 3.8g); PROTEIN 12.1g; CARB 34.3g; FIBER 10.8g; CHOL 106mg; IRON 3.5mg; SODIUM 450mg; CALC 116mg

Running a marathon? Here's your carbo-load: a classic Egyptian street food of rice, pasta, and lentils topped with spicy-sweet tomato sauce and deeply savory caramelized onions. The recipe comes courtesy of Anissa Helou, native Lebanese food writer and author of Mediterranean Street Food.

KOSHARI

HANDS-ON TIME: 35 MIN. TOTAL TIME: 1 HR. 45 MIN.

Sauce:
1 tablespoon extra-virgin olive oil
1 cup finely chopped onion
1½ tablespoons minced fresh garlic
½ teaspoon sea salt
½ teaspoon freshly ground black pepper
½ teaspoon crushed red pepper
2 (14.5-ounce) cans diced tomatoes, undrained

Koshari:
3 tablespoons extra-virgin olive oil
3 cups thinly sliced onion
½ cup uncooked vermicelli, broken into 1-inch pieces
5 cups water
1¼ cups dried lentils or yellow split peas
2½ cups hot cooked long-grain rice
1 teaspoon sea salt

1. To prepare sauce, heat a large saucepan over medium heat. Add 1 tablespoon oil to pan; swirl to coat. Add chopped onion to pan, and cook 15 minutes or until golden, stirring occasionally. Add garlic; cook 2 minutes. Stir in ½ teaspoon salt, peppers, and tomatoes; cook 10 minutes or until slightly thick. Transfer tomato mixture to a food processor; process 1 minute or until smooth. Keep warm. Wipe skillet dry with paper towels.

2. To prepare koshari, heat pan over medium heat. Add 3 tablespoons oil to pan; swirl to coat. Add sliced onion; cook 15 minutes or until deep golden brown, stirring frequently. Remove onion with a slotted spoon to several layers of paper towels; set aside. Return pan to medium heat. Add vermicelli; sauté 2 minutes or until golden brown, stirring frequently. Set aside.

3. Combine 5 cups water and lentils in a medium saucepan; bring to a boil. Cover, reduce heat, and simmer 30 minutes or until lentils are tender. Remove from heat; add vermicelli, stirring well to combine. Wrap a clean kitchen towel around lid, and cover lentil mixture; let stand 10 minutes or until vermicelli is tender. Add rice and 1 teaspoon salt to lentil mixture; fluff with a fork. Serve immediately with sauce and onions. Serves 8 (serving size: ¾ cup lentil mixture, ⅓ cup sauce, and 2 tablespoons onion mixture)

CALORIES 292; FAT 7.7g (sat 1g, mono 5g, poly 0.8g); PROTEIN 10.2g; CARB 47.5g; FIBER 7.6g; CHOL 0mg; IRON 3mg; SODIUM 569mg; CALC 53mg

A PLACE AT THE TABLE

*t*hroughout Africa and the Middle East, food is served family-style from a communal bowl or plate. "Family meals are a huge part of Middle Eastern culture," says Michael Solomonov, owner of the Israeli restaurant, Zahav. "The communal plate means that everyone shares."

Over the years, I've learned the benefits of sharing a table with strangers and loved ones. When families eat together, they tend to eat more fruits and vegetables, and drink less soda. Children are less likely to be overweight. Research from Columbia University found that eating a family dinner helps kids get better grades and keeps them away from drugs and alcohol. One study even found that eating a family dinner can help working moms unwind.

Beyond all that, eating as a group is just more fun. It helps you stay connected to your community, stimulates conversation, and makes mealtime about more than just nourishment of the body—it's sustenance for the soul.

In America, they're called meatballs. In the Middle East, they go by kofta. Sometimes the meat mixture gets formed onto skewers and grilled; sometimes it's simmered in spicy gravy. These easy kofta hail from Morocco. They get pan-seared, and then served over saffron rice with a garlicky yogurt sauce.

QUICK LAMB KOFTA
with Harissa Yogurt Sauce

HANDS-ON TIME: 20 MIN. TOTAL TIME: 20 MIN.

1 (3½-ounce) bag boil-in-bag jasmine rice
1 teaspoon saffron threads
2 tablespoons thinly sliced green onions
2 tablespoons minced fresh cilantro
2 tablespoons grated fresh onion
2 tablespoons 2% Greek-style plain yogurt
1 teaspoon ground cumin
1 teaspoon ground coriander
1 teaspoon turmeric
2 teaspoons bottled minced garlic
½ teaspoon salt
¼ teaspoon freshly ground black pepper
1 pound lean ground lamb
Cooking spray
½ cup 2% Greek-style plain yogurt
¼ cup chopped bottled roasted red bell pepper
1 teaspoon ground cumin
1 teaspoon ground coriander
2 teaspoons bottled minced garlic
½ teaspoon crushed red pepper
¼ teaspoon salt

1. Cook boil-in-bag jasmine rice and saffron in boiling water according to package directions. Drain; fluff rice with a fork. Sprinkle with green onions.

2. While rice cooks, combine cilantro and next 9 ingredients (through lamb); shape into 12 oblong patties.

3. Heat a large nonstick skillet over medium-high heat. Coat pan with cooking spray. Add patties to pan; cook 10 minutes or until done, turning occasionally to brown on all sides.

4. While kofta cooks, combine ½ cup yogurt and remaining ingredients. Serve sauce with kofta and rice. Serves 4 (serving size: 3 patties, about ¼ cup sauce, and about ⅓ cup rice)

CALORIES 344; FAT 16.3g (sat 6.9g, mono 6.4g, poly 1.1g); PROTEIN 24.8g; CARB 24.4g; FIBER 0.8g; CHOL 77mg; IRON 2.9mg; SODIUM 563mg; CALC 72mg

how to: SHAPE KOFTA

Whether formed solely by hand or molded around a skewer for grilling, what distinguishes kofta from meatballs and burgers is their oblong shape. If forming onto skewers for grilling, slide skewer through center of kofta lengthwise, molding meat firmly around skewer to retain oblong shape.

1 Place about ½ cup of meat mixture in the palm of your hand.

2 Form into an oblong football shape about 2 inches in diameter and 3 to 4 inches long.

Iran takes rice to new heights. For chelo, the rice is parboiled, and then fried in a pan, covered with a cloth, and steamed with butter and salt, creating a crispy, golden crust on the bottom. I cut back on the butter and salt, but the rice still forms a good crust, known as tah dig. Use a nonstick pan here so you can invert the whole pan of rice and show the golden brown crust.

CHELO KEBAB

HANDS-ON TIME: 60 MIN. TOTAL TIME: 9 HR. 20 MIN.

Kebabs:
2 onions, coarsely chopped
2 garlic cloves, chopped
3 tablespoons fresh lemon juice
3 tablespoons olive oil
¼ teaspoon salt
¼ teaspoon freshly ground black pepper
1½ pounds boneless leg of lamb, trimmed and cut into 1-inch cubes
18 grape tomatoes
Cooking spray
Chelo:
1½ cups uncooked basmati rice
6 cups water
2 teaspoons salt
3 tablespoons unsalted butter, melted and divided
1 tablespoon olive oil
¼ teaspoon saffron threads, crushed
2 tablespoons chopped green onions
2 tablespoons chopped fresh mint
2 tablespoons chopped fresh cilantro
1 lemon, cut into 6 wedges

1. To prepare kebabs, place onions and garlic in food processor; process 2 to 3 minutes or until pureed. Combine pureed onion mixture, lemon juice, 3 tablespoons oil, ¼ teaspoon salt, and pepper in a large zip-top plastic bag. Add lamb; seal and marinate in refrigerator 8 hours, turning bag occasionally.

2. Preheat grill to medium-high heat or broiler.

3. Remove lamb from bag; discard marinade. Thread lamb onto 6 (10-inch) metal skewers; thread tomatoes onto 2 or 3 (10-inch) metal skewers. Place skewers on grill rack or broiler pan coated with cooking spray; cook tomatoes 4 to 5 minutes and lamb 10 to 12 minutes or until desired degree of doneness, turning occasionally.

4. To prepare chelo, place rice in a fine sieve; rinse 1 to 2 minutes with warm running water. Drain. Bring 6 cups water and 2 teaspoons salt to a boil in a large, heavy nonstick skillet over high heat. Add rice; boil, uncovered, 5 to 7 minutes, stirring occasionally. (Rice will be slightly crunchy.) Drain rice through a sieve into a bowl, reserving rice and cooking liquid. Rinse rice with warm running water.

5. Combine 2 tablespoons reserved rice cooking liquid, 2 tablespoons melted butter, 1 tablespoon oil, and saffron in nonstick skillet; place over high heat. Add one-third of rice, stirring to coat. Spread evenly over bottom of pan. Add remaining rice (do not stir), spreading evenly. Drizzle with remaining 1 tablespoon melted butter. Place a clean dish towel over rice, folding towel to fit within perimeter of pan. Cover pan with lid. Cook over high heat 3 to 4 minutes or until rice begins to brown on bottom. Reduce heat to low, and cook 20 minutes or until rice is tender and a crisp, browned layer forms on bottom of pan. Remove lid and towel; invert rice onto a plate.

6. Spoon about ½ cup rice onto each of 6 plates. Remove tomatoes from skewers. Place a lamb skewer and 3 tomatoes on each plate. Combine green onions, mint, and cilantro; sprinkle 1 tablespoon over each serving. Serve with lemon wedges. Serves 6

CALORIES 441; FAT 16.3g (sat 6.3g, mono 7.5g, poly 1.3g); PROTEIN 26.7g; CARB 49g; FIBER 2.4g; CHOL 88mg; IRON 3.8mg; SODIUM 654mg; CALC 21mg

Beginning in the 17th century, slaves from Indonesia and India were brought to work the farms of Cape Town, South Africa, and became known as Cape Malays. As a result of their influence, Malay curry dishes are now enjoyed all over South Africa, combining sweet flavors like dried fruit, ginger, and cinnamon with garlic and onions.

CAPE MALAY CURRY

HANDS-ON TIME: 20 MIN. TOTAL TIME: 2 HR. 20 MIN.

1½ teaspoons ground turmeric
1½ teaspoons ground cumin
1½ teaspoons ground coriander
1½ teaspoons chili powder
¾ teaspoon ground cinnamon
½ teaspoon salt
2 teaspoons canola oil
2 cups chopped onion
1½ tablespoons minced peeled fresh ginger
2 bay leaves
1 garlic clove, minced
1 pound beef stew meat, cut into bite-sized pieces
1¼ cups fat-free, lower-sodium beef broth
1 cup water
1 cup chopped green bell pepper (about 1 medium)
⅓ cup chopped dried apricots
⅓ cup apricot spread
2 teaspoons red wine vinegar
¼ cup low-fat buttermilk
2 cups cooked long-grain rice

1. Combine first 6 ingredients in a small bowl, stirring well.
2. Heat a Dutch oven over medium-high heat. Add oil; swirl to coat. Add spice mixture; cook 15 seconds, stirring constantly. Add onion; sauté 2 minutes. Add ginger, bay leaves, and garlic; sauté 15 seconds. Add beef; sauté 3 minutes. Add broth and next 5 ingredients (through vinegar); bring to a boil. Cover, reduce heat, and simmer 1½ hours. Uncover; discard bay leaves, if desired. Simmer 30 minutes or until beef is very tender. Remove from heat; stir in buttermilk. Serve over rice. Serves 4 (serving size: 1¼ cups beef mixture and ½ cup cooked rice)

CALORIES 349; FAT 11.5g (sat 3.4g, mono 5.1g, poly 1.2g); PROTEIN 25.7g; CARB 35.3g; FIBER 3.9g; CHOL 71mg; IRON 4.3mg; SODIUM 396mg; CALC 77mg

A salad of parsley, bulgur, and tomato, tabbouleh is traditionally served as part of mezze, the Middle East's version of tapas. Here, sautéed chicken thighs and a creamy sesame sauce turn the bulgur salad into a main dish. This healthy meal-in-a-bowl comes from Mark Bittman, author of How to Cook Everything.

CHICKEN TABBOULEH
with Tahini Drizzle

HANDS-ON TIME: 26 MIN. TOTAL TIME: 37 MIN.

1¼ cups water

1 cup uncooked bulgur, rinsed and drained

2 tablespoons olive oil, divided

1 teaspoon kosher salt, divided

½ pound skinless, boneless chicken thighs

½ teaspoon freshly ground black pepper

3 cups chopped tomato

1 cup chopped fresh parsley

1 cup chopped fresh mint

1 cup chopped green onions

1 teaspoon minced fresh garlic

¼ cup tahini (roasted sesame seed paste)

¼ cup plain 2% reduced-fat Greek yogurt

3 tablespoons fresh lemon juice

1 tablespoon water

1. Combine 1¼ cups water, bulgur, 1 tablespoon olive oil, and ½ teaspoon salt in a medium saucepan; bring to a boil. Reduce heat; simmer 10 minutes (do not stir) or until liquid almost evaporates. Remove from heat; fluff with a fork. Place bulgur in a medium bowl; let stand 10 minutes.

2. Heat a large nonstick skillet over medium-high heat. Add remaining 1 tablespoon oil to pan; swirl to coat. Add chicken to pan; sprinkle with ¼ teaspoon salt and black pepper. Sauté 4 minutes on each side or until done; shred chicken. Combine bulgur, chicken, tomato, and next 4 ingredients (through garlic) in a large bowl; toss gently.

3. Combine remaining ¼ teaspoon salt, tahini, and remaining ingredients in a small bowl, stirring with a whisk. Drizzle over salad. Serves 4 (serving size: about 1½ cups)

CALORIES 395; FAT 18.2g (sat 3g, mono 8.8g, poly 5.1g); PROTEIN 21.5g; CARB 41g; FIBER 10.9g; CHOL 48mg; IRON 4.2mg; SODIUM 573mg; CALC 127mg

Bulgur

In the Arab world, bulgur—boiled, dried, and ground wheat berries—is a staple food used like rice. A high-fiber whole grain, it is typically simmered in water. Coarser grinds take longer to cook, but you'll know the bulgur is done when little holes form on top. In the United States, bulgur is ground extra-coarse (#4), coarse (#3), medium (#2), and fine (#1). Medium grind is the most common and most versatile, but if you have a choice, choose extra-coarse for pilafs, coarse or medium for salads and soups, and fine for *kibbeh*. Don't confuse bulgur with cracked wheat, which is similar but not parboiled like bulgur, so it takes longer to cook. Freekeh also belongs to the wheat family, but it's made by roasting and grinding young green wheat.

Popular in West Africa, Chicken Yassa calls for simply marinating chicken in lemon juice, broiling the chicken, and then stewing it in the boiled-down marinade. "It's the first West African dish I tasted," says food writer Jessica B. Harris. "Now, it's my good luck dish."

SENEGALESE LEMON CHICKEN *(Chicken Yassa)*

HANDS-ON TIME: 25 MIN. TOTAL TIME: 4 HR. 25 MIN.

6 cups sliced onion (about 3 pounds)
⅓ cup fresh lemon juice
1 teaspoon salt
½ teaspoon freshly ground black pepper
1 jalapeño pepper, seeded and minced
4 bone-in chicken breast halves (about 2 pounds), skinned
4 bone-in chicken leg quarters (about 2 pounds), skinned
Cooking spray
1½ tablespoons peanut oil
2 cups thinly sliced carrot
1½ cups fat-free, lower-sodium chicken broth
½ cup pimiento-stuffed olives
½ cup water
1 tablespoon Dijon mustard
1 Scotch bonnet pepper, pierced with a fork
4 cups hot cooked long-grain rice

1. Combine first 5 ingredients in a large bowl; divide evenly between 2 (1-gallon) heavy-duty zip-top plastic bags. Divide chicken evenly between bags; seal bags. Toss each bag well to coat. Refrigerate 3 hours, turning bags occasionally.
2. Preheat broiler.
3. Remove chicken from bags, reserving marinade. Place chicken on a broiler rack coated with cooking spray; broil 6 minutes on each side or until lightly browned.
4. Strain marinade through a colander over a bowl, reserving marinade and onion. Heat a Dutch oven over medium-high heat. Add oil to pan; swirl to coat. Add onion; sauté 5 minutes. Add reserved marinade; bring to a boil. Cook 1 minute; add chicken, carrot, and next 5 ingredients (through Scotch bonnet pepper). Bring to a boil; cover, reduce heat, and simmer 1 hour or until chicken is done. Discard Scotch bonnet. Serve over rice. Serves 8 (serving size: 1 chicken breast half or 1 chicken leg quarter, ⅔ cup stew, and ½ cup rice)

CALORIES 422; FAT 13.6g (sat 3g, mono 5.5g, poly 3.6g); PROTEIN 32.7g; CARB 40.4g; FIBER 3.6g; CHOL 99mg; IRON 3mg; SODIUM 704mg; CALC 48mg

The Indian spice trade carried curried dishes throughout East Africa. Combined with traditional African braising techniques, curried dishes like this aromatic chicken braised in broth with dates and raisins became popular. To save money, start with a whole bird (3 to 4 pounds), and remove the bone-in breasts, thighs, and drumsticks yourself.

EAST AFRICAN BRAISED CHICKEN

HANDS-ON TIME: 24 MIN. TOTAL TIME: 1 HR. 24 MIN.

2 bone-in chicken breast halves
  (about ¾ pound), skinned
2 bone-in chicken thighs
  (about ½ pound), skinned
2 chicken drumsticks
  (about ½ pound), skinned
½ teaspoon salt
½ teaspoon black pepper
1 tablespoon olive oil
3 cups vertically sliced onion
1 tablespoon chopped peeled
  fresh ginger
1 teaspoon curry powder
½ teaspoon ground cinnamon
½ teaspoon ground cardamom
¼ teaspoon ground red pepper
2 large garlic cloves, thinly
  sliced
½ cup fat-free, lower-sodium
  chicken broth
½ cup dry white wine
3 tablespoons chopped pitted
  dates
3 tablespoons golden raisins

1. Preheat oven to 350°.
2. Sprinkle chicken with salt and black pepper. Heat a Dutch oven over medium-high heat. Add oil to pan; swirl to coat. Add chicken; cook 4 minutes on each side or until golden brown. Remove chicken from pan.
3. Add onion to pan; reduce heat to medium-low, and cook 10 minutes, stirring frequently. Add ginger and next 5 ingredients (through garlic); cook 1 minute. Stir in chicken, broth, and remaining ingredients, and bring to a boil. Cover and bake at 350° for 1 hour. Serves 4 (serving size: 1 chicken breast half or 1 chicken thigh and 1 drumstick and about ¼ cup sauce)

CALORIES 279; FAT 8.9g (sat 2g, mono 4.4g, poly 1.6g); PROTEIN 28.1g; CARB 21.9g; FIBER 3g; CHOL 79mg; IRON 2mg; SODIUM 423mg; CALC 48mg

Golden Raisins

Also known as sultanas, golden raisins are made by drying Thompson seedless grapes and treating them with sulfur dioxide to retain their golden color. They tend to be moister and plumper than dark raisins and show up in both Middle Eastern and African dishes like couscous, rice pilafs, and stews. Plump the raisins in hot liquid to melt any crystallized sugars.

According to chef Marcus Samuelsson, "A brief Italian occupation from 1936 to 1941 left a European presence evident in Ethiopia's cathedrals and in dishes like pasta saltata." Here is the chef's modern version of the now-classic Ethiopian dish—minus all the butter and oil.

RED WHOLE-WHEAT PENNE
(Pasta Saltata)

HANDS-ON TIME: 22 MIN. TOTAL TIME: 52 MIN.

1 pound peeled Yukon gold
   potatoes (about 2)
¼ cup extra-virgin olive oil,
   divided
½ cup blanched whole
   almonds
¼ cup thinly sliced shallots
   (about 1 large)
2 garlic cloves, minced
¼ cup fresh lemon juice
2 tablespoons grated fresh
   Parmesan cheese
2 tablespoons harissa
1 teaspoon salt
6 cups hot cooked whole-
   wheat penne (about 12
   ounces uncooked tube-
   shaped pasta)
¼ cup chopped arugula
¼ cup chopped fresh basil

1. Place potatoes in a saucepan; cover with water. Bring to a boil. Reduce heat, and simmer 15 minutes or until tender. Drain potatoes in a colander over a bowl, reserving 1½ cups liquid. Cool potatoes slightly, and cut into ½-inch pieces.
2. Heat a small skillet over low heat. Add 1 tablespoon oil to pan; swirl to coat. Add almonds, shallots, and garlic to pan; cook 8 minutes or until almonds are golden, stirring often. Remove from heat; cool.
3. Place almond mixture in a food processor; add remaining 3 tablespoons oil, juice, cheese, harissa, and salt; process 1 minute or until well blended and almost smooth. With processor on, slowly pour 1½ cups reserved cooking liquid through food chute; process 1 minute or until smooth.
4. Combine pasta, potatoes, and almond mixture in a large bowl, tossing gently. Fold in arugula; sprinkle with basil. Serves 4 (serving size: about 2 cups)

CALORIES 318; FAT 13.6g (sat 1.6g, mono 8g, poly 3.3g); PROTEIN 9.3g; CARB 47.6g; FIBER 6.7g; CHOL 1mg; IRON 2.3mg; SODIUM 325mg; CALC 71mg

Persian traders brought mangoes to East Africa in the 10th century. Serve this simple mango salad with any East African meal of stewed or braised meat. Jalapeños, coriander, cumin, cinnamon, and cloves spice it up, and peanuts give it crunch. If you can't find red jalapeños, double up on the green ones.

CUCUMBER-MANGO SALAD

HANDS-ON TIME: 12 MIN. TOTAL TIME: 52 MIN.

2 cups thinly sliced English cucumber (about 1)
1½ cups finely chopped red onion
½ teaspoon salt
1 garlic clove, minced
1 teaspoon peanut oil
2 cups chopped seeded tomato (about 1 pound)
3 tablespoons chopped unsalted, dry-roasted peanuts
1 tablespoon finely chopped seeded red jalapeño pepper (about 1)
1 tablespoon finely chopped seeded green jalapeño pepper (about 1)
¼ teaspoon coriander seeds, crushed
¼ teaspoon ground cumin
⅛ teaspoon ground red pepper
Dash of ground cinnamon
Dash of ground cloves
1¾ cups diced peeled ripe mango (about 1)
1 tablespoon chopped fresh cilantro
3 tablespoons fresh lime juice

1. Combine first 4 ingredients in a colander; toss gently. Let stand at least 20 minutes.

2. Heat a large skillet over medium-high heat. Add oil to pan; swirl to coat. Add tomato and next 8 ingredients (through ground cloves) to pan; sauté 5 minutes or until tomato is tender. Remove from heat; cool to room temperature (about 20 minutes).

3. Combine drained cucumber mixture, tomato mixture, and remaining ingredients in a medium bowl; toss gently to combine. Serves 6 (serving size: ⅔ cup)

CALORIES 95; FAT 3.4g (sat 0.5g, mono 1.5g, poly 1.1g); PROTEIN 2.8g; CARB 15.9g; FIBER 2.9g; CHOL 0mg; IRON 0.7mg; SODIUM 204mg; CALC 31mg

Bulgur forms the basis of many Middle Eastern salads. This Turkish one, from cultural anthropologist Claudia Roden, requires no cooking and fewer than 10 minutes of hands-on time. The bulgur softens as it absorbs the juice of the fresh tomatoes.

BULGUR SALAD
with Nuts (Batrik)

HANDS-ON TIME: 7 MIN. TOTAL TIME: 67 MIN.

1 pound coarsely chopped plum
  tomato
¾ cup uncooked bulgur
1 teaspoon tomato paste
1 tablespoon olive oil
¼ teaspoon salt
Dash of crushed red pepper
½ cup finely chopped green
  onions
⅓ cup finely chopped walnuts

1. Place tomato in a food processor; process until smooth. Combine tomato, bulgur, and tomato paste in a large bowl. Cover and let stand 1 hour. Stir in oil, salt, and pepper. Stir in onions and nuts immediately before serving. Serves 4 (serving size: ¾ cup)

CALORIES 218; **FAT** 10.7g (sat 1.2g, mono 3.5g, poly 5.3g); **PROTEIN** 6g; **CARB** 28.6g; **FIBER** 7.1g; **CHOL** 0mg; **IRON** 1.5mg; **SODIUM** 163mg; **CALC** 29mg

In the Kenyan language of Kikuyu, irio just means "food." But in daily use, it means a quick dish of the region's staples: mashed potatoes, corn, peas, and greens. Irio is perfectly at home alongside roasted or grilled meats, but if you want some meatless protein, stir about a cup of frozen and thawed lima beans directly into the mash.

MASHED PEAS AND POTATOES
with Corn (Irio)
HANDS-ON TIME: 29 MIN. TOTAL TIME: 40 MIN.

1½ pounds baking potatoes, peeled and coarsely chopped
2½ cups water
1½ teaspoons salt
2 cups frozen green peas
1 tablespoon butter
¾ cup finely chopped onion
4 cups chopped spinach, kale, or watercress (about 4 ounces)
1½ cups frozen whole-kernel corn

1. Combine potatoes, 2½ cups water, and salt in medium saucepan; cover and bring to a boil over high heat. Reduce heat to medium; simmer, covered, 7 minutes. Add peas; cover and cook 5 minutes or until potatoes are tender. Drain potato mixture in a colander over a bowl, reserving 1 cup cooking liquid.
2. Melt butter in saucepan over medium heat. Add onion; sauté 4 minutes or until tender. Add spinach and corn; cook 3 to 4 minutes or until spinach wilts and corn is thoroughly heated. Remove from heat.
3. Pass potatoes and peas through a ricer or food mill or mash with a potato masher. Stir potato mixture and enough of reserved cooking liquid into spinach mixture to create a creamy texture. Serves 10 (serving size: about ½ cup)

Note: If you have leftovers, you can refrigerate them, and then the next day form them into patties and pan-fry.

CALORIES 123; FAT 1.7g (sat 0.8g, mono 0.4g, poly 0.2g); PROTEIN 3.8g; CARB 24g; FIBER 3.1g; CHOL 3mg; IRON 1mg; SODIUM 88mg; CALC 24mg

Dishes in Morocco tend be heavily spiced, and this soup is no exception. It features ras el hanout, a "top of the shop" spice blend of the merchant's best spices. Ras el hanout is a classic seasoning for grilled lamb, tagines, and couscous, so keep the extras in a tightly sealed jar for later use. Pumpkin is traditional for this soup, but butternut squash works well, too.

MOROCCAN PUMPKIN SOUP
(Chorbat al Qara'a)
HANDS-ON TIME: 25 MIN. TOTAL TIME: 25 MIN.

3½ cups (1-inch) cubed peeled fresh pumpkin or butternut squash (about 1¼ pounds)
2 cups organic vegetable broth
1¾ cups diced yellow onion
1 cup water
1 teaspoon Ras El Hanout
¾ teaspoon kosher salt
½ teaspoon ground coriander
½ cup whole milk
1 tablespoon butter
8 teaspoons plain yogurt
¼ cup fresh cilantro leaves

1. Combine first 7 ingredients in a large saucepan; bring to a boil. Cover, reduce heat, and simmer 10 minutes or until vegetables are tender.
2. Place half of squash mixture in a blender. Remove center piece of blender lid (to allow steam to escape); secure blender lid on blender. Place a clean towel over opening in blender lid (to avoid splatters). Blend until smooth. Pour pureed mixture into a large bowl. Repeat procedure with remaining squash mixture. Return pureed mixture to pan over low heat. Add milk and butter to pan; cook 3 minutes or until thoroughly heated. Serve with yogurt and cilantro. Serves 8 (serving size: about ⅔ cup soup, 1 teaspoon yogurt, and 1½ teaspoons cilantro)

CALORIES 91; FAT 2.3g (sat 1.3g, mono 0.6g, poly 0.1g); PROTEIN 2.2g; CARB 17.4g; FIBER 2.8g; CHOL 6mg; IRON 0.9mg; SODIUM 392mg; CALC 84mg

RAS EL HANOUT
HANDS-ON TIME: 5 MIN. TOTAL TIME: 5 MIN.

2½ teaspoons kosher salt
2 teaspoons ground cumin
2 teaspoons ground ginger
2 teaspoons freshly ground black pepper
1½ teaspoons ground cinnamon
1 teaspoon ground coriander
1 teaspoon ground red pepper
1 teaspoon ground allspice
1 teaspoon saffron threads, crushed
½ teaspoon ground cloves
¼ teaspoon freshly ground nutmeg

1. Combine all ingredients in a small bowl. Store in an airtight container for up to 1 month. Serves 48 (serving size: ¼ teaspoon)

CALORIES 2; FAT 0.1g (sat 0g, mono 0g, poly 0g); PROTEIN 0.1g; CARB 0.3g; FIBER 0.1g; CHOL 0mg; IRON 0.1mg; SODIUM 98mg; CALC 3mg

Berbere, Ethiopia's signature spice blend, includes garlic, ginger, coriander, fenugreek, and allspice in addition to a big pinch of ground chiles. Look for it at well-stocked supermarkets. For a change of pace, skip the rice and serve the wat with Teff Injera Flatbread (page 122).

SPICY RED LENTIL STEW
(Mesir Wat)

HANDS-ON TIME: 22 MIN. TOTAL TIME: 1 HR. 10 MIN.

2 teaspoons canola oil
2 cups chopped red onion
1 tablespoon minced peeled fresh ginger
3 garlic cloves, minced
3 tablespoons tomato paste
1½ tablespoons berbere spice
3 cups organic vegetable broth
1 cup dried small red lentils
¼ teaspoon salt
¼ cup finely chopped fresh cilantro
4 cups hot cooked basmati rice

1. Heat a large Dutch oven over medium heat. Add oil; swirl to coat. Add onion to pan; cook 15 minutes or until tender, stirring occasionally. Add ginger and garlic; cook 5 minutes, stirring frequently. Stir in tomato paste and berbere spice; cook 1 minute, stirring to combine. Gradually add broth, stirring with a whisk until blended. Increase heat to medium-high; bring to a simmer.
2. Rinse lentils until cold water; drain. Add lentils to broth mixture; simmer, partially covered, 35 minutes or until lentils are tender, stirring occasionally. Stir in salt. Sprinkle with cilantro; serve over rice. Serves 4 (serving size: 1 cup lentils and 1 cup rice)

CALORIES 454; FAT 3.9g (sat 0.3g, mono 1g, poly 1g); PROTEIN 19g; CARB 85.5g; FIBER 9.5g; CHOL 0mg; IRON 5.1mg; SODIUM 867mg; CALC 43mg

Moroccan tagine is both a piece of cookware and a slow-cooked stew. Traditionally made of clay, the cookware consists of a shallow round base and a tall, cone-shaped lid. The stew develops a rich, concentrated flavor because the lid traps steam and sends it back down to the stew, eliminating the need for much added water.

LAMB AND CHICKPEA TAGINE

HANDS-ON TIME: 23 MIN. TOTAL TIME: 1 HR. 13 MIN.

1 tablespoon olive oil
1 pound lamb stew meat
1 cup chopped onion
1/2 teaspoon salt
1/4 teaspoon ground red
    pepper
1/4 teaspoon ground cumin
5 garlic cloves, minced
1 tablespoon tomato paste
2 teaspoons honey
2 1/2 cups fat-free, lower-
    sodium chicken broth
1/2 cup golden raisins
1 (15-ounce) can chickpeas
    (garbanzo beans), rinsed
    and drained
1/3 cup chopped pistachios
2 tablespoons small fresh
    cilantro leaves

1. Heat a large saucepan over medium-high heat. Add oil to pan; swirl to coat. Add lamb; sauté 4 minutes, turning to brown on all sides. Remove lamb with a slotted spoon. Add onion, salt, pepper, and cumin to pan; sauté 4 minutes, stirring occasionally. Add garlic; sauté 1 minute, stirring constantly. Return lamb to pan; stir in tomato paste and honey. Cook 30 seconds, stirring constantly. Add broth, raisins, and chickpeas; bring to a boil. Reduce heat to medium; cover and cook 50 minutes or until lamb is tender, stirring occasionally. Sprinkle with pistachios and cilantro. Serves 5 (serving size: about 2/3 cup lamb mixture, 4 teaspoons pistachios, and 1 1/2 teaspoons cilantro)

CALORIES 432; FAT 15.6g (sat 3.9g, mono 7.5g, poly 2.6g); PROTEIN 37.9g; CARB 36.2g; FIBER 5.4g; CHOL 98mg; IRON 4.8mg; SODIUM 729mg; CALC 81mg

Europe
& Eurasia

ALMONDS:
Toast almonds and other nuts in a hot pan or oven to intensify their flavor.

BEER:
Used in place of water as a steaming liquid and in sauces, batters, yeast breads, and cakes.

PAPRIKA:
Powdered mild chiles show up in Hungarian paprikash as well as Spanish chorizo, which features smoked pimentón (Spanish paprika).

The Flavors of Europe & Eurasia

OLIVE OIL:
Popular throughout the Mediterranean, particularly Greece; use delicate extra-virgin olive oil for drizzling and virgin oil for cooking.

Remarkably, the European continent covers only 2 percent of the Earth's surface but includes 50 countries. That gives the region an incredibly varied set of cuisines. On the eastern side, Russia borders northwest Asia and spans nine time zones. A little south of there, the cuisines of the Caucasus—with their love of lamb and eggplant—have more in common with Middle Eastern countries than they do with European countries like Belgium.

With so many cultures and such a diverse landscape, it's very difficult to generalize. But wine and beer are popular across the entire European continent. You also find lemons in everything from British lemon curd to Polish lemon cake. The further west you go in Europe, the more prominent meat and dairy products become. For instance, cured sausage and aged cheese loom large in the cuisines of Italy and Spain. Here's a peek at some of the key flavors and aromas in the many different cuisines of Europe.

CURED SAUSAGE:
Before refrigeration, salting and drying meat was the primary method of preserving, providing salty, savory, meaty satisfaction.

AGED CHEESE:
From cheddar to Parmigiano-Reggiano (the king of cheeses), aged cheese brings umami (savory) flavor to many cuisines of Europe.

VINEGAR:
From red wine and balsamic to sherry and malt vinegars, the high acidity of vinegar provides spark in dressings, dips, and sauces.

PARSLEY:
Fresh herbs like parsley, basil, sage, rosemary, thyme, and oregano lend fresh, inviting aromas.

LEMONS:
To avoid discoloring green vegetables like asparagus, use only lemon zest instead of the acidic juice.

WINE:
Often added to hot pans to dissolve browned bits of food and lend deep flavor to sauces.

A platter of Greek mezze (little dishes) typically includes grape leaves stuffed with seasoned rice. "This classic Mediterranean dish makes a great party hors d'oeuvre," says Joanne Weir, James Beard Award-winning cookbook author and television personality.

STUFFED GRAPE LEAVES

HANDS-ON TIME: 37 MIN. TOTAL TIME: 4 HR. 42 MIN.

42 bottled large grape leaves (about 6 ounces)
2 tablespoons extra-virgin olive oil, divided
1½ cups minced yellow onion (about 1 medium)
1 cup thinly sliced green onions (about 1 bunch)
⅓ cup sliced almonds, chopped
3 cups water, divided
¾ cup uncooked long-grain rice
½ teaspoon salt
¼ teaspoon freshly ground black pepper
¼ teaspoon ground cinnamon
4 ounces crumbled feta cheese (about 1 cup)
3 tablespoons chopped fresh flat-leaf parsley
3 tablespoons chopped fresh mint
2 tablespoons chopped fresh dill
3 tablespoons fresh lemon juice, divided
Lemon wedges (optional)
Fat-free Greek-style plain yogurt (optional)

1. Rinse grape leaves with cold water; drain well. Pat dry with paper towels. Remove stems; discard.
2. Heat a saucepan over medium heat. Add 1 tablespoon oil to pan; swirl to coat. Add yellow onion; cook 10 minutes or until tender, stirring occasionally. Add green onions and almonds; cook 3 minutes. Stir in 2 cups water; bring to a boil. Add rice, salt, pepper, and cinnamon; cover, reduce heat, and simmer 22 minutes or until rice is tender. Remove from heat; cool. Stir in cheese, parsley, mint, and dill.
3. Spoon 1½ heaping tablespoons rice mixture onto center of 1 grape leaf. Bring 2 opposite points of leaf to center; fold over filling. Beginning at 1 short side, roll up leaf tightly. Repeat procedure with remaining rice mixture and 35 grape leaves. Place 12 stuffed grape leaves, seam sides down, in a large saucepan lined with 3 grape leaves. Drizzle with 1 teaspoon oil and 1 tablespoon juice. Top with 12 stuffed grape leaves; drizzle with 1 teaspoon oil and 1 tablespoon juice. Repeat procedure with remaining stuffed grape leaves, oil, and juice. Cover with remaining 3 grape leaves; pour 1 cup water over leaves. Invert a small heatproof plate on top of leaves. Bring to a boil. Cover, reduce heat, and simmer 1½ hours. Remove from heat, and let stand in saucepan 2 hours. Serve at room temperature with lemon wedges and yogurt, if desired. Serves 12 (serving size: 3 stuffed grape leaves)

CALORIES 128; FAT 6.5g (sat 1.9g, mono 3.4g, poly 0.8g); PROTEIN 4g; CARB 14.4g; FIBER 1.2g; CHOL 8.4mg; IRON 2.1mg; SODIUM 210mg; CALC 175mg

how to: STUFF GRAPE LEAVES
Look for brined grape leaves packed in tall glass jars.

1 Spoon a mound of filling onto center of grape leaf. Do not pat it down.

2 Fold 2 opposite points of leaf over filling. The points should barely touch.

3 Beginning at the short side closest to you, roll up tightly.

Multiple layers of paper-thin phyllo dough make these ubiquitous Greek spinach pastries shatteringly crisp. To get a jump on prep before a party, prepare the filling up to a day ahead and keep it refrigerated. You can also let the filled pastries stand at room temperature for up to 1 hour. Then pop them in the oven 20 minutes before guests arrive.

SPANAKOPITAS

HANDS-ON TIME: 60 MIN. TOTAL TIME: 1 HR. 20 MIN.

1 (10-ounce) package fresh spinach, coarsely chopped

1½ ounces feta cheese, crumbled (about ⅓ cup)

¼ cup 1% low-fat cottage cheese

2 tablespoons grated fresh Parmesan cheese

5 teaspoons olive oil, divided

1½ cups chopped green onions

3 large egg whites, divided and lightly beaten

1½ tablespoons chopped fresh dill or 1½ teaspoons dried dill

1 tablespoon fresh lemon juice

½ teaspoon salt, divided

¼ teaspoon freshly ground black pepper

5 sheets frozen phyllo dough, thawed

1. Preheat oven to 350°.

2. Place spinach in a large skillet or Dutch oven. Place over medium heat; cook until spinach wilts. Place spinach in a colander, pressing until barely moist. Combine spinach and cheeses in a bowl; set aside.

3. Heat a nonstick skillet over medium-high heat. Add 2 teaspoons olive oil to pan; swirl to coat. Add green onions; sauté 2 minutes or until soft. Stir green onions, 2 beaten egg whites, dill, lemon juice, ¼ teaspoon salt, and black pepper into spinach mixture.

4. Combine remaining 1 tablespoon olive oil, remaining ¼ teaspoon salt, and remaining 1 egg white in a small bowl, stirring with a whisk. Working with 1 phyllo sheet at a time, cut each sheet lengthwise into 4 (3½-inch-wide) strips; lightly brush phyllo sheet with egg mixture (cover remaining phyllo dough to keep it from drying). Spoon about 1 tablespoon spinach mixture onto one end of each strip. Fold 1 corner of the opposite end over mixture, forming a triangle; keep folding back and forth into a triangle to end of strip. Place triangles, seam sides down, on a baking sheet. Bake at 350° for 20 minutes or until golden. Serves 20 (serving size: 1 triangle)

CALORIES 43; FAT 2.1g (sat 0.6g, mono 1.1g, poly 0.3g); PROTEIN 2.3g; CARB 4g; FIBER 0.8g; CHOL 2mg; IRON 0.8mg; SODIUM 147mg; CALC 44mg

Americans love fries with ketchup. Spaniards love fries with brava sauce, a "fierce" tomato sauce with chiles and vinegar. I use three types of peppers—roasted piquillo peppers, smoked paprika, and ground red pepper for heat. I chill the spuds and steam them before roasting, both of which make the patatas creamy inside and crispy outside.

FIERCE POTATOES
(Patatas Bravas)

HANDS-ON TIME: 20 MIN. TOTAL TIME: 3 HR. 29 MIN.

2 pounds baking potatoes
3 tablespoons olive oil,
  divided
¼ teaspoon saffron threads,
  finely crushed
¾ teaspoon salt, divided
½ cup chopped yellow onion
2 large garlic cloves, minced
1 bay leaf
2 bottled roasted piquillo
  peppers or 1 bottled roasted
  red bell pepper, drained and
  chopped (½ cup)
1½ cups unsalted tomato
  puree (fresh or canned)
1 tablespoon Spanish smoked
  paprika
¼ teaspoon ground red
  pepper
1 tablespoon sherry vinegar
2 tablespoons chopped fresh
  chives

1. Soak whole potatoes in ice water in refrigerator 2 hours; drain. Cut potatoes into 1-inch cubes. Steam potatoes, covered, 9 minutes or until just tender. Rinse with cold water; drain and pat dry.

2. Preheat oven to 450°.

3. Combine 1½ tablespoons olive oil and saffron in center of a jelly-roll pan. Bake at 450° for 3 to 4 minutes to bloom saffron. Scrape oil and saffron into a medium bowl using a rubber spatula. Return pan to oven. Add potatoes and ½ teaspoon salt to saffron oil, tossing to coat.

4. Spread potatoes on preheated pan; bake at 450° for 45 minutes or until golden brown and crisp, stirring twice.

5. While potatoes cook, heat a small saucepan over medium heat. Add remaining 1½ tablespoons oil to pan; swirl to coat. Add onion; sauté 4 minutes or until tender. Add garlic and bay leaf; sauté 1 minute. Add roasted pepper, tomato puree, paprika, and ground red pepper; bring to a boil over high heat. Reduce heat to low; cover and simmer 20 minutes, stirring occasionally.

6. Remove from heat; discard bay leaf. Place pepper mixture, remaining ¼ teaspoon salt, and vinegar in a blender. Remove center piece of blender lid (to allow steam to escape); secure blender lid on blender. Place a clean towel over opening in blender lid (to avoid splatters). Blend until smooth. Spoon sauce onto plates or a platter. Top with potatoes, and sprinkle with chives. Serves 8 (serving size: ⅔ cup potatoes and ¼ cup sauce)

CALORIES 165; FAT 5.4g (sat 0.8g, mono 3.7g, poly 0.7g); PROTEIN 3.7g; CARB 27.4g; FIBER 3.9g; CHOL 0mg; IRON 2.2mg; SODIUM 275mg; CALC 29mg

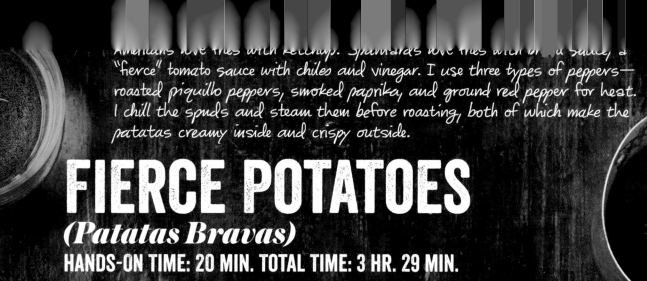

Unlike yeast-risen breads, soda bread can be mixed and baked immediately. Buttermilk usually provides the acid required to activate the baking soda, forming bubbles that inflate the dough. Packed with whole grains like steel-cut oats, wheat germ, and whole-wheat flour, this version of the Irish classic comes from Margaret M. Johnson, author of Flavors of Ireland.

BROWN SODA BREAD

HANDS-ON TIME: 15 MIN. TOTAL TIME: 1 HR. 40 MIN.

Cooking spray
11.25 ounces whole-wheat flour (about 2½ cups)
2.25 ounces all-purpose flour (about ½ cup)
½ cup steel-cut oats
2 tablespoons brown sugar
1 tablespoon wheat germ
1 teaspoon baking soda
1 teaspoon baking powder
½ teaspoon salt
2 cups low-fat buttermilk
1 large egg, lightly beaten

1. Preheat oven to 325°.
2. Coat a 9 x 5–inch loaf pan with cooking spray. Line pan with parchment paper, and coat with cooking spray.
3. Weigh or lightly spoon flours into dry measuring cups; level with a knife. Combine flours and next 6 ingredients (through salt). Combine buttermilk and egg; add to flour mixture. Stir just until combined.
4. Spoon mixture into prepared pan. Bake at 325° for 1 hour and 5 minutes or until a wooden pick inserted in center comes out clean. Invert bread onto a wire rack; cool completely. Remove parchment; slice bread into 12 slices. Serves 12 (serving size: 1 slice)

CALORIES 160; **FAT** 1.8g (sat 0.5g, mono 0.2g, poly 0.3g); **PROTEIN** 7.2g; **CARB** 30.8g; **FIBER** 4g; **CHOL** 18mg; **IRON** 1.7mg; **SODIUM** 286mg; **CALC** 86mg

A popular pastry for centuries, strudel is all about the dough. It's traditionally made with flour, eggs, water, and butter or oil, and then stretched thin on the backs of your hands. Then, it's rolled around the filling multiple times, and baked to create layer upon layer of crisp, flaky goodness. Here, puff pastry makes a similar flaky crust, and it's conveniently available frozen.

APPLE STRUDEL

HANDS-ON TIME: 9 MIN. TOTAL TIME: 54 MIN.

2 tablespoons butter
1/4 cup packed brown sugar
2 tablespoons fresh lemon juice
1/2 teaspoon ground cinnamon
1/8 teaspoon salt
6 medium Granny Smith apples, peeled and thinly sliced (about 2 1/2 pounds)
1 sheet frozen puff pastry dough, thawed
1/4 cup chopped walnuts
2 tablespoons granulated sugar

1. Preheat oven to 400°.
2. Melt butter in a large skillet over medium-high heat. Stir in brown sugar, juice, cinnamon, salt, and apples. Cover, reduce heat, and cook 10 minutes or until apples are tender, stirring occasionally. Remove apples from pan; cool.
3. Roll pastry to a 15 x 12–inch rectangle on a lightly floured surface. Spoon apple mixture along 1 long edge of pastry; roll up jelly-roll fashion. Gently press seam to seal. Cut slits in top.
4. Place nuts and granulated sugar in a food processor; pulse until finely ground. Sprinkle strudel with nut mixture, pressing gently. Place strudel on a baking sheet lined with parchment paper. Bake at 400° for 25 minutes or until golden. Let stand 5 minutes; slice. Serves 8 (serving size: 1 slice)

CALORIES 318; FAT 17g (sat 5g, mono 7.6g, poly 3.4g); PROTEIN 3.2g; CARB 41.6g; FIBER 2.6g; CHOL 8mg; IRON 1.2mg; SODIUM 135mg; CALC 23mg

how to: FILL AND FOLD STRUDEL

For the best flavor, look for all-butter puff pastry such as Dufour.

1 It's important to thaw the puff pastry just as the package instructs before rolling into a 15 x 12–inch rectangle.

2 Spoon filling along 1 long edge. In the final product, this line of filling will be in the center of the strudel.

3 Roll up strudel jelly-roll fashion. As you roll, the filling will spread over the surface of the rectangle.

4 Seal. Cut slits in top, then sprinkle with nut mixture. Sealing the dough keeps the filling from bubbling out while baking.

SIP AND SAVOR

europeans are the world's ultimate wine connoisseurs. On my first trip to Greece and Italy in 1985, I was struck by the recurring customs that come with drinking wine. For instance, wine glasses were filled only one-third full. That allows enough room to swirl the wine in the glass, which aerates the wine and heightens its aromas. I also saw Europeans holding their wineglasses by the stem instead of the bowl. Why? Because the hand itself can warm up the wine and negatively affect the taste. Not to mention it can block the view of the wine's color and clarity.

Many Americans have come to enjoy a glass of wine with dinner, and it's now considered beneficial for health. But to keep from going overboard, sip it slowly and make the wine last throughout the meal. "Drinking water intermittently while dining is a great way to savor the wine without going overboard on calories," explains Sidney Fry, *Cooking Light* Nutrition Editor. "Split glasses among friends, swirl your glass, and enjoy each sip. Consider the beverage a part of your meal—something to heighten, enhance, and complement flavors."

Halibut stands in for salmon in this twist on the Swedish delicacy. For food safety, it's best to use thawed frozen-at-sea (FAS) halibut. Depending on the size of the fillets, you may end up using two to five pieces. But don't use one large fillet; it will have thick and thin sections, so the salt mixture won't seep evenly throughout the fish.

FENNEL-CURED HALIBUT GRAVLAX

HANDS-ON TIME: 7 MIN. TOTAL TIME: 24 HR. 7 MIN.

⅓ cup coarse sea salt
⅓ cup sugar
⅓ cup chopped fennel fronds
¼ cup olive oil
1 teaspoon freshly ground
   black pepper
2 pounds halibut fillets,
   skinned
3 tablespoons finely chopped
   fresh dill

1. Place first 5 ingredients in a food processor; process until finely ground.
2. Arrange fish in a single layer in a 13 x 9-inch baking dish. Rub salt mixture evenly over surface of fish. Cover and refrigerate fish 24 hours.
3. Rinse fish thoroughly under cold water; pat dry. Pat dill onto fish. Cut fish into ¼-inch slices. Store in an airtight container in refrigerator up to 3 days. Serves 12 (serving size: about 2½ ounces)

CALORIES 95; FAT 2.3g (sat 0.3g, mono 1.1g, poly 0.6g); PROTEIN 14.8g; CARB 2.8g; FIBER 0g; CHOL 23mg; IRON 0.6mg; SODIUM 631mg; CALC 34mg

Italians call it baccalà. The Spanish, bacalao. In Portuguese, it's bacalhau. Salted cod is a fantastic ingredient to keep in your fridge. It keeps for months and can be stirred into scrambled eggs and fried potatoes to make this Portuguese specialty, bacalhau à la brás. This savory, rustic dish makes the perfect brunch, as it's served family-style in a big pan.

SALTED COD À LA BRÁS

HANDS-ON: 56 MIN. TOTAL: 25 HR. 26 MIN.

1 pound boneless, skinless dried salted cod loin
1 pound baking potatoes, peeled and cut into (2 x ¼-inch) sticks
¼ cup olive oil, divided
1 small onion, halved lengthwise and thinly sliced crosswise (1½ cups)
¼ teaspoon saffron threads, finely crushed
1 garlic clove, minced
6 large eggs
¼ teaspoon salt
¼ teaspoon ground black pepper
⅓ cup chopped oil-cured olives
2 tablespoons chopped fresh parsley

Rinse fish with cold water; place, skin side up, in a shallow baking dish. Cover with water to ¼ inch above fish. Cover and chill 24 hours, changing water 4 times.

Drain fish. Place fish in a large saucepan; cover with water. Bring to a boil, reduce heat to medium-low, and simmer 12 to 15 minutes or until fish begins to flake apart. Drain. Flake fish into bite-sized pieces with a fork.

While fish cooks, place potato sticks in a large bowl. Cover with cold water to 1 inch above potatoes; let stand 30 minutes to draw out starch. Drain and pat dry with paper towels.

Heat a large nonstick skillet over medium-high heat. Add 2 tablespoons oil to pan; swirl to coat. Add half of potatoes; cook 5 minutes or until golden brown. Remove potatoes from pan; drain on paper towels. Add 1 tablespoon oil to pan; swirl to coat. Repeat procedure with remaining potatoes. Reduce heat to medium.

Add 1½ teaspoons oil to pan; swirl to coat. Add onion, saffron, and garlic; sauté 6 to 8 minutes or until onion is golden brown. Add remaining 1½ teaspoons oil and fish; cook 3 minutes, stirring occasionally. Add potatoes; cook 2 minutes.

Combine eggs, salt, and pepper in a large bowl; stir well with a whisk. Pour eggs over potato mixture, and cook 3 minutes or until eggs are soft-scrambled, stirring occasionally. Sprinkle with olives and parsley. Serves 6 (serving size: about 1 cup)

CALORIES 329; FAT 17g (sat 3.1g, mono 8.9g, poly 2.6g); PROTEIN 26.6g; CARB 19g; FIBER 2.4g; CHOL 226mg; IRON 1.8mg; SODIUM 423mg; CALC 124mg

Before refrigeration, salting cod helped preserve the fish. Lower-quality salted cod comes from thinner fillets and tends be so dried out that it lacks flavor. Look for salted cod that's about ½-inch thick, preferably from the loin section, and at least a little pliable. To remove the salt and rehydrate the fish, soak it in cold water for a day or two, changing the water three to four times a day (change the water more often if you soak the fish for less time).

Greek versions of this baked casserole layer a tomato-based meat sauce with sautéed or roasted eggplant and a topping of creamy béchamel (white) sauce. In this meatless rendition, bulgur wheat stands in for the traditional ground lamb. To get a touch of smoke in the mix, grill the eggplant instead of roasting it.

VEGETARIAN MOUSSAKA

HANDS-ON TIME: 60 MIN. TOTAL TIME: 2 HR. 30 MIN.

3 peeled eggplants, cut into ½-inch-thick slices (about 2½ pounds)
2 tablespoons extra-virgin olive oil, divided
Cooking spray
2 cups chopped onion
4 garlic cloves, minced
½ cup uncooked bulgur
¼ teaspoon ground allspice
¼ teaspoon ground cinnamon
⅛ teaspoon ground cloves
2 cups organic vegetable broth
2 teaspoons chopped fresh oregano
1 (14.5-ounce) can no-salt-added diced tomatoes, undrained
1 tablespoon butter
2 tablespoons all-purpose flour
1 cup 1% low-fat milk
2 tablespoons finely grated fresh Romano cheese
¼ teaspoon salt
1 large egg, lightly beaten
Chopped fresh parsley leaves (optional)

1. Preheat broiler to high.

2. Brush eggplant slices with 1 tablespoon oil. Place half of eggplant on a foil-lined baking sheet coated with cooking spray; broil 5 inches from heat 5 minutes on each side or until browned. Repeat procedure with remaining eggplant. Set eggplant aside.

3. Heat a large skillet over medium-high heat. Add remaining 1 tablespoon oil to pan; swirl to coat. Add chopped onion to pan; sauté 8 minutes. Add garlic; sauté 1 minute. Add bulgur; cook 3 minutes or until bulgur is lightly toasted, stirring frequently. Add allspice, cinnamon, and cloves; cook 1 minute, stirring constantly. Stir in broth, oregano, and tomatoes. Bring to a boil; reduce heat, and simmer 20 minutes or until thickened, stirring occasionally.

4. Melt butter in a saucepan over medium heat. Add flour; cook 1 minute, stirring constantly with a whisk until well blended. Gradually add milk, stirring constantly with a whisk. Bring to a boil; reduce heat to medium-low, and simmer 5 minutes or until thickened, stirring frequently. Stir in cheese and salt. Remove from heat, and cool slightly. Add egg, stirring well with a whisk.

5. Preheat oven to 350°.

6. Arrange half of eggplant in an 11 x 7–inch glass or ceramic baking dish coated with cooking spray. Spread bulgur mixture evenly over eggplant; arrange remaining eggplant over bulgur mixture. Top with milk mixture. Bake at 350° for 40 minutes, and remove from oven. Increase oven temperature to 475°. Return dish to oven for 4 minutes or until top is browned. Let stand 10 minutes before serving. Garnish with parsley, if desired. Serves 4 (serving size: ¼ of casserole)

CALORIES 343; FAT 13.1g (sat 4.2g, mono 6.4g, poly 1.3g); PROTEIN 11.4g; CARB 47.8g; FIBER 13.4g; CHOL 57mg; IRON 2.3mg; SODIUM 583mg; CALC 203mg

What's the difference between cottage pie and shepherd's pie? Not much, except that shepherd's pie is a newer term used mostly when ground lamb is the meat of choice. Made with beef or lamb, the pie has become standard British pub fare, not least because it's a filling meal and goes swimmingly with a pint of ale.

ENGLISH COTTAGE PIE
HANDS-ON TIME: 30 MIN. TOTAL TIME: 50 MIN.

1 tablespoon all-purpose flour
1 tablespoon butter, softened
Cooking spray
1½ cups chopped onion
½ cup chopped carrot
1 (8-ounce) package cremini or button mushrooms, thinly sliced
1 pound extra-lean ground beef
2 tablespoons no-salt-added tomato paste
1 cup fat-free, lower-sodium beef broth
¼ teaspoon freshly ground black pepper
¼ cup chopped fresh parsley
1 tablespoon fresh thyme leaves
½ teaspoon salt
3 cups leftover mashed potatoes
3 ounces shredded reduced-fat sharp white cheddar cheese (about ¾ cup), divided
Paprika (optional)

1. Preheat oven to 350°.
2. Combine flour and butter; stir well. Heat a large nonstick skillet over medium-high heat. Coat pan with cooking spray. Add onion and carrot; sauté 5 minutes. Add mushrooms; sauté 5 minutes or until lightly browned. Remove vegetables from pan. Add beef to pan; cook 5 minutes or until browned, stirring to crumble. Stir in tomato paste, and cook 3 minutes. Stir in broth and pepper. Return vegetables to pan, and bring to a simmer. Stir in parsley, thyme, and salt. Add flour mixture, and cook 1 minute or until thick, stirring constantly.
3. Spoon meat mixture into an 8-inch square glass or ceramic baking dish coated with cooking spray, spreading evenly. Combine potatoes and half of cheese; spread potato mixture evenly over meat mixture. Top with remaining cheese. Sprinkle with paprika, if desired. Bake at 350° for 20 minutes or until bubbly. Serves 6 (serving size: ⅔ cup)

CALORIES 288; FAT 10g (sat 5.6g, mono 2.3g, poly 0.5g); PROTEIN 24.1g; CARB 29.9g; FIBER 4g; CHOL 60mg; IRON 2.8mg; SODIUM 626mg; CALC 164mg

To Hungarians, goulash typically means paprika-spiced beef soup. But in America, Hungarian goulash refers to a thicker stew that more closely resembles Hungarian paprikash and is served with noodles. Nomenclature aside, the dish is delicious. A thick stew of spiced lean pork gets ladled over buttered egg noodles and topped with sour cream.

HUNGARIAN GOULASH
HANDS-ON TIME: 28 MIN. TOTAL TIME: 1 HR. 28 MIN.

1 garlic clove, crushed
1 teaspoon kosher salt, divided
¼ teaspoon caraway seeds, crushed
¼ teaspoon freshly ground black pepper, divided
Cooking spray
1 tablespoon paprika
1 (1-pound) pork tenderloin, trimmed and cut into 1-inch pieces
2 cups coarsely chopped onion
1 bacon slice, finely chopped
1¾ cups water, divided
1 cup chopped seeded tomato
¾ cup beer
⅛ teaspoon crushed red pepper
3 Hungarian wax chiles, seeded and cut into 1-inch pieces
1½ tablespoons all-purpose flour
8 ounces uncooked egg noodles
1 tablespoon butter
3 tablespoons sour cream
Fresh parsley leaves (optional)

1. Place garlic in a small bowl; mash with the back of a spoon to form a paste. Add ¼ teaspoon salt, caraway seeds, and ⅛ teaspoon black pepper.

2. Heat a large Dutch oven over high heat. Coat pan with cooking spray. Combine paprika, ¼ teaspoon salt, remaining ⅛ teaspoon black pepper, and pork in a medium bowl; toss. Add pork to pan; sauté 6 minutes, browning on all sides. Remove pork from pan.

3. Reduce heat to medium-high; return pan to heat. Add onion and bacon; sauté 7 minutes or until bacon is done, stirring frequently. Stir in garlic mixture; cook 1 minute, stirring constantly. Add 1½ cups water, tomato, and beer; bring to a boil. Reduce heat, and simmer 30 minutes, stirring occasionally. Stir in red pepper and chiles; simmer 15 minutes. Add pork to pan; simmer 15 minutes, stirring occasionally. Combine remaining ¼ cup water and flour in a small bowl; stir with a whisk. Stir flour mixture and remaining ½ teaspoon salt into pork mixture. Bring to a boil; cook 1 minute, stirring constantly.

4. Cook noodles according to package directions, omitting salt and fat. Combine noodles and butter in a medium bowl, stirring until butter melts. Place 1 cup noodles in each of 4 shallow bowls; top with 1 cup pork mixture. Top each serving with about 2 teaspoons sour cream. Garnish with parsley, if desired. Serves 4

CALORIES 476; FAT 11.3g (sat 5g, mono 2.4g, poly 1g); PROTEIN 35g; CARB 56.1g; FIBER 5.4g; CHOL 154mg; IRON 3.9mg; SODIUM 626mg; CALC 69mg

Caraway Seed

From a plant in the carrot family, caraway "seeds" (actually the dried fruit of the plant), have an earthy, sweet anise aroma that helps to flavor everything from Eastern European rye breads to North African spice blends. The taste pairs well with cabbage, so caraway often shows up in sauerkraut and cabbage soups. If you don't have it, use dill seeds, anise seeds, and/or fennel seeds for a similar aroma.

In her recipe for Boeuf Bourguignon, Julia Child hails the stew as "one of the most delicious beef dishes concocted by man." Here's a pretty faithful rendition with some judicious shortcuts like skipping the blanched bacon rind.

BEEF BOURGUIGNON
with Egg Noodles

HANDS-ON TIME: 30 MIN. TOTAL TIME: 2 HR. 15 MIN.

⅓ cup all-purpose flour
2 teaspoons salt, divided
¾ teaspoon freshly ground black pepper, divided
2¼ pounds beef stew meat
3 bacon slices, chopped and divided
1 cup chopped onion
1 cup sliced carrot
4 garlic cloves, minced
1½ cups dry red wine
1 (14-ounce) can lower-sodium beef broth
8 cups halved mushrooms (about 1½ pounds)
2 tablespoons tomato paste
2 teaspoons chopped fresh thyme
2 bay leaves
1 (16-ounce) package frozen pearl onions
7 cups hot cooked medium egg noodles (about 6 cups uncooked noodles)
3 tablespoons chopped fresh flat-leaf parsley

1. Combine flour, 1 teaspoon salt, and ¼ teaspoon pepper in a large zip-top plastic bag. Add beef; seal and shake to coat.

2. Cook half of bacon in a large Dutch oven over medium-high heat until crisp. Remove bacon from pan with a slotted spoon; set aside. Add half of beef mixture to drippings in pan; cook 5 minutes, browning on all sides. Remove beef from pan; cover and keep warm. Repeat procedure with remaining bacon and beef mixture. Remove beef from pan; cover and keep warm.

3. Add onion, carrot, and garlic to pan; sauté 5 minutes. Stir in wine and broth, scraping pan to loosen browned bits. Add bacon, beef, remaining 1 teaspoon salt, remaining ½ teaspoon pepper, mushrooms, and next 4 ingredients (through pearl onions); bring to a boil. Cover, reduce heat, and simmer 45 minutes. Uncover and cook 1 hour or until beef is tender. Discard bay leaves. Serve beef mixture over noodles; sprinkle with parsley. Serves 9 (serving size: about 1 cup beef mixture, ¾ cup noodles, and 1 teaspoon parsley)

CALORIES 447; FAT 14.6g (sat 5.1g, mono 6.1g, poly 1.5g); PROTEIN 32.7g; CARB 45.7g; FIBER 3.9g; CHOL 117mg; IRON 6mg; SODIUM 677mg; CALC 47mg

In Eastern Europe, cabbage rolls are stuffed with all manner of pork, beef, rice, and buckwheat. Also known as halupki and parkkas, Jewish-American versions are popular throughout the United States. This lightened Polish version uses turkey sausage, lean ground beef, and medium-grain white rice.

POLISH CABBAGE ROLLS
(Golumpki)

HANDS-ON TIME: 45 MIN. TOTAL TIME: 2 HR. 45 MIN.

1 tablespoon canola oil
2¼ cups finely chopped onion
⅔ cup finely chopped carrot
½ cup finely chopped celery
1¼ cups uncooked medium-grain rice
3 garlic cloves, minced
1 pound bulk turkey Italian sausage
1 pound 93% lean ground beef
3 tablespoons chopped fresh parsley
¾ teaspoon ground black pepper, divided
1 large egg, lightly beaten
18 large green cabbage leaves
1 (28-ounce) can crushed tomatoes, undrained
1½ cups fat-free, lower-sodium chicken broth
1 tablespoon brown sugar
⅛ teaspoon salt

1. Preheat oven to 350°.
2. Heat a large Dutch oven over medium heat. Add oil to pan; swirl to coat. Add onion, carrot, and celery; sauté 6 minutes. Add rice and garlic; cook 3 minutes, stirring to coat rice with oil. Spoon rice mixture into a large bowl; crumble sausage and beef into bowl. Add parsley, ½ teaspoon pepper, and egg; stir well.
3. Steam cabbage leaves, covered, 6 to 8 minutes or until tender and pliable. Remove cabbage from steamer. Let cool slightly.
4. Working with 1 cabbage leaf at a time, place about ⅓ cup meat mixture in center of leaf. Fold in edges of leaf; roll up. Repeat procedure with remaining cabbage leaves and meat mixture to form 18 cabbage rolls; set aside.
5. Combine crushed tomatoes, broth, brown sugar, salt, and remaining ¼ teaspoon pepper in Dutch oven; bring to a simmer over medium, and cook 15 minutes, stirring occasionally. Remove from heat. Add cabbage rolls to pan, nestling them into sauce and spoon sauce over rolls. Cover pan with lid, and bake at 350° for 1½ to 2 hours or until rice is tender and meat mixture is no longer pink. Serve sauce over cabbage rolls. Serves 9 (serving size: 2 golumpki and 6 tablespoons sauce)

CALORIES 364; FAT 11.1g (sat 4g, mono 3.9g, poly 2.1g); PROTEIN 29.1g; CARB 38.8g; FIBER 4.8g; CHOL 103mg; IRON 4.5mg; SODIUM 707mg; CALC 135mg

In Italian, saltimbocca means "jump in the mouth," an apt description for a quick dish layered with rich, salty prosciutto. The classic version consists of pounded veal rolled up with prosciutto and sage, and then cooked in a Marsala butter sauce. The only difference here is chicken instead of veal and a lighter, brighter lemon sauce.

LEMONY CHICKEN SALTIMBOCCA

HANDS-ON TIME: 15 MIN. TOTAL TIME: 15 MIN.

4 (4-ounce) chicken cutlets
⅛ teaspoon salt
12 fresh sage leaves
2 ounces very thinly sliced prosciutto, cut into 8 thin strips
4 teaspoons extra-virgin olive oil, divided
⅓ cup fat-free, lower-sodium chicken broth
¼ cup fresh lemon juice
½ teaspoon cornstarch
Lemon wedges (optional)

1. Sprinkle chicken evenly with salt. Place 3 sage leaves on each cutlet; wrap 2 prosciutto slices around each cutlet, securing sage leaves in place.
2. Heat a large skillet over medium heat. Add 1 tablespoon oil to pan; swirl to coat. Add chicken to pan; cook 2 minutes on each side or until done. Remove chicken from pan; keep warm.
3. Combine broth, lemon juice, and cornstarch in a small bowl; stir with a whisk until smooth. Add cornstarch mixture and remaining 1 teaspoon olive oil to pan; bring to a boil, stirring constantly. Cook 1 minute or until slightly thickened, stirring constantly with a whisk. Spoon sauce over chicken. Serve with lemon wedges, if desired. Serves 4 (serving size: 1 cutlet and 2 tablespoons sauce)

CALORIES 202; **FAT** 7.5g (sat 1.5g, mono 4.3g, poly 0.9g); **PROTEIN** 30.5g; **CARB** 2.3g; **FIBER** 0.2g; **CHOL** 77mg; **IRON** 1.1mg; **SODIUM** 560mg; **CALC** 18mg

This French braised dish is dressed to impress. You brown chicken parts in bacon drippings, and then braise the chicken in a Dutch oven with vegetables and herbs. The braising liquid is spiked with brandy and Champagne, and then enriched with browned butter to create a luxurious sauce.

CHAMPAGNE—BROWNED BUTTER CHICKEN

HANDS-ON TIME: 50 MIN. TOTAL TIME: 1 HR. 45 MIN.

2 center-cut bacon slices

²/₃ cup all-purpose flour

6 bone-in chicken thighs, skinned (about 1³/₄ pounds)

6 bone-in chicken drumsticks, skinned (about 1¹/₂ pounds)

1¹/₄ teaspoons kosher salt, divided

³/₄ teaspoon freshly ground black pepper, divided

2 tablespoons canola oil, divided

1 pound red-skinned potatoes, quartered

1 pound button mushrooms, halved

¹/₄ cup brandy

4 shallots, halved

³/₄ cup unsalted chicken stock

1 tablespoon black peppercorns

3 thyme sprigs

1 bay leaf

¹/₂ bunch fresh flat-leaf parsley

12 baby carrots with tops

1 cup brut Champagne

3 tablespoons butter

1 teaspoon all-purpose flour

2 tablespoons chopped fresh flat-leaf parsley

2 teaspoons chopped fresh thyme

1. Preheat oven to 300°.

2. Cook bacon in a large Dutch oven over medium heat until crisp; remove bacon from pan, reserving drippings in pan. Reserve bacon for another use. Place ⅔ cup flour in a shallow dish. Sprinkle chicken evenly with ¾ teaspoon salt and ½ teaspoon pepper. Dredge chicken lightly in flour; shake off excess flour. Increase heat to medium-high. Add 1 tablespoon oil to drippings in pan; swirl to coat. Add half of chicken to pan; cook 5 minutes or until browned. Turn chicken over; cook 2 minutes. Remove from pan. Repeat procedure with remaining 1 tablespoon oil and chicken.

3. Add potatoes to pan; cook 3 minutes or until browned, stirring occasionally. Add mushrooms; sprinkle with ¼ teaspoon salt. Cook 3 minutes, stirring occasionally. Stir in brandy. Cook until liquid almost evaporates (about 30 seconds), stirring occasionally. Return chicken to pan. Add shallots and stock; bring to a boil. Place peppercorns and next 3 ingredients on a double layer of cheesecloth. Gather edges; tie with butcher's twine. Add bundle to pan. Bake, uncovered, at 300° for 15 minutes.

4. Trim carrot tops to 1-inch; scrub carrots. Add carrots to pan. Bake an additional 45 minutes or until vegetables are tender and chicken is done. Remove chicken and vegetables from pan; keep warm. Discard herb bundle. Place pan over medium-high heat. Add Champagne to pan; bring to a boil, scraping pan to loosen browned bits. Cook until mixture reduces to ⅔ cup (about 11 minutes).

5. Melt butter in a saucepan over medium heat. Cook butter 3 minutes or until browned, shaking pan occasionally. Stir in 1 teaspoon flour; cook 1 minute, stirring with a whisk. Gradually add butter mixture to reduced Champagne mixture, stirring with a whisk. Cook 1 minute or until slightly thick. Stir in ¼ teaspoon salt and ¼ teaspoon pepper. Serve with chicken and vegetables. Garnish with chopped fresh parsley and thyme. Serves 6 (serving size: 1 drumstick, 1 thigh, 2 carrots, about ⅔ cup mushroom mixture, and about 2 tablespoons sauce)

CALORIES 464; **FAT** 16.9g (sat 5.7g, mono 6.5g, poly 3.1g); **PROTEIN** 35.9g; **CARB** 39.2g; **FIBER** 3.1g; **CHOL** 123mg; **IRON** 4.2mg; **SODIUM** 658mg; **CALC** 40mg

Souvlaki is Greek for "little skewers." Cubes of pork are traditional, but chicken also takes well to the marinade of lemon juice, garlic, olive oil, and oregano. A little zucchini on the skewers adds color, and the tzatziki (cucumber-yogurt sauce) is like a Greek version of Ranch dressing.

CHICKEN SOUVLAKI WITH TZATZIKI

HANDS-ON TIME: 12 MIN. TOTAL TIME: 46 MIN.

3 tablespoons fresh lemon
   juice
1½ teaspoons chopped
   fresh or ½ teaspoon dried
   oregano
2 teaspoons olive oil
½ teaspoon salt
4 garlic cloves, minced
½ pound skinless, boneless
   chicken breast, cut into
   1-inch pieces
1 medium zucchini, quartered
   lengthwise and cut into
   (½-inch-thick) slices
Cooking spray
½ cup shredded, seeded,
   peeled cucumber
½ cup plain low-fat yogurt
1 tablespoon fresh lemon juice
¼ teaspoon salt
1 garlic clove, minced

1. Combine first 5 ingredients in a zip-top plastic bag; seal and shake to combine. Add chicken to bag; seal and shake to coat. Marinate chicken in refrigerator 30 minutes, turning once.
2. Remove chicken from bag; discard marinade. Thread chicken and zucchini alternately onto each of 4 (8-inch) skewers.
3. Heat a grill pan over medium-high heat. Coat pan with cooking spray. Add skewers; cook 8 minutes or until chicken is done, turning once.
4. While chicken cooks, combine cucumber, yogurt, 1 tablespoon lemon juice, ¼ teaspoon salt, and 1 garlic clove, stirring well. Serve tzatziki with souvlaki. Serves 2 (serving size: 2 skewers and about ¼ cup tzatziki)

CALORIES 219; FAT 4.7g (sat 1.3g, mono 2.3g, poly 0.6g); PROTEIN 30.9g; CARB 12.3g; FIBER 2.4g; CHOL 69mg; IRON 1.4mg; SODIUM 705mg; CALC 161mg

In this old-school Italian pizza, the crust is thin and crisp, the sauce is a minimal tomato sauté, and the cheese is sliced from a fresh ball of mozzarella. To help blister the top of the pizza, turn on your oven's convection feature. Or, heat a second pizza stone over the pie so it can radiate heat onto the cheese.

PIZZA MARGHERITA

HANDS-ON TIME: 36 MIN. TOTAL TIME: 26 HR. 42 MIN.

1 cup warm water (100° to 110°), divided
10 ounces bread flour (about 2 cups plus 2 tablespoons)
1 package dry yeast (about 2¼ teaspoons)
4 teaspoons olive oil
¾ teaspoon kosher salt, divided
Cooking spray
1 tablespoon yellow cornmeal
¾ cup Basic Pizza Sauce
5 ounces thinly sliced fresh mozzarella cheese (about 1¼ cups)
⅓ cup small fresh basil leaves

1. Pour ¾ cup warm water in the bowl of a stand mixer with dough hook attached. Weigh or lightly spoon flour into dry measuring cups and spoons; level with a knife. Add flour to ¾ cup water; mix until combined. Cover and let stand 20 minutes. Combine remaining ¼ cup water and yeast in a small bowl; let stand 5 minutes or until bubbly. Add yeast mixture, oil, and ½ teaspoon salt to flour mixture; mix 5 minutes or until a soft dough forms. Place dough in a large bowl coated with cooking spray; cover surface of dough with plastic wrap lightly coated with cooking spray. Refrigerate 24 hours.
2. Remove dough from refrigerator. Let stand, covered, 1 hour or until dough comes to room temperature. Punch dough down. Press dough out to a 12-inch circle on a lightly floured baking sheet sprinkled with cornmeal. Crimp edges to form a ½-inch border. Cover dough loosely with plastic wrap.
3. Position an oven rack in lowest setting. Place a pizza stone on lowest rack. Preheat oven to 550°. Preheat pizza stone 30 minutes before baking dough.
4. Remove plastic wrap from dough. Sprinkle dough with remaining ¼ teaspoon salt. Spread Basic Pizza Sauce evenly over dough, leaving a ½-inch border. Arrange cheese slices evenly over pizza. Slide pizza onto preheated pizza stone, using a spatula as a guide. Bake at 550° for 11 minutes or until crust is golden. Cut pizza into 10 wedges, and sprinkle evenly with basil. Serves 5 (serving size: 2 wedges)

CALORIES 360; FAT 13.6g (sat 4.9g, mono 6.3g, poly 1.2g); PROTEIN 13.3g; CARB 45.8g; FIBER 2.4g; CHOL 23mg; IRON 2.1mg; SODIUM 424mg; CALC 17mg

BASIC PIZZA SAUCE

HANDS-ON TIME: 9 MIN. TOTAL TIME: 39 MIN.

2 tablespoons extra-virgin olive oil
5 garlic cloves, minced
1 (28-ounce) can tomatoes, preferably San Marzano
½ teaspoon kosher salt
½ teaspoon dried oregano

1. Heat a medium saucepan over medium heat. Add oil to pan; swirl to coat. Add garlic to pan; cook 1 minute, stirring frequently. Remove tomatoes from can using a slotted spoon, reserving juices. Crush tomatoes. Stir tomatoes, juices, salt, and oregano into garlic mixture; bring to a boil. Reduce heat, and simmer 30 minutes, stirring occasionally. Serves 32 (serving size: 1 tablespoon)

CALORIES 13; FAT 0.9g (sat 0.1g, mono 0.7g, poly 0.1g); PROTEIN 0.5g; CARB 1g; FIBER 0.2g; CHOL 0mg; IRON 0.6mg; SODIUM 49mg; CALC 1mg

SMALL BITES, BIG FLAVORS

pain's tradition of tapas began hundreds of years ago when wise bar owners realized that serving patrons a glass of vino topped with a small plate of savory food would ward off hunger. The simple custom took off and coincided with similar phenomena throughout the Mediterranean. In France, they are called *hors d'oeuvres,* and in Italy *antipasti.* In Greece, they use the word *meze,* in Morocco, *mukabalatt.* Even Venice has a tapas equivalent called *cicheti.*

The civilized practice of gathering with friends in the evening for drinks and nibbles isn't exclusive to the Mediterranean. Americans, too, have come to love small-plate dining while eating out and entertaining at home. There is a dizzying array of delicious recipes to prepare, so you can entertain healthfully, with ease and continental charm. But offering simple plates of ready-mades like olives, cheese, crudités, and smoked meats will save you time and still satisfy. Either way, small-bite meals promote portion control and keep your taste buds happy and your hunger satisfied with exotic and exciting flavors.

According to Jacques Médecin, author of Cuisine Niçoise, hard-cooked eggs are the only cooked ingredients in traditional salad Niçoise. The fish is usually salted anchovies, not tuna, and the salad does not include potatoes. However, popular versions feature both tuna and potatoes.

SEARED TUNA NIÇOISE

HANDS-ON TIME: 19 MIN. TOTAL TIME: 36 MIN.

3 large eggs
1¹⁄₂ cups quartered small red potatoes
1 cup haricots verts, trimmed
1 (15-ounce) can cannellini beans, rinsed and drained
2 tablespoons sliced green onions
2 tablespoons chopped fresh parsley
Cooking spray
2 (6-ounce) tuna steaks
¹⁄₂ teaspoon kosher salt, divided
¹⁄₄ teaspoon freshly ground black pepper
2 tablespoons extra-virgin olive oil
3 tablespoons red wine vinegar
1 teaspoon Dijon mustard
²⁄₃ cup grape tomatoes, halved
¹⁄₄ cup pitted and quartered niçoise olives

1. Place eggs in a large saucepan. Cover with water to 1 inch above eggs. Bring just to a boil. Remove from heat; cover and let stand 15 minutes. Drain; cool in ice water 5 minutes. Peel eggs; cut each egg into 4 slices.
2. Place potatoes in pan; cover with water. Bring to a boil. Reduce heat; simmer 12 minutes. Add green beans, and cook 3 minutes. Drain; plunge green beans into ice water for 1 minute. Drain well.
3. Partially mash cannellini beans; stir in green onions and parsley. Set aside.
4. Heat a large cast-iron skillet over medium-high heat. Coat pan with cooking spray. Sprinkle tuna with ¼ teaspoon salt and pepper. Add tuna to pan; cook 2 minutes on each side or until desired degree of doneness. Cut thinly across the grain.
5. Combine remaining ¼ teaspoon salt, oil, vinegar, and mustard in a small bowl, stirring with a whisk. Add tomatoes and olives; toss.
6. Place eggs, potatoes, green beans, cannellini bean mixture, tuna, and tomato mixture on each of 4 plates. Serves 4 (serving size: about 2 ounces tuna, 3 egg slices, ⅓ cup potatoes, ¼ cup green beans, ¼ cup cannellini bean mixture, and 2 tablespoons tomato mixture)

CALORIES 404; **FAT** 17.3g (sat 3.5g, mono 9.7g, poly 3g); **PROTEIN** 32.2g; **CARB** 28.8g; **FIBER** 6.8g; **CHOL** 172mg; **IRON** 3.9mg; **SODIUM** 619mg; **CALC** 99mg

Since their introduction to Italy in the 1500s, potatoes have become the main ingredient in gnocchi. Browned butter with fresh herbs has also become the preferred sauce. Here's a dependable recipe inspired by Lidia Bastianich, owner of several acclaimed New York City restaurants and author of numerous cookbooks on Italian and Italian-American cuisine.

POTATO GNOCCHI
with Browned Butter

HANDS-ON TIME: 35 MIN. TOTAL TIME: 1 HR. 52 MIN.

- 2 (12-ounce) baking potatoes, unpeeled
- 1 teaspoon kosher salt
- 4.5 ounces all-purpose flour (about 1 cup)
- 2 tablespoons chopped fresh chives
- 1/4 teaspoon freshly ground black pepper
- 2 large eggs, lightly beaten
- 3 tablespoons butter
- 1 large garlic clove, crushed
- 1/4 cup coarsely chopped walnut halves
- 1/2 ounce fresh Parmigiano-Reggiano or Grana Padano cheese, grated
- Sliced fresh chives

Place potatoes in a saucepan; cover with water. Bring to a boil over medium-high heat. Cook 40 minutes; drain. Cool slightly; peel. Press potato flesh through a ricer. Spread potatoes on a baking sheet; sprinkle with salt. Cool.

Scoop potatoes into a large bowl. Weigh or lightly spoon flour into a dry measuring cup; level with a knife. Add flour to potatoes, and toss. Form a well in center. Add chopped chives, pepper, and eggs; stir. Turn dough out onto a lightly floured surface. Gently knead just until dough comes together (about 1 minute).

Cut dough into 4 equal portions; roll each into a 22-inch-long rope. Cut each rope into 22 pieces. Score gnocchi with a fork. Cook half of gnocchi 3 minutes in boiling water. Remove with a slotted spoon. Repeat with remaining gnocchi; drain.

Melt butter in a large skillet over medium heat. Add garlic; cook 2 minutes. Add nuts; cook 2 minutes or until butter browns. Discard garlic. Set aside half of butter mixture. Add half of gnocchi to pan; toss. Cook 1 minute or until browned. Transfer gnocchi to a bowl. Repeat with reserved butter and remaining gnocchi. Place gnocchi in each of 4 shallow bowls. Sprinkle evenly with cheese and sliced fresh chives. Serves 4 (serving size: about 22 gnocchi)

CALORIES 398; FAT 15.2g (sat 6.8g, mono 3.5g, poly 3.7g); PROTEIN 3.7g; CARB 56.4g; FIBER 3.6g; CHOL 78mg; IRON 3.4mg; SODIUM 606mg; CALC 73mg

Gnocchi

The dough for making gnocchi is similar to pasta dough, but it's shaped into dumplings instead. The dough may include potatoes, squash, spinach, or other vegetables, and the flour could be wheat or semolina. Gnocchi varies from region to region in Italy, but potato gnocchi has become the most well known. Starchy baking potatoes give you the fluffiest results. Spreading out the cooked potatoes to evaporate excess moisture allows you to use less flour, resulting in lighter-textured dumplings. To shape them, roll the dough into ropes, then cut each rope crosswise into puffy squares and flatten the squares slightly (as shown left) or score the squares with a fork to make a rounder-textured pillow (as shown right).

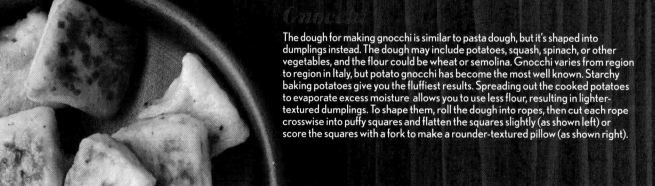

Lasagna from Bologna, Italy, is a casserole consisting of sheets of fresh pasta layered with a meat sauce and a white béchamel sauce. Italian-American lasagna uses dried noodles, ricotta cheese instead of béchamel, and a topping of mozzarella. This Italian-American version is lightened up with leaner meat in the sauce, plus a little pancetta for porky goodness.

CLASSIC LIGHT LASAGNA

HANDS-ON TIME: 40 MIN. TOTAL TIME: 1 HR. 35 MIN.

1½ cups coarsely chopped onion
¾ cup coarsely chopped celery
½ cup coarsely chopped carrot
4 garlic cloves, peeled
1 tablespoon olive oil
1 tablespoon unsalted tomato paste
1 ounce diced pancetta
1 pound ground turkey breast
¼ cup white wine
¾ teaspoon kosher salt
¾ teaspoon crushed red pepper
½ teaspoon dried oregano
½ teaspoon freshly ground black pepper
1 cup 1% low-fat milk
½ cup chopped fresh basil
1 (28-ounce) can crushed tomatoes, undrained
1½ cups part-skim ricotta cheese
6 ounces shredded part-skim mozzarella cheese, divided (about 1½ cups)
1 large egg, lightly beaten
Cooking spray
6 cooked lasagna noodles

1. Place first 4 ingredients in a food processor; pulse until coarsely ground. Heat a medium saucepan over medium-high heat. Add oil to pan; swirl to coat. Add tomato paste and pancetta; cook 1 minute, stirring constantly. Add turkey, and cook 4 minutes, stirring to crumble. Add wine; cook 2 minutes or until liquid evaporates, scraping pan to loosen browned bits. Add onion mixture, salt, and next 3 ingredients (through black pepper) to pan, and cook 3 minutes, stirring occasionally. Add milk and basil; cook 3 minutes, stirring occasionally. Stir in tomatoes; reduce heat, and simmer 20 minutes.

2. Preheat oven to 425°.

3. Combine ricotta, 1 cup mozzarella cheese, and egg in a small bowl.

4. Spread ¾ cup turkey mixture in bottom of a 13 x 9–inch glass or ceramic baking dish coated with cooking spray. Arrange 3 noodles over turkey mixture; top with half of remaining turkey mixture and half of ricotta mixture. Repeat layers once, ending with ricotta mixture. Sprinkle remaining ½ cup mozzarella evenly over top. Bake at 425° for 35 minutes.

5. Preheat broiler to high. (Keep lasagna in oven.)

6. Broil lasagna 2 minutes or until cheese is golden brown and sauce is bubbly. Let stand 10 minutes before serving. Serves 8 (serving size: ⅛ of casserole)

CALORIES 364; **FAT** 13.2g (sat 6g, mono 3.7g, poly 0.7g); **PROTEIN** 30.9g; **CARB** 31.4g; **FIBER** 3.8g; **CHOL** 75mg; **IRON** 2.4mg; **SODIUM** 644mg; **CALC** 381mg

In the Greek version of baked ziti, the noodles are mixed with two sauces: a lamb-and-tomato sauce and a milk-and-cheese sauce. I lightened the cream sauce by using 2% milk and fewer eggs. The casserole keeps for days in the refrigerator and cuts into neat little squares for reheating.

GREEK BAKED ZITI
(Pastitsio)

HANDS-ON TIME: 51 MIN. TOTAL TIME: 1 HR. 55 MIN.

1 tablespoon olive oil
1¾ cups chopped onion
1 large garlic clove, minced
½ pound lean ground lamb
½ pound ground sirloin
3 (14.5-ounce) cans unsalted diced tomatoes, undrained
1 teaspoon dried oregano
1 teaspoon salt, divided
½ teaspoon ground cinnamon
2 tablespoons butter
¼ cup all-purpose flour
3 cups 2% reduced-fat milk, divided
3 large eggs, lightly beaten
¾ cup crumbled feta cheese, divided
10 ounces uncooked ziti (short tube-shaped pasta)
Cooking spray
¼ cup dry breadcrumbs
Fresh oregano leaves (optional)

1. Heat a large skillet over medium heat. Add oil to pan; swirl to coat. Add onion; sauté 5 minutes or until tender. Add garlic; sauté 1 minute. Add lamb and beef; cook 4 minutes or until browned, stirring to crumble. Add tomatoes, oregano, ½ teaspoon salt, and cinnamon; bring to a simmer over medium-high heat. Reduce heat to low, and cook 20 minutes, stirring occasionally and mashing with a spatula or flat side of a wooden spoon. Remove from heat; set aside.
2. While sauce cooks, melt butter in medium saucepan over medium heat. Add flour, stirring with a whisk. Cook 1 minute, stirring constantly. Add ½ cup milk, stirring with a whisk until smooth. Gradually add remaining 2½ cups milk and remaining ½ teaspoon salt, stirring until smooth. Bring to boil over medium-high heat, and cook 1 minute or until slightly thick. Remove from heat. Gradually add hot milk to eggs, stirring constantly with a whisk. Stir in ½ cup cheese. Keep warm.
3. Preheat oven to 350°.
4. Cook pasta in boiling water 9 minutes or until al dente, omitting salt and fat. Drain. Stir 3 cups pasta into tomato sauce; stir remaining 3 cups pasta into white sauce.
5. Spoon tomato-sauced pasta into a 13 x 9–inch glass or ceramic baking dish coated with cooking spray. Top with white-sauced pasta, spreading evenly. Sprinkle with remaining ¼ cup cheese and breadcrumbs. Bake at 350° for 30 minutes or until bubbly. Let stand 5 minutes; sprinkle with oregano leaves, if desired. Serves 10 (serving size: ⅒ of casserole)

CALORIES 383; FAT 16.8g (sat 7.9g, mono 6.2g, poly 1.2g); PROTEIN 19.8g; CARB 38g; FIBER 3.7g; CHOL 108mg; IRON 2.9mg; SODIUM 532mg; CALC 199mg

In Italy, wild mushrooms are so cherished that you need a mushroom hunting license to forage for them. Porcini are king. Dried porcini make this easy to prepare, but if you're lucky enough to find some fresh porcini, sauté them and mix into the risotto near the end of cooking.

RISOTTO
with Porcini Mushrooms and Mascarpone
HANDS-ON TIME: 47 MIN. TOTAL TIME: 1 HR. 17 MIN.

2 cups boiling water
1 cup dried porcini
  mushrooms (about 1
  ounce)
1 (14-ounce) can fat-free,
  lower-sodium beef broth
Cooking spray
1 cup uncooked Arborio rice
  or other short-grain rice
³/₄ cup chopped shallots
2 garlic cloves, minced
¹/₂ cup dry white wine
1 ounce grated Parmigiano-
  Reggiano cheese (about
  ¹/₄ cup)
1 tablespoon chopped fresh
  thyme
¹/₂ teaspoon salt
¹/₂ teaspoon freshly ground
  black pepper
1 ounce mascarpone cheese
  (about ¹/₄ cup)
Fresh thyme leaves
  (optional)

1. Combine 2 cups boiling water and mushrooms; let stand 30 minutes or until soft. Drain through a colander over a bowl. Reserve 1½ cups soaking liquid; chop mushrooms. Bring soaking liquid and broth to a simmer in a small saucepan (do not boil). Keep broth mixture warm over low heat.
2. Heat a large saucepan over medium-high heat. Coat pan with cooking spray. Add rice, shallots, and garlic; sauté 5 minutes. Add wine, and cook until liquid evaporates (about 2 minutes).
3. Add 1 cup broth mixture to rice mixture; cook over medium heat 5 minutes or until liquid is nearly absorbed, stirring constantly. Add remaining broth mixture, ½ cup at a time, stirring frequently until each portion of broth mixture is absorbed before adding the next (about 25 minutes total). Add mushrooms, Parmigiano-Reggiano, chopped thyme, salt, and pepper; stir until cheese melts. Spoon 1 cup risotto into each of 4 bowls. Top each serving with 1 tablespoon mascarpone and thyme leaves, if desired. Serves 4 (serving size: 1 cup)

CALORIES 312; FAT 6g (sat 3g, mono 0.6g, poly 0.1g); PROTEIN 10.8g; CARB 48.5g; FIBER 4g; CHOL 15mg; IRON 2.1mg; SODIUM 595mg; CALC 109mg

Make Authentic Risotto

Risotto rice is high in starch, which helps make it creamy. Stirring throughout the process while intermittently adding stock releases the starch and thickens the liquid. "The key is at the end when you stir the risotto like crazy," says Marc Vetri, author of *Rustic Italian Cooking*. "You want to emulsify the stock, the starch from the rice, and any added fats to create a creamy sauce."

Unlike most other recipes using rice, a Spanish paella is cooked completely uncovered. The rice in the finished dish should be tender and al dente with the characteristic crisp crust at the base of the pan called a socarrat.

PAELLA WITH POBLANOS, CORN, AND CLAMS

HANDS-ON TIME: 35 MIN. TOTAL TIME: 1 HR. 40 MIN.

2 tablespoons olive oil
2 cups chopped yellow onion
3 garlic cloves, minced
2 poblano chiles, seeded and chopped
1¼ teaspoons kosher salt, divided
½ teaspoon freshly ground black pepper, divided
¾ cup uncooked short-grain brown rice
¼ teaspoon saffron threads, crushed
2 cups water
⅛ teaspoon ground red pepper
1½ cups fresh corn kernels (about 2 ears)
1 cup halved cherry tomatoes
2 pounds littleneck clams
2 tablespoons chopped fresh flat-leaf parsley
8 lemon wedges

1. Preheat oven to 450°.

2. Heat a 12-inch ovenproof skillet over medium-high heat. Add oil to pan; swirl to coat. Add onion, garlic, poblanos, ½ teaspoon salt, and ¼ teaspoon black pepper; sauté 3 minutes. Add rice and saffron. Cook 2 minutes, stirring constantly. Add 2 cups water, remaining ¾ teaspoon salt, remaining ¼ teaspoon black pepper, and red pepper; bring to a boil.

3. Bake at 450° for 50 minutes or until rice is done. Stir in corn and tomatoes. Nestle clams into rice mixture. Bake at 450° for 12 minutes or until shells open, and discard unopened shells.

4. Return pan to medium-high heat, and cook without stirring 10 minutes or until liquid evaporates and rice browns. (It should smell toasty but not burned.) Top evenly with parsley; serve with lemon wedges. Serves 4 (serving size: 1¼ cups rice mixture, about 7 clams, and 2 lemon wedges)

CALORIES 340; FAT 9.1g (sat 1.1g, mono 5.2g, poly 1.3g); PROTEIN 14.8g; CARB 52.7g; FIBER 5.6g; CHOL 21mg; IRON 10mg; SODIUM 651mg; CALC 68mg

The rich, malty flavor of Guinness Stout makes a perfect match for beef. In this classic Irish stew, the ingredients simmer for awhile, during which time the beef chuck, onions, carrots, parsnips, and turnips all soak up the earthy broth. Thanks to Margaret M. Johnson, author of seven cookbooks on Irish cuisine, for sharing this classic recipe.

BEEF AND GUINNESS STEW

HANDS-ON TIME: 33 MIN. TOTAL TIME: 3 HR. 3 MIN.

3 tablespoons canola oil, divided
¼ cup all-purpose flour
2 pounds boneless chuck roast, trimmed and cut into 1-inch cubes
1 teaspoon salt, divided
5 cups chopped onion (about 3 onions)
1 tablespoon tomato paste
4 cups fat-free, lower-sodium beef broth
1 (11.2-ounce) bottle Guinness Stout
1 tablespoon raisins
1 teaspoon caraway seeds
½ teaspoon black pepper
1½ cups (½-inch-thick) diagonal slices carrot (about 8 ounces)
1½ cups (½-inch-thick) diagonal slices parsnip (about 8 ounces)
1 cup (½-inch) cubed peeled turnip (about 8 ounces)
2 tablespoons finely chopped fresh flat-leaf parsley

1. Heat a Dutch oven over medium-high heat. Add 1½ tablespoons oil to pan; swirl to coat. Place flour in a shallow dish. Sprinkle beef with ½ teaspoon salt; dredge beef in flour. Add half of beef to pan; cook 5 minutes, turning to brown on all sides. Remove beef from pan with a slotted spoon. Repeat procedure with remaining 1½ tablespoons oil and beef.

2. Add onion to pan; cook 5 minutes or until tender, stirring occasionally. Stir in tomato paste; cook 1 minute, stirring frequently. Stir in broth and beer, scraping pan to loosen browned bits. Return meat to pan. Stir in remaining ½ teaspoon salt, raisins, caraway seeds, and pepper; bring to a boil. Cover, reduce heat, and simmer 1 hour, stirring occasionally. Uncover and bring to a boil. Cook 50 minutes, stirring occasionally. Add carrot, parsnip, and turnip. Cover, reduce heat to low, and simmer 30 minutes, stirring occasionally. Uncover and bring to a boil; cook 10 minutes or until vegetables are tender. Sprinkle with parsley. Serves 8 (serving size: about 1 cup)

CALORIES 365; FAT 19.4g (sat 5.7g, mono 9.6g, poly 1.7g); PROTEIN 25.3g; CARB 18.8g; FIBER 3.6g; CHOL 62mg; IRON 2.6mg; SODIUM 454mg; CALC 52mg

This French stew of beans, pork, and poultry is traditionally cooked in an earthenware cassole, a sort of inverted cone that provides a wide surface area on top for maximum crust. A Dutch oven or wide braising pan works well, too.

CASSOULET

HANDS-ON TIME: 38 MIN. TOTAL TIME: 5 HR. 33 MIN.

¼ cup salt
6 (8-ounce) duck leg quarters
1½ tablespoons canola oil
4 thick-cut bacon slices, sliced crosswise into (½-inch-thick) strips
1 (¾-pound) boneless leg of lamb, trimmed and cut into (1-inch) cubes
1½ cups chopped onion
¼ teaspoon freshly ground black pepper
¼ cup no-salt-added tomato puree
3 garlic cloves, minced
2 cups fat-free, lower-sodium chicken broth
2 cups water
4 (15-ounce) cans organic Great Northern beans, drained and divided
8 ounces cooked spicy Italian sausage or Polish kielbasa, diagonally sliced
¼ cup dry breadcrumbs
Chopped fresh thyme (optional)

1. Rub salt evenly over duck; cover and refrigerate 30 minutes.
2. Heat a large Dutch oven over medium heat. Add oil to pan; swirl to coat. Add bacon to pan; cook 7 minutes or until crisp, stirring occasionally. Remove bacon from pan using a slotted spoon; set aside. Increase heat to medium-high. Add lamb to drippings in pan; cook 8 minutes, turning to brown on all sides. Remove lamb from pan, and set aside.
3. Preheat oven to 300°.
4. Rinse duck with cold water; pat dry with paper towels. Add half of duck, skin side down, to pan; cook over medium heat 15 minutes or until golden brown. Turn duck over, and cook 10 minutes or until browned and fat under skin is melted. Remove duck from pan. Repeat procedure with remaining duck, reserving 1 tablespoon duck fat; set duck aside. Add onion and pepper to duck fat in pan; cook 7 minutes or until lightly browned, stirring occasionally. Stir in tomato puree and garlic; cook 1 minute. Return lamb to pan. Nestle duck into lamb mixture; add broth and 2 cups water. Cover and bake at 300° for 2½ hours or until lamb and duck are very tender. Remove duck from pan; let stand until tepid. Remove skin from duck; discard. Cut duck legs in half through the joint. Return duck to lamb mixture.
5. Increase oven temperature to 375°.
6. Stir 2 cans of beans into lamb mixture. Add bacon and sausage; top mixture with remaining 2 cans of beans. Sprinkle breadcrumbs evenly over top. Cover and cook 1 hour and 10 minutes. Uncover and cook 20 minutes or until browned and bubbly. Sprinkle with chopped thyme, if desired. Serves 12 (serving size: 1 drumstick or thigh and about ¾ cup bean mixture)

CALORIES 323; FAT 14.4g (sat 4.6g, mono 4.4g, poly 1.2g); PROTEIN 27.1g; CARB 20g; FIBER 7.1g; CHOL 79mg; IRON 2.9mg; SODIUM 821mg; CALC 88mg

Duck

Game birds that fly long distances, like ducks and geese, store fat beneath the skin for sustained energy. But domesticated ducks no longer migrate, so they retain that fat. To crisp the skin and keep it from tasting flabby, you need to melt away the excess fat. It helps to slash the skin to give the fat an escape hatch. When buying duck, you'll find two main species, mallard and Muscovy. Wild mallards have been bred to produce domestic Pekin (Peking) or Long Island ducks. Muscovy ducks grow a bit larger and have stronger-tasting meat and about 30 percent less fat. A third type, the Moulard duck, is a Pekin-Muscovy hybrid that's used primarily to make foie gras. However, Moulards also develop rich breast meat that makes an excellent choice for a dish of pan-seared or grilled duck breast.

Traditional Spanish garlic soup has very few ingredients: water, garlic, bread, and paprika. It's a brew of humble origins. Poaching eggs in the broth makes it a bit more filling. You could also add a few thin strips of Serrano ham if you like. Either way, the soup is said to help hangovers.

GARLIC SOUP
(Sopa de Ajo)
HANDS-ON TIME: 10 MIN. TOTAL TIME: 40 MIN.

2 teaspoons olive oil
5 tablespoons minced fresh garlic
1 teaspoon smoked paprika
3 cups organic vegetable broth
1 cup water
¼ teaspoon salt
¼ teaspoon freshly ground black pepper
2 (1-ounce) slices rustic bread, cut into 1-inch cubes
8 large eggs
2 tablespoons fresh flat-leaf parsley leaves

1. Preheat broiler.
2. Heat a large saucepan over medium heat. Add oil to pan; swirl to coat. Add garlic to pan; cook 5 minutes or until tender (do not brown). Stir in paprika. Add broth, 1 cup water, salt, and pepper; bring to a boil. Reduce heat, and simmer 10 minutes.
3. Arrange bread cubes in a single layer on a baking sheet; broil 4 minutes or until golden, stirring once halfway through cooking. Reduce oven temperature to 350°.
4. Place about ¼ cup bread cubes in each of 8 ovenproof soup bowls. Break one egg into each bowl; ladle about ½ cup broth mixture into each bowl. Arrange bowls on a baking sheet; bake at 350° for 20 minutes or until egg whites are set but yolks are still runny. Sprinkle evenly with chopped parsley. Serves 8

CALORIES 114; FAT 5.2g (sat 1.3g, mono 2.7g, poly 0.9g); PROTEIN 7.3g; CARB 7.6g; FIBER 0.3g; CHOL 180mg; IRON 1.3mg; SODIUM 398mg; CALC 38mg

Most Eastern European countries have a version of borshch (borscht). Sometimes it's a vegetarian soup served cold. Sometimes it's a carnivore's dream served hot. Bright red beets are the one constant. Wear gloves when grating the beets to avoid staining your hands.

UKRAINIAN BORSHCH

HANDS-ON TIME: 40 MIN. TOTAL TIME: 11 HR. 15 MIN.

½ cup dried navy beans

¾ pound beef chuck top blade steak, cubed, or beef stew meat

6 cups fat-free, lower-sodium beef broth, divided

1 smoked ham hock (about 10 ounces)

1 bay leaf

2 onions

2 large carrots

1 celery stalk

2 teaspoons canola oil

1½ cups diced seeded peeled tomato

¼ cup tomato paste

4 large beets, peeled and grated

1 baking potato, peeled and cut into ½-inch pieces

1 parsnip, cut into ½-inch pieces

2 cups shredded green cabbage

½ cup chopped fresh dill, divided

2 garlic cloves, minced

¼ cup red wine vinegar

½ teaspoon salt

½ teaspoon freshly ground black pepper

½ cup light sour cream

Sort and wash beans; place in a large bowl. Cover with water to 2 inches above beans; cover and let stand 8 hours.

Heat a large Dutch oven over medium-high heat. Add beef to pan; cook 5 to 6 minutes, browning on all sides. Add 1 cup broth, scraping pan to loosen browned bits. Add remaining 5 cups broth, ham hock, and bay leaf. Cut 1 onion, 1 carrot, and celery stalk in half; add to soup. Bring to boil over medium-high heat. Cover, reduce heat to low, and simmer 1 hour.

Drain beans; add to soup. Cover and simmer 40 to 50 minutes or until beef and ham hock are tender. Remove ham hock to a cutting board to cool. Remove and discard bay leaf, onion, carrot, and celery. Strain soup through a sieve into a large bowl, reserving stock. Set beef and beans aside. Remove meat from ham hock, and chop; discard skin, fat, and bone.

Place a large zip-top plastic bag inside a 2-quart glass measure. Pour stock into bag; let stand 10 minutes (fat will rise to the top). Seal bag; carefully snip off 1 bottom corner of bag. Drain stock into bowl, stopping before fat layer reaches opening; discard fat.

Finely chop remaining onion and carrot. Heat Dutch oven over medium heat. Add oil to pan; swirl to coat. Add onion and carrot; sauté 5 minutes or until tender. Add tomato and tomato paste; cook 5 minutes or until tomato breaks down. Mash tomato with a wooden spoon. Add stock, beets, potato, and parsnip; bring to boil over high heat. Cover, reduce heat to medium-low, and simmer 30 minutes until potato and parsnip are tender.

Return beef, beans, and ham hock meat to soup. Add cabbage, 6 tablespoons dill, and garlic; cook 15 to 20 minutes or until cabbage is tender. Remove from heat; stir in vinegar, salt, and pepper. Serve soup with remaining 2 tablespoons dill and sour cream. Serves 10 (serving size: 1¼ cups soup and about 2½ teaspoons sour cream)

CALORIES 200; FAT 5.7g (sat 1.9g, mono 2.5g, poly 0.7g); PROTEIN 13.8g; CARB 24g; FIBER 3.4g; CHOL 32mg; IRON 2.2mg; SODIUM 539mg; CALC 64mg

Dill

A member of the parsley family, dill leaves and seeds lend subtle aromas of caraway and lemon to countless Eastern European dishes like pickles, salads, soups, and stews. To make fresh dill last longer, wrap the stems in a damp paper towel in a produce bag or stand the herbs upright in a tall glass of water, and refrigerate.

The Spanish port city of Alicante sits just south of Valencia on the Mediterranean Sea. Very little wheat grows there, but almond trees abound, so local desserts like these cookies often use ground almonds in place of flour. Freshly ground almonds yield the best flavor, but if you want to save time, look for almond flour (or meal) in a well-stocked supermarket.

FLOURLESS ALMOND COOKIES
(Almendrados)
HANDS-ON TIME: 20 MIN. TOTAL TIME: 60 MIN.

2 cups whole blanched almonds
²/₃ cup sugar
4 teaspoons grated lemon rind
Dash of salt
1 large egg
Cooking spray
1 teaspoon ground cinnamon
24 whole blanched almonds

1. Preheat oven to 350°.
2. Place 2 cups almonds in a food processor; process until finely ground. Add sugar, lemon rind, salt, and egg; pulse 10 times or until dough forms a ball.
3. Shape dough into 24 balls, about 1 tablespoon each. Place 1 inch apart on baking sheets coated with cooking spray. Sprinkle evenly with cinnamon. Gently press one whole almond into the center of each dough ball. Bake at 350° for 16 minutes or until edges are golden brown. Cool 5 minutes on pans. Remove from pans; cool on wire racks. Serves 24 (serving size: 1 cookie)

CALORIES 103; FAT 7g (sat 0.6g, mono 4.4g, poly 1.6g); PROTEIN 3.2g; CARB 8.5g; FIBER 1.5g; CHOL 8mg; IRON 0.6mg; SODIUM 13mg; CALC 32mg

South America

The Flavors of South America

While Spanish conquistadors sought gold in the New World, they discovered an even greater treasure in the food: chocolate, vanilla, chiles, avocados, corn, tomatoes, potatoes, beans, and squash. They brought their fortunes back to Europe, and many of these New World foods have since become staples around the globe. The culinary cross-pollination continued as Spain and Portugal colonized South America, and ingredients like olive oil were quickly adopted. "South America is now a vast and varied universe," says Maricel Presilla, food historian and author of the James Beard Award–winning cookbook *Gran Cocina Latina*. "And the food is not difficult to make. Explore your local markets. Everything you need is there for the taking."

You'll find other important foods in specific regions of South America, such as quinoa in the Andean highlands and annatto seeds in the tropical lowlands. But corn, beans, and squash (known as the three sisters) and onions, garlic, and olive oil (the beginning of many stocks and stews) still form the backbone of the cuisine. Here's a look at some other distinctive flavors in the South American culinary landscape.

AVOCADO:
Added to salsas and used as a topping for rich flavor; to speed ripening, store in a paper bag with a banana.

CHILES & CHILE PASTE:
Various fresh and dried chiles add heat and flavor; one of the most distinctive is Peruvian aji amarillo, a bright yellow, medium-hot chile; look for aji amarillo paste from brands such as Goya.

CAPERS:
Pickled flower buds from a bush native to the Mediterranean; provides acidity; often combined with raisins and olives.

OLIVES:
Brined-cured Spanish green olives or purple Peruvian alfonso olives are most popular; often combined with raisins in empanadas.

COFFEE:
This isn't a native plant, but South America produces about 45 percent of the world's coffee; it's primarily brewed into a beverage.

RAISINS:
Source of sweetness in empanada fillings, casseroles, and grain puddings.

BEEF:
It's the bedrock of asado and churrasco, grilled meat cooked over an open fire in Argentina, Uruguay, Paraguay, Brazil, Chile, Peru, and Colombia.

SWEET POTATOES:
Pale-fleshed, less sweet varieties called camote provide subtle nutty taste in stews and as an accompaniment to Peruvian ceviche.

CINNAMON:
Known as canela in Mexico, Ceylon cinnamon is more complex, softer, and more easily ground than the cassia cinnamon sold in most North American markets (and pictured here).

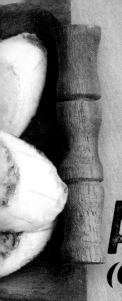

Salsa is Spanish for "sauce," and every Latin American country has a few. In Venezuela, they favor this mixture of avocados, onions, peppers, herbs, and vinegar. Unlike Mexican guacamole, guasacaca keeps the avocados chunky. The recipe comes from Ecuadorian-born Maria Baez Kijac, author of the award-winning cookbook The South American Table.

AVOCADO SALSA
(Guasacaca)

HANDS-ON TIME: 10 MIN. TOTAL TIME: 3 HR. 10 MIN.

2 cups finely chopped onion

¾ cup finely chopped red bell pepper (1 small)

3 tablespoons finely chopped seeded jalapeño pepper

3 tablespoons extra-virgin olive oil

3 tablespoons white wine vinegar

1 teaspoon Dijon mustard

¾ teaspoon sea salt

¼ teaspoon freshly ground black pepper

1 large garlic clove, minced

1½ cups chopped peeled avocado (about 2)

1½ cups chopped seeded plum tomato (about 1 pound)

2 tablespoons chopped fresh cilantro

¼ teaspoon hot pepper sauce

1. Combine first 9 ingredients in a large bowl; toss mixture gently. Cover and refrigerate 3 hours. Stir in avocado and remaining ingredients just before serving. Serves 24 (serving size: ¼ cup)

CALORIES 46; FAT 3.7g (sat 0.5g, mono 2.5g, poly 0.5g); PROTEIN 0.8g; CARB 3.5g; FIBER 1g; CHOL 0mg; IRON 0.3mg; SODIUM 77mg; CALC 6mg

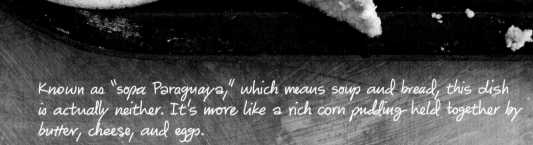

Known as "sopa Paraguaya," which means soup and bread, this dish is actually neither. It's more like a rich corn pudding held together by butter, cheese, and eggs.

PARAGUAYAN CORN BREAD

HANDS-ON TIME: 30 MIN. TOTAL TIME: 1 HR. 10 MIN.

Cooking spray
2 tablespoons grated fresh Parmesan cheese
1 tablespoon butter
1 tablespoon canola oil
1 cup chopped onion
⅓ cup chopped green bell pepper
2 cups fresh corn kernels (about 4 ears), divided
½ cup 1% low-fat cottage cheese
1½ cups yellow cornmeal
3 ounces shredded Muenster cheese (about ¾ cup)
½ cup fat-free milk
1 teaspoon salt
½ teaspoon freshly ground black pepper
4 large egg whites
½ teaspoon cream of tartar

1. Preheat oven to 400°.
2. Coat a 9-inch round cake pan with cooking spray. Sprinkle with Parmesan cheese, and set aside.
3. Heat a medium skillet over medium heat. Add butter and oil to pan; swirl to coat. Add onion and bell pepper; cook 5 minutes or until soft. Place onion mixture in a food processor. Add 1½ cups corn and cottage cheese; process until almost smooth, scraping sides of bowl occasionally. Place pureed mixture in a large bowl. Stir in remaining ½ cup corn, cornmeal, Muenster cheese, milk, salt, and black pepper.
4. Place egg whites and cream of tartar in a large bowl; beat with a mixer at high speed until stiff peaks form. Gently stir one-fourth of egg white mixture into batter; gently fold in remaining egg white mixture. Spoon into prepared pan.
5. Bake at 400° for 30 minutes or until a wooden pick inserted in center comes out clean (cover loosely with foil if it becomes too brown). Cool in pan 10 minutes on a wire rack. Place a plate upside down on top of bread; invert onto plate. Cut into wedges. Serves 8 (serving size: 1 wedge)

CALORIES 235; FAT 79g (sat 3.7g, mono 2.2g, poly 1.5g); PROTEIN 10.9g; CARB 31g; FIBER 3.4g; CHOL 16mg; IRON 0.7mg; SODIUM 503mg; CALC 133mg

BOLIVIAN EMPANADAS
(Salteñas)

HANDS-ON TIME: 1 HR. 40 MIN. TOTAL TIME: 10 HR. 43 MIN.

1 (8-ounce) skinless, boneless chicken breast half

½ teaspoon freshly ground black pepper, divided

¼ teaspoon salt, divided

1 tablespoon canola oil, divided

½ cup finely chopped yellow onion

2 tablespoons finely chopped green onions

2 teaspoons aji amarillo paste or powder, or 2 teaspoons paprika plus ¼ to ½ teaspoon ground red pepper

¾ teaspoon ground cumin

¾ teaspoon dried oregano

2 cups fat-free, lower-sodium chicken broth

2 teaspoons sugar

1½ teaspoons red wine vinegar

1 Yukon gold potato, diced

¼ cup frozen green peas

1 tablespoon chopped fresh parsley

2 teaspoons unflavored gelatin

¼ cup water

½ cup pitted Sicilian green olives, chopped

¼ cup raisins

⅓ cup butter

1 tablespoon annatto (achiote) seeds

9 ounces all-purpose flour (about 2 cups)

3 tablespoons sugar

¼ teaspoon salt

½ cup warm water

1 large egg

1 teaspoon warm water

1 large egg white, lightly beaten

1. Place chicken breast half between 2 sheets of heavy-duty plastic wrap; pound to ¼-inch thickness using a meat mallet or small heavy skillet. Sprinkle chicken with ¼ teaspoon pepper and ⅛ teaspoon salt.

2. Heat a Dutch oven over medium-high heat. Add 2 teaspoons oil; swirl. Add chicken; cook 4 to 5 minutes on each side or until done. Remove chicken; shred.

3. Reduce heat to medium; add 1 teaspoon oil and yellow onion to pan. Cook 4 minutes or until tender, stirring occasionally. Add green onions, aji amarillo paste, cumin, and oregano; cook 1 minute, stirring constantly. Add ¼ teaspoon pepper, ⅛ teaspoon salt, broth, sugar, vinegar, and potato; bring to a boil over high heat, stirring occasionally. Reduce heat to medium, and simmer 10 minutes or until potato is almost tender, stirring occasionally. Add shredded chicken, peas, and parsley; cook an additional 5 minutes or until potato is tender, stirring occasionally.

4. Sprinkle gelatin over ¼ cup water in a small bowl; let stand 1 minute. Add gelatin mixture, olives, and raisins to potato mixture; cook 5 minutes, stirring occasionally. Spoon into a bowl; cool 15 minutes. Cover and chill at least 8 hours or overnight.

5. Combine butter and annatto seeds in a saucepan; cook over low heat 5 minutes or until butter melts. Remove from heat; let stand 10 minutes. Discard annatto.

6. Weigh or lightly spoon flour into dry measuring cups; level with a knife. Combine flour, sugar, and ¼ teaspoon salt in bowl of a stand mixer; beat at low speed using paddle attachment. Add ¼ cup annatto butter, ½ cup warm water, and 1 egg; beat at medium speed 2 minutes or until dough is sticky and stretchy. Turn dough out onto a sheet of plastic wrap; shape into a rectangle. Cover and chill 30 minutes.

7. Preheat oven to 450°. Shape dough into 16 (1¼-inch) balls. Working with 1 portion of dough at a time (cover remaining dough to prevent drying), roll each portion into a 5-inch circle on a floured surface. Spoon 2 tablespoons filling into center of each circle, compacting into an oval shape. Fold dough over filling to make a half-moon shape; press edges together to seal. Hold upright so seam is on top. Starting at 1 end, pinch dough seam between finger and thumb and twist seam into rope against filling, continuing to pinch and twist until you reach other end to seal. Sealed salteña should resemble a 4-inch-long football with roped crimping on top. Place on baking sheets lined with parchment paper. Repeat procedure with remaining dough and filling (cover salteñas to prevent drying).

8. Add 1 teaspoon warm water and egg white to remaining annatto butter, scraping pan to remove as much butter as possible. Brush mixture over salteñas. Bake at 450° for 18 to 20 minutes or until crust is set and filling is thoroughly heated. Let stand 5 minutes before serving. Serves 16 (serving size: 1 empanada)

CALORIES 162; FAT 5.9g (sat 2.7g, mono 1.8g, poly 0.6g); PROTEIN 6.5g; CARB 21g; FIBER 1.3g; CHOL 31mg; IRON 1.2mg; SODIUM 278mg; CALC 15mg

Annatto Seeds and Oil

Also known as achiote, annatto is the natural orange food coloring of South and Central America. It also colors food products from Velveeta cheese to packaged Spanish yellow rice. The pebbly reddish seeds come from a tropical tree and, in Mexico, are often soaked in water and ground to a paste with garlic and spices to make achiote paste. In South America, the seeds are more often heated in oil to extract their rich orange-red hue and earthy, musky aromas. To make annatto oil, combine 1 part annatto seeds and 2 parts oil (such as 1 tablespoon seeds and 2 tablespoons oil) in a small saucepan; cook over low heat for 8 to 10 minutes or until the oil turns a deep orange color. Remove from the heat, and let stand 10 minutes. Remove and discard the seeds with a slotted spoon.

Flans—sweet custards baked in caramel-coated dishes—came to South America via Spain. They have a built-in sauce of caramelized sugar. In Argentina, Chile, and Uruguay, they like to up the ante by serving flan with dulce de leche, a sweet, creamy paste made by cooking down sweetened milk until it's thick but still pourable.

DULCE DE LECHE FLAN

HANDS-ON TIME: 13 MIN. TOTAL TIME: 5 HR. 5 MIN.

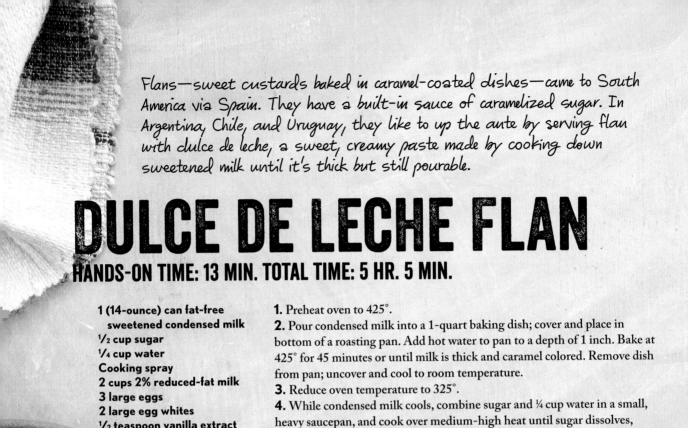

1 (14-ounce) can fat-free
   sweetened condensed milk
1/2 cup sugar
1/4 cup water
Cooking spray
2 cups 2% reduced-fat milk
3 large eggs
2 large egg whites
1/2 teaspoon vanilla extract

1. Preheat oven to 425°.
2. Pour condensed milk into a 1-quart baking dish; cover and place in bottom of a roasting pan. Add hot water to pan to a depth of 1 inch. Bake at 425° for 45 minutes or until milk is thick and caramel colored. Remove dish from pan; uncover and cool to room temperature.
3. Reduce oven temperature to 325°.
4. While condensed milk cools, combine sugar and 1/4 cup water in a small, heavy saucepan, and cook over medium-high heat until sugar dissolves, stirring frequently. Continue cooking 5 minutes or until golden, stirring constantly. Immediately pour into a 9-inch round cake pan coated with cooking spray, tipping quickly until caramelized sugar coats bottom of pan.
5. Spoon thickened condensed milk into a large bowl. Add 2% milk and remaining ingredients; stir with a whisk until well blended. Strain milk mixture through a fine sieve into prepared pan, and discard solids.
6. Place cake pan in bottom of roasting pan; add hot water to pan to a depth of 1 inch. Bake at 325° for 40 minutes or until a knife inserted in center comes out clean. Remove from oven, and cool flan to room temperature in water bath (this allows the flan to gradually reach room temperature, which helps prevent cracking). Remove cake pan from water bath, and cover and chill at least 3 hours or overnight. Loosen edges of flan with a knife or rubber spatula. Place a plate, upside down, on top of cake pan; invert flan onto plate. Drizzle any remaining caramelized syrup over flan. Serves 8 (serving size: 1 wedge)

CALORIES 250; **FAT** 3.2g (sat 1.3g, mono 1.1g, poly 0.3g); **PROTEIN** 9.6g; **CARB** 45.7g; **FIBER** 0g; **CHOL** 88mg; **IRON** 0.3mg; **SODIUM** 120mg; **CALC** 223mg

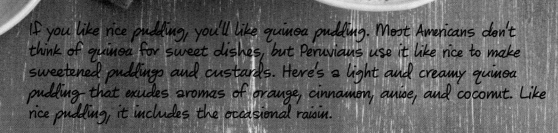

If you like rice pudding, you'll like quinoa pudding. Most Americans don't think of quinoa for sweet dishes, but Peruvians use it like rice to make sweetened puddings and custards. Here's a light and creamy quinoa pudding that exudes aromas of orange, cinnamon, anise, and coconut. Like rice pudding, it includes the occasional raisin.

QUINOA PUDDING

HANDS-ON TIME: 15 MIN. TOTAL TIME: 1 HR. 17 MIN.

¾ cup uncooked quinoa
½ vanilla bean, split
   lengthwise
1½ cups water
1 teaspoon grated orange rind
⅛ teaspoon salt
1 (3-inch) cinnamon stick
1 star anise
4 cups 2% reduced-fat milk
½ cup packed dark brown
   sugar
¼ cup finely shredded
   reduced-fat unsweetened
   dehydrated coconut
¼ cup raisins
1 large egg, lightly beaten
Grated orange rind (optional)

1. Place quinoa in a fine sieve; place sieve in a large bowl. Cover quinoa with water. Using your hands, rub grains together for 30 seconds; rinse and drain. Repeat procedure twice. Drain well, and place in a large saucepan.

2. Scrape seeds from vanilla bean; add seeds and bean to quinoa. Add 1½ cups water, orange rind, salt, cinnamon, and star anise. Bring to boil over high heat. Cover, reduce heat to medium-low, and simmer 15 minutes or until liquid is absorbed.

3. Stir in milk and sugar; bring to a boil over high heat. Reduce heat to medium-low, and simmer, uncovered, 22 minutes, stirring occasionally. Stir in coconut and raisins; simmer, uncovered, an additional 20 minutes or until mixture is thick and creamy, stirring frequently.

4. Remove from heat; discard vanilla bean, cinnamon, and star anise. Gradually add 1 cup hot pudding to egg, stirring constantly with a whisk. Return mixture to pan, stirring until well blended.

5. Garnish each serving with orange rind, if desired. Serves 6 (serving size: about ¾ cup)

Note: Substitute 1½ teaspoons vanilla extract for the vanilla bean, if desired. Add the vanilla extract after cooking the pudding (at the end of step 3).

CALORIES 274; FAT 6.3g (sat 3.3g, mono 1.6g, poly 1g); PROTEIN 9.8g; CARB 45.7g; FIBER 2.1g; CHOL 44mg; IRON 1.4mg; SODIUM 144mg; CALC 229mg

Born and raised in Lima, chef Ricardo Zarate knows a thing or two about Peruvian cuisine. He calls this puckery ceviche criollo ("Creole") because the method used to make it is indigenous to Peru rather than Spain. The "tiger's milk" sauce is the milky liquid that forms when the fish marinates for ceviche.

CEVICHE WITH TIGER'S MILK SAUCE
(Ceviche Criollo con Leche de Tigre)

HANDS-ON TIME: 20 MIN. TOTAL TIME: 40 MIN.

1 rocoto chile pepper, stem removed
25¼ ounces striped sea bass, cut into cubes and divided
¼ cup chopped red onion
¾ cup fresh lime juice (about 5 limes)
½ teaspoon kosher salt
2 garlic cloves
1 (2-inch) piece celery
1 (1-inch) length peeled fresh ginger, sliced
1 cup thinly vertically sliced red onion
1 tablespoon chopped fresh cilantro

1. Boil rocoto pepper 1 minute; drain. Repeat twice. Place 1¼ ounces rocoto pepper flesh (reserve remaining pepper for another use), 1 teaspoon rocoto pepper seeds, 1¼ ounces fish, ¼ cup chopped red onion, juice, salt, garlic, celery, and ginger in a blender. Process until smooth. Chill rocoto mixture 20 minutes.

2. Combine chilled rocoto mixture, remaining 24 ounces sea bass, sliced red onion, and cilantro in a bowl; toss to combine. Serve in chilled bowls or glasses. Serves 8 (serving size: ½ cup)

CALORIES 150; FAT 2.5g (sat 0.6g, mono 0.5g, poly 0.9g); PROTEIN 22.9g; CARB 9.3g; FIBER 1g; CHOL 49mg; IRON 0.6mg; SODIUM 249mg; CALC 32.7mg

Two of the most popular dishes in Brazil's Bahia state are bobo camarones (shrimp in yuca cream sauce) and moqueca (seafood coconut stew). This recipe combines both. Coconut milk flavors the sauce, while mashed yuca adds creaminess. Dendê oil (bright orange palm oil) is usually stirred in at the end to lend the sauce color, but I've used annatto oil instead.

SHRIMP IN BAHIA SAUCE

HANDS-ON TIME: 56 MIN. TOTAL TIME: 1 HR. 21 MIN.

8 ounces fresh or frozen yuca (cassava), thawed

3 garlic cloves, peeled

2 pounds large shrimp, peeled and deveined

2 tablespoons fresh lime juice

½ teaspoon salt, divided

2 tablespoons olive oil

2 teaspoons annatto (achiote) seeds

1 large onion, halved lengthwise and sliced crosswise (2¼ cups)

1 red bell pepper, halved lengthwise and sliced crosswise (1 cup)

3 cups diced seeded peeled tomato

½ cup light coconut milk

1 tablespoon chopped seeded Scotch bonnet or habanero pepper

2 tablespoons chopped fresh cilantro, divided

1 lime, cut into 8 wedges

1. Peel yuca, and cut into ½-inch cubes to measure 1¼ cups. Place yuca in a medium saucepan; cover with water. Bring to boil over high heat. Cover, reduce heat to medium-low, and simmer 25 minutes or until tender. Drain yuca in a colander over a bowl, reserving ½ cup cooking liquid. Return yuca and reserved ½ cup cooking liquid to pan; mash with a potato masher until smooth. Discard any tough fibers.

2. Place garlic on a cutting board; mash to a paste by dragging and pressing broad side of knife over garlic several times. Combine garlic, shrimp, lime juice, and ¼ teaspoon salt in a medium bowl. Let stand at room temperature 30 minutes.

3. Heat a large skillet over medium-low heat. Add oil to pan; swirl to coat. Stir in annatto seeds, and cook 5 minutes or until oil turns deep orange in color, shaking pan frequently. Remove from heat; let stand 10 minutes. Discard annatto seeds, reserving oil in pan.

4. Heat pan over medium heat until annatto oil is hot. Add onion and bell pepper; cook 6 minutes or until tender. Add tomato; cook 10 minutes or until tomato breaks down, stirring occasionally. Mash mixture with a wooden spoon. Add shrimp with marinade, coconut milk, and Scotch bonnet. Reduce heat to low, and simmer 3 minutes, stirring occasionally. Stir in reserved mashed yuca, remaining ¼ teaspoon salt, and 1 tablespoon cilantro; cook 2 minutes or until shrimp are done. Spoon shrimp mixture into shallow bowls; sprinkle evenly with remaining 1 tablespoon cilantro, and serve with lime wedges. Serves 8 (serving size: about 1 cup shrimp mixture and 1 lime wedge)

CALORIES 225; FAT 6.6g (sat 1.5g, mono 2.6g, poly 0.6g); PROTEIN 22.4g; CARB 19g; FIBER 19g; CHOL 193mg; IRON 0.8mg; SODIUM 371mg; CALC 105mg

Originally from the Ecuadorian highlands, llapingachos have become popular all over the country. They're like thick potato pancakes stuffed with cheese and cooked in a hot pan until crisp and golden brown. A simple tomato salad usually comes on the side, but you could add some chopped avocado for more richness.

ECUADORIAN POTATO AND CHEESE PATTIES
(Llapingachos Ecuatorianos)

HANDS-ON TIME: 19 MIN. TOTAL TIME: 64 MIN.

1³/₄ teaspoons kosher salt, divided

2 medium baking potatoes (about 1¹/₄ pounds), peeled and quartered

1¹/₂ ounces shredded queso fresco or Monterey Jack cheese (about 6 tablespoons)

2 tablespoons minced green onions

¹/₄ teaspoon freshly ground black pepper

1 tablespoon olive oil

³/₄ cup diced tomato

¹/₂ cup julienne-cut red onion

1. Place 1½ teaspoons salt and potatoes in a saucepan, and cover with water. Bring to a boil; reduce heat, and simmer 15 minutes or until tender. Drain, and mash with a potato masher until smooth. Cool.

2. Add cheese, green onions, remaining ¼ teaspoon salt, and pepper to potato mixture, stirring well. Divide potato mixture into 6 balls (about ½ cup per ball). Flatten balls into ½-inch-thick patties (about 3-inch diameter). Place on a baking sheet; cover and refrigerate 20 minutes or until firm.

3. Heat large nonstick skillet over medium heat. Add oil to pan; swirl to coat. Place patties in pan; cook 5 minutes or until bottoms are browned. Turn patties; cook 3 minutes. Top patties with tomato and red onion. Serves 6 (serving size: 1 patty, 2 tablespoons tomato, and 4 teaspoons red onion)

CALORIES 157; **FAT** 4.6g (sat 1.8g, mono 1.3g, poly 1.2g); **PROTEIN** 4.2g; **CARB** 24.9g; **FIBER** 2.1g; **CHOL** 6mg; **IRON** 0.6mg; **SODIUM** 279mg; **CALC** 64mg

Potatoes

The potato varieties available in U.S. markets represent only a tiny fraction of the 4,000 varieties grown worldwide. But in the spud's native country of Peru, cooks still use thousands of varieties. Potatoes are the staple starch of the South American highlands. However, very starchy varieties like russets are less popular than medium-starch types like Peruvian Perricholi (similar to Yukon gold) and Purpura (purple-flesh). High up in the chilly, windy Andes Mountains, cooks leave bitter-tasting varieties outside to be naturally freeze-dried, which reduces bitterness and preserves the potatoes for later use. The best way to store fresh potatoes is in a cool, dark, well-ventilated place where they can last for months and even improve in flavor as enzymes gradually break down lipids in the cell membranes.

START WITH SOFRITO

*M*any Latin American specialties start with a flavor base called sofrito, which consists of minced onions, peppers, tomatoes, garlic, and herbs. Across Central and South America, the ingredients vary according to region, but its preparation is similar. The ingredients are cooked in oil (or sometimes lard) to release their flavor. As the liquid evaporates, the natural sugars begin to caramelize, adding a slight sweetness and intriguing depth of flavor to the finished dish. The more caramelization, the deeper the flavor.

If this simple technique sounds familiar, it should. Some say it first appeared in a cookbook published circa 1324 in Spain, and many cuisines that originated in Europe start with a similar base. In France, it's called a *mirepoix* and consists of onions, celery, and carrots. The same combination is called a *soffritto* in Italy. Many Portuguese dishes gain their flavor from *refogado,* which is a combination of onions, garlic and tomato. In America, Creole and Cajun dishes often start with the "holy trinity"—onions, peppers, and celery.

Sweet Potato and Black Bean

EMPANADAS

HANDS-ON TIME: 24 MIN. TOTAL TIME: 2 HR. 3 MIN.

9 ounces all-purpose flour
  (about 2 cups)
¾ teaspoon kosher salt
⅓ cup canola oil
¼ cup cold water
1 tablespoon cider vinegar
1 large egg, lightly beaten
1 poblano chile
1 tablespoon cumin seeds
1 cup mashed cooked sweet
  potatoes
1 cup canned black beans,
  rinsed and drained
⅓ cup chopped green onions
2 tablespoons chopped fresh
  cilantro
1 teaspoon ancho chile
  powder
½ teaspoon kosher salt
1 egg white, lightly beaten
Cooking spray

1. Weigh or lightly spoon flour into dry measuring cups, and level with a knife. Combine flour and ¾ teaspoon salt in a large bowl, stirring with a whisk. Combine canola oil, ¼ cup cold water, vinegar, and egg in a medium bowl. Gradually add oil mixture to flour mixture, stirring just until moist. Knead lightly until smooth. Shape dough into a ball, and wrap in plastic wrap. Chill 1 hour.

2. Preheat broiler. Place chile on a foil-lined baking sheet; broil 8 minutes or until blackened, turning after 6 minutes. Place in a paper bag; close tightly. Let stand 15 minutes. Peel chile; cut in half lengthwise. Discard seeds and membranes; finely chop.

3. Preheat oven to 400°. Cook cumin seeds in a large saucepan over medium heat 1 minute or until toasted, stirring constantly. Place cumin in a clean spice grinder; process until ground. Combine cumin, poblano, sweet potatoes, and next 5 ingredients (through ½ teaspoon salt) in a large bowl; mash with a fork until almost smooth.

4. Divide dough into 10 equal portions, shaping each into a ball. Roll each dough portion into a 5-inch circle on a lightly floured surface. Working with 1 portion at a time (cover remaining dough to keep from drying), spoon 3 tablespoons poblano mixture into center of each circle. Moisten edges of dough with egg white; fold dough over filling. Press edges together to seal. Place on a large baking sheet coated with cooking spray. Cut 3 diagonal slits across top of each empanada. Bake at 400° for 16 minutes or until lightly browned. Serves 10 (serving size: 1 empanada)

CALORIES 209; FAT 8.4g (sat 0.7g, mono 5g, poly 2.3g); PROTEIN 5.1g; CARB 29g; FIBER 2.9g; CHOL 18mg; IRON 2.3mg; SODIUM 359mg; CALC 32mg

how to: FILL AND FOLD EMPANADAS

Let empanada dough rest so it is more pliable for shaping.

1 While rolling the dough, depend on a ruler to ensure the circle is 5 inches in diameter. Measure the diameter by placing a ruler at the widest part of the circle.

2 Accurately measure the filling with a measuring spoon so the empanadas will be uniform in size and bake evenly.

3 Beaten egg white brushed around the edges of the dough acts as a glue to seal the pastry together when it's folded.

4 Fold dough over filling, and carefully match edges together before pressing edges to seal.

Street vendors in Peru sell anticuchos (grilled meat skewers) made with beef hearts. If you're not feeling that adventurous, sirloin works well, too. Either way, the real star is ground aji amarillo, made from Peru's medium-hot, sunny-yellow chile pepper. It shows up in both the spice rub and the sauce for the beef, lending a subtle floral aroma and radiant yellow color.

PERUVIAN BEEF KEBABS

Anticuchos with Roasted Yellow Pepper Sauce

HANDS-ON TIME: 17 MIN. TOTAL TIME: 3 HR. 53 MIN.

1½ pounds boneless sirloin steak, trimmed and cut into ½-inch pieces
3 tablespoons red wine vinegar
4 teaspoons ground aji amarillo or hot paprika, divided
1¾ teaspoons freshly ground black pepper, divided
1¾ teaspoons salt, divided
1½ teaspoons ground cumin, divided
1¼ teaspoons ground turmeric, divided
1 large yellow bell pepper
¼ cup finely chopped green onions
2 tablespoons white vinegar
1 tablespoon water
1 tablespoon olive oil
1 tablespoon fresh lemon juice
1 garlic clove, minced
3 tablespoons chopped fresh flat-leaf parsley
Cooking spray

1. Combine steak, red wine vinegar, 2 teaspoons aji amarillo, 1 teaspoon black pepper, ½ teaspoon salt, ½ teaspoon cumin, and ½ teaspoon turmeric in a large bowl; toss well. Cover and chill 3 hours.

2. Preheat broiler.

3. Cut bell pepper in half lengthwise, discarding seeds and membranes. Place pepper halves, skin sides up, on a foil-lined baking sheet; flatten with hand. Broil 15 minutes or until blackened. Place in a paper bag, and fold to close tightly. Let stand 10 minutes. Peel and coarsely chop. Place bell pepper, green onions, white vinegar, 1 tablespoon water, olive oil, lemon juice, 1 teaspoon cumin, 1 teaspoon aji amarillo, ½ teaspoon turmeric, ¼ teaspoon black pepper, ¼ teaspoon salt, and garlic in a blender; process until smooth. Set aside.

4. Combine parsley, 1 teaspoon salt, 1 teaspoon aji amarillo, ½ teaspoon black pepper, and ¼ teaspoon turmeric.

5. Prepare grill to medium-high heat.

6. Remove beef from bowl; thread beef onto each of 6 (10-inch) skewers. Press rub onto beef. Place kebabs on grill rack coated with cooking spray; grill 6 minutes or until desired degree of doneness, turning once. Serve with sauce. Serves 6 (serving size: 3 ounces meat and about 2½ tablespoons sauce)

CALORIES 188; FAT 7g (sat 2.7g, mono 3g, poly 0.3g); PROTEIN 26.3g; CARB 3.4g; FIBER 0.8g; CHOL 76mg; IRON 3.6mg; SODIUM 612mg; CALC 23mg

Chimichurri is like a loose herb pesto spiked with vinegar. It probably originated in Spain, but has since become the preferred condiment for grilled beef in Argentina and Uruguay. This recipe uses fresh parsley and cilantro, along with ground cumin and red pepper flakes, to flavor grilled pork tenderloin.

ARGENTINEAN PORK
with Chimichurri

HANDS-ON TIME: 20 MIN. TOTAL TIME: 1 HR. 30 MIN.

6 tablespoons olive oil, divided
1 cup fresh parsley leaves, divided
²/₃ cup fresh cilantro leaves, divided
½ teaspoon ground cumin
¼ teaspoon crushed red pepper
1 (1-pound) pork tenderloin, trimmed
³/₄ teaspoon kosher salt, divided
½ teaspoon freshly ground black pepper
Cooking spray
1 tablespoon fresh oregano leaves
1 tablespoon fresh lemon juice
1 tablespoon sherry vinegar
2 garlic cloves, chopped
1 shallot, chopped

1. Combine 2 tablespoons oil, ¼ cup parsley, ⅓ cup cilantro, cumin, and red pepper in a shallow dish. Add pork. Cover with plastic wrap, and refrigerate 1 hour, turning once.

2. Preheat grill to medium-high.

3. Sprinkle pork with ½ teaspoon salt and black pepper. Place pork on grill rack coated with cooking spray, and grill 8 minutes. Turn pork over, and grill 7 minutes or until a thermometer registers 145°. Remove pork from grill. Let stand 5 minutes. Slice pork crosswise.

4. Place remaining ¾ cup parsley, ⅓ cup cilantro, ¼ teaspoon salt, oregano, and remaining ingredients in a food processor; pulse 10 times. Drizzle remaining ¼ cup olive oil through food chute with food processor on. Serve with pork. Serves 4 (serving size: 3 ounces pork and 2 tablespoons sauce)

Note: Chimichurri can be made ahead of time and refrigerated for a few days. Add vinegar just before serving to avoid discoloration.

CALORIES 319; FAT 23g (sat 3.6g, mono 15.7g, poly 2.6g); PROTEIN 24.5g; CARB 2.9g; FIBER 0.7g; CHOL 74mg; IRON 2.4mg; SODIUM 430mg; CALC 39mg

Churrasco means different things in different parts of Latin America: a particular cut of beef in Argentina, a general term for barbecue in Brazil, and a flat beef tenderloin in Nicaragua. For this dish, the beef steak is cut in the Nicaraguan style, seasoned with Salvadoran spices, and accented with pebre, Chile's spicy version of chimichurri.

BROILED BEEF TENDERLOIN
with Chilean Cilantro Sauce

HANDS-ON TIME: 40 MIN. TOTAL TIME: 40 MIN.

Cooking spray
4 cups sliced onion
1/2 teaspoon sugar
1 (1 1/2-pound) center-cut beef tenderloin
1/2 teaspoon salt
1/2 teaspoon garlic powder
1/2 teaspoon dried oregano
1/2 teaspoon freshly ground black pepper
1/4 teaspoon ground cumin
Chilean Cilantro Sauce (Pebre)

1. Heat a large skillet over medium heat. Coat pan with cooking spray. Add onion and sugar; cover and cook 10 minutes or until golden brown, stirring frequently.
2. Preheat broiler.
3. Cut tenderloin lengthwise with the grain into 6 even steaks. Place 1 steak between 2 sheets of heavy-duty plastic wrap; flatten to an even thickness using a meat mallet or rolling pin. Repeat procedure with remaining steaks. Combine salt and next 4 ingredients (through cumin). Rub salt mixture over both sides of steaks. Place steaks on a broiler pan coated with cooking spray. Broil 2 minutes on each side or until desired degree of doneness. Top each steak with onion mixture; drizzle each with 1 tablespoon Chilean Cilantro Sauce. Serves 6 (serving size: 3 ounces steak, 1/2 cup onion mixture, and 1 tablespoon sauce)

CALORIES 167; FAT 7.3g (sat 2.3g, mono 3.4g, poly 0.5g); PROTEIN 17.1g; CARB 8.2g; FIBER 1.7g; CHOL 48mg; IRON 2.5mg; SODIUM 329mg; CALC 27mg

CHILEAN CILANTRO SAUCE (Pebre)

HANDS-ON TIME: 5 MIN. TOTAL TIME: 5 MIN.

2/3 cup organic vegetable broth
1/2 cup minced fresh cilantro
1/2 cup minced onion
1/2 cup minced red bell pepper
1/4 cup white vinegar
1/4 cup extra-virgin olive oil
1 teaspoon salt
1 teaspoon dried oregano
1 teaspoon crushed red pepper
1/2 teaspoon freshly ground black pepper
4 garlic cloves, minced

1. Combine all ingredients, stirring with a whisk until well blended. Serves 32 (serving size: 1 tablespoon)
Note: Store remaining sauce in an airtight container in the refrigerator for up to 2 weeks.

CALORIES 18; FAT 1.8g (sat 0.2g, mono 1.3g, poly 0.2g); PROTEIN 0.1g; CARB 0.8g; FIBER 0.2g; CHOL 0mg; IRON 0.1mg; SODIUM 95mg; CALC 4mg

Think of this dish as Chilean shepherd's pie, except the top crust is made with fresh pureed corn instead of potatoes. It is traditionally baked in individual clay dishes, but the directions here call for one large casserole. To use individual dishes, just decrease the cooking time by 5 to 10 minutes.

MEAT AND CORN PIE
(Pastel de Choclo)

HANDS-ON TIME: 50 MIN. TOTAL TIME: 1 HR. 42 MIN.

8 ears yellow corn
½ cup 2% reduced-fat milk
¼ cup yellow cornmeal
1 teaspoon sugar
¼ teaspoon salt
1 tablespoon butter
1 tablespoon chopped fresh basil
2 (6-ounce) skinless, boneless chicken breast halves
½ teaspoon salt, divided
½ teaspoon freshly ground black pepper, divided
Cooking spray
½ cup raisins
1 cup hot water
1 tablespoon canola oil
2 cups finely chopped onion
½ teaspoon dried oregano
½ teaspoon ground cumin
½ teaspoon paprika
¼ teaspoon ground red pepper
2 large garlic cloves, minced
¾ pound 95% lean ground beef
1 tablespoon all-purpose flour
½ cup fat-free, lower-sodium beef broth
2 hard-cooked large eggs, thinly sliced
½ cup pitted green olives, chopped
Fresh basil leaves (optional)

1. Remove husks from corn, and scrub silks from corn. Cut kernels from ears of corn to measure 6 cups. Place corn kernels, milk, cornmeal, sugar, and salt in a blender or food processor; process until pureed.

2. Melt butter in large saucepan over medium heat. Add corn puree, and cook 10 to 12 minutes or until mixture is thick like oatmeal, stirring frequently. Remove from heat; stir in basil.

3. Preheat broiler.

4. Place each chicken breast half between 2 sheets of heavy-duty plastic wrap; pound to ¼-inch thickness using a meat mallet or small heavy skillet. Sprinkle chicken with ¼ teaspoon salt and ¼ teaspoon pepper. Place chicken on a jelly-roll pan coated with cooking spray. Broil chicken 5 to 6 minutes on each side or until chicken is done. Cool slightly; shred chicken with 2 forks.

5. Preheat oven to 375°.

6. Combine raisins and 1 cup hot water in a bowl. Let stand 10 minutes.

7. While raisins stand, heat a large skillet over medium heat. Add oil to pan; swirl to coat. Add onion; sauté 4 minutes. Add oregano and next 4 ingredients (through garlic); sauté 1 minute. Add beef; cook 5 to 7 minutes or until browned, stirring to crumble. Sprinkle with flour; cook 2 minutes, stirring constantly. Stir in remaining ¼ teaspoon salt, remaining ¼ teaspoon pepper, and broth; cook 1 minute or until slightly thick, stirring constantly.

8. Drain raisins; discard liquid. Spread beef mixture in an 8-inch square glass or ceramic baking dish coated with cooking spray. Top with shredded chicken, sliced eggs, raisins, and olives. Pour corn puree over casserole, spreading to cover filling. Bake at 375° for 30 to 35 minutes or until corn puree is lightly browned and forms a crust. Garnish with basil, if desired. Serves 6 (serving size: ⅙ of casserole)

CALORIES 449; FAT 14.4g (sat 4.4g, mono 5.9g, poly 2.3g); PROTEIN 32.6g; CARB 52.5g; FIBER 5.2g; CHOL 136mg; IRON 3.7mg; SODIUM 552mg; CALC 80mg

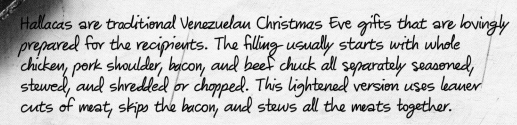

Hallacas are traditional Venezuelan Christmas Eve gifts that are lovingly prepared for the recipients. The filling usually starts with whole chicken, pork shoulder, bacon, and beef chuck all separately seasoned, stewed, and shredded or chopped. This lightened version uses leaner cuts of meat, skips the bacon, and stews all the meats together.

VENEZUELAN TAMALES
(Hallacas)

HANDS-ON TIME: 3 HR. 7 MIN. TOTAL TIME: 4 HR. 48 MIN.

¼ cup plus 2 tablespoons olive oil, divided
1 (8-ounce) skinless, boneless chicken breast half, chopped
6 ounces beef sirloin, chopped
6 ounces pork tenderloin, finely chopped
1½ cups finely chopped leek
1 cup finely chopped onion
⅓ cup chopped green onions
2 garlic cloves, minced
1⅔ cups chopped green or red bell pepper
½ cup chopped seeded Cubanelle or Anaheim chile
¾ cup chopped seeded tomato
2½ cups fat-free, lower-sodium chicken broth, divided
⅓ cup red wine vinegar
2 tablespoons brown sugar
1 teaspoon smoked paprika
½ teaspoon salt
½ teaspoon ground red pepper
¼ teaspoon black pepper
½ cup sliced shallots

1. Heat a large nonstick skillet over medium-high heat. Add 1 tablespoon oil to pan; swirl to coat. Add chicken; cook 5 minutes or until done, stirring occasionally. Remove from skillet. Add 1½ teaspoons oil to pan; add beef and pork, and cook 5 minutes or until done, stirring occasionally. Remove from skillet. Reduce heat to medium; add 1½ teaspoons oil. Add leek, onion, green onions, and garlic; sauté 5 minutes. Add bell pepper and chile; sauté 5 minutes. Add tomato; cook 5 minutes or until tomato breaks down. Mash with a wooden spoon. Add 1 cup broth, vinegar, and next 5 ingredients (through black pepper); bring to simmer over high heat. Return meats to pan; reduce heat to medium-low, and simmer 30 minutes or until liquid almost evaporates and mixture is slightly thick. Remove from heat; cool slightly, and stir in next 8 ingredients (shallots through cilantro).
2. Combine ¼ cup oil and annatto seeds in small saucepan; cook over low heat 4 minutes or until oil is deep orange in color and seeds just begin to darken. Remove from heat; let stand 10 minutes.
3. Place remaining 1½ cups broth in a large glass measure. Microwave at HIGH 1 to 2 minutes or until warm.
4. Discard annatto seeds; reserve 1 tablespoon annatto oil. Scrape remaining annatto oil into a food processor using a rubber spatula. Add warm broth, squash puree, corn flour, and ½ teaspoon salt; process 2 minutes or until well blended and dough forms. Let stand in food processor, covered, 30 minutes.
5. Shape dough into 16 (2-inch) balls with moist hands; place on a cutting board lined with damp paper towels (cover with plastic wrap to prevent drying).

- ½ cup sliced roasted red bell pepper
- ½ cup raisins
- ⅓ cup sliced pimiento-stuffed olives
- ½ cup finely chopped sweet pickles
- ½ cup small capers
- ½ cup sliced almonds
- ¼ cup chopped fresh cilantro
- 1 tablespoon annatto (achiote) seeds
- 1⅓ cups butternut squash puree (canned or fresh)
- 3 cups precooked white corn flour (such as P.A.N.)
- ½ teaspoon salt
- 16 (12-inch) squares foil
- 3 hard-cooked large eggs, thinly sliced lengthwise
- Reduced-fat sour cream, fresh cilantro leaves (optional)

6. For each tamale, place 1 foil square, shiny side up, on work surface; lightly brush annatto oil down center of square. Place 1 dough ball in center of square over oil; pat dough into a 6-inch circle with moist fingers. Spoon about ⅓ cup filling onto dough circle, leaving a ½-inch. Top with an egg slice. Use foil to fold dough over filling, top to bottom then side to side, using moist fingers to seal the edges. Wrap foil over tamales top to bottom then side to side like a package. Steam tamales, covered, 1 to 1½ hours or until dough is firm. Unwrap hallacas. Garnish with sour cream and cilantro, if desired. Serves 16 (serving size: 1 hallaca)

CALORIES 266; FAT 10.2g (sat 1.7g, mono 5.9g, poly 1.8g); PROTEIN 13.2g; CARB 32g; FIBER 3.5g; CHOL 58mg; IRON 3.1mg; SODIUM 548mg; CALC 83mg

In Colombia and Venezuela, arepas are the daily bread—seared in a hot skillet, and then finished in the oven. Arepas are eaten every which way—with a spread of jam, a savory or sweet topping, or split open like pita breads and stuffed with all manner of tasty fillings.

COLOMBIAN TURKEY FLATBREAD SANDWICHES
(Turkey Arepas)

HANDS-ON TIME: 32 MIN. TOTAL TIME: 54 MIN.

7.5 ounces (1½ cups) yellow arepa flour (masarepa, such as P.A.N.)
1 teaspoon salt, divided
2 cups hot water
2 tablespoons canola oil, divided
1 cup finely chopped onion
1 cup finely chopped green bell pepper
2 teaspoons minced seeded jalapeño pepper
½ teaspoon cumin seeds
2 garlic cloves, minced
2 cups chopped leftover cooked turkey breast
¼ cup chopped fresh cilantro
½ teaspoon freshly ground black pepper
⅓ cup (3 ounces) shredded reduced-fat sharp white cheddar cheese

1. Preheat oven to 400°.
2. Weigh or lightly spoon flour into dry measuring cups; level with a knife. Combine flour and ½ teaspoon salt; stir well. Add 2 cups hot water; stir until well combined and smooth. Let stand 10 minutes. Divide dough into 12 equal portions, shaping each into a ball. (Dough should be moist.) Working with 1 portion at a time, roll each portion into a 3-inch circle (about ½ inch thick).
3. Heat 1½ teaspoons canola oil in a large nonstick skillet over medium-high heat. Add 6 arepas to pan; cook 2 minutes on each side or until browned and crisp. Place on a baking sheet. Repeat procedure with 1½ teaspoons oil and remaining arepas. Bake at 400° for 20 minutes or until arepas sound hollow when lightly tapped.
4. While arepas bake, heat a large nonstick skillet over medium heat. Add remaining 1 tablespoon oil to pan; swirl to coat. Add onion and bell pepper; cook 5 minutes, stirring occasionally. Add jalapeño, cumin seeds, and garlic; cook 2 minutes, stirring occasionally. Stir in remaining ½ teaspoon salt, turkey, cilantro, and black pepper; cook 1 minute. Remove from heat; stir in cheese.
5. Remove arepas from oven; let stand 2 minutes. Cut a 3-inch pocket in the side of each arepa; spoon turkey mixture into arepas. Serves 6 (serving size: 2 filled arepas)

CALORIES 282; FAT 10.4g (sat 3g, mono 3.3g, poly 2.3g); PROTEIN 20.8g; CARB 26.5g; FIBER 4.8g; CHOL 42mg; IRON 3mg; SODIUM 547mg; CALC 162mg

KNOW YOUR CORN

Corn (maize) is to the Americas what rice is to Asia. It's the most widely grown food crop in the New World and a staple of Central and South American meals. Most South American dishes don't use sweet corn. Instead, they use field corn, a starchy variety that is processed to make arepa flour, hominy, and masa.

Arepa flour is field corn that has been hulled, ground, and partially cooked. It can be quickly made into the Central and South American flatbreads called arepas, which are like thick pancakes and perfect for a hearty snack. You can find arepa flour under the brand name P.A.N., which is widely available in supermarkets.

Hominy is field corn that has been soaked in a strong alkali such as calcium hydroxide or lye and heated to remove the tough outer hull, which makes the corn easier to digest. This ancient process is called *nixtamalization* because it results in nixtamal, the Mexican term for hominy. Nixtamalization also makes the niacin, calcium, and iron in field corn more available to the body.

Fresh masa is hominy that is ground into a paste so it can be flattened into corn tortillas with a press. For masa harina, the paste is dried into a flour that can be reconstituted to quickly make masa dough for dishes like Chipotle Pork Tamales (page 300) and Pupusa Casserole (page 296).

A common condiment in Peru, sarsa is a salsa or relish of chopped fresh onions, herbs, and citrus juice. Some versions include tomatoes. Some toss in radishes. As long as the base of the relish remains crisp and puckery, you can add what you like. This version from chef Douglas Rodriguez is a fuller salad including lima beans, hominy, and farmer's cheese.

PERUVIAN SARSA SALAD

HANDS-ON TIME: 7 MIN. TOTAL TIME: 7 MIN.

1 cup thinly sliced red onion
1/2 cup sliced radishes
1/2 cup frozen lima beans, thawed
1/2 cup canned white hominy, drained
1 ounce crumbled farmer's cheese or feta cheese (about 1/4 cup)
1/4 cup chopped bottled roasted red bell peppers
2 tablespoons chopped fresh mint
2 tablespoons chopped fresh cilantro
3 tablespoons fresh lemon juice
1 tablespoon olive oil
1/4 teaspoon salt
1/4 teaspoon freshly ground black pepper
3 garlic cloves, minced

1. Combine first 8 ingredients in a large bowl. Combine lemon juice and remaining ingredients in a small bowl, stirring with a whisk. Drizzle dressing over salad, and toss gently to combine. Serves 6 (serving size: 1/2 cup)

CALORIES 77; FAT 3.6g (sat 1.1g, mono 1.9g, poly 0.3g); PROTEIN 2.6g; CARB 9.5g; FIBER 1.3g; CHOL 4mg; IRON 0.8mg; SODIUM 198mg; CALC 44mg

In Uruguay and Argentina, this salad belongs to a roster of side dishes that accompany cocktails and steaks. It's traditionally made with porotos, small dark, rectangular beans with an earthy flavor. Fava beans come closest in flavor, but you can also use kidney or pinto beans.

URUGUAYAN BEAN SALAD
HANDS-ON TIME: 6 MIN. TOTAL TIME: 6 MIN.

3 cups canned fava or kidney
  beans, drained and rinsed
1 cup chopped seeded tomato
¾ cup finely chopped onion
¼ cup chopped fresh flat-leaf
  parsley
3 tablespoons red wine vinegar
2 tablespoons extra-virgin
  olive oil
1 teaspoon dried oregano
½ teaspoon crushed red
  pepper
½ teaspoon freshly ground
  black pepper
¼ teaspoon salt

1. Combine all ingredients in a bowl, and toss gently. Serves 6 (serving size: ⅔ cup)

CALORIES 167, **FAT** 5.2g (sat 0.6g, mono 3.3g, poly 0.5g); **PROTEIN** 6.7g; **CARB** 23.7g; **FIBER** 6g; **CHOL** 0mg; **IRON** 2mg; **SODIUM** 353mg; **CALC** 34mg

This salad of boiled potatoes and thick, custardy chile-cheese sauce gets its bright yellow color from aji amarillo, a yellow chile that's become an edible symbol of Peru. Huancaína sauce means that it is made in the style of people from Huancayo, the Peruvian highlands.

POTATOES with Huancaína Sauce (Papa a la Huancaína)

HANDS-ON TIME: 54 MIN. TOTAL TIME: 1 HR. 34 MIN.

2 pounds Yukon gold or blue potatoes
1¼ teaspoons salt, divided
1 red bell pepper
2 tablespoons olive oil, divided
¼ cup chopped onion
2 garlic cloves, minced
⅓ cup evaporated fat-free milk
¼ cup aji amarillo paste, or 3 peeled and seeded aji amarillo peppers
6 ounces queso fresco or sheep's milk feta cheese
4 cups shredded iceberg lettuce
2 hard-cooked large eggs, each sliced into 6 wedges
¼ cup kalamata or black olives, pitted and halved lengthwise

1. Place unpeeled potatoes and 1 teaspoon salt in a large saucepan; cover with water. Bring to boil over high heat. Cover, reduce heat to medium-low, and cook 25 minutes or until potatoes are tender. Drain and cool slightly. Peel potatoes, and cut lengthwise into ¼-inch-thick slices.

2. Preheat broiler.

3. Cut bell pepper in half lengthwise; discard seeds and membranes. Place pepper halves, skin sides up, on a foil-lined baking sheet; flatten with hand. Broil 6 to 8 minutes or until blackened. Place in a paper bag; fold to close tightly. Let stand 5 minutes. Peel and coarsely chop to measure ⅓ cup.

4. Heat a small nonstick skillet over medium heat. Add 1 teaspoon oil to pan; swirl to coat. Add onion; sauté 5 minutes or until lightly browned. Add garlic; sauté 1 minute.

5. Place onion mixture, ⅓ cup roasted red bell pepper, milk, aji amarillo paste, cheese, remaining 5 teaspoons oil, and remaining ¼ teaspoon salt in a blender; process 3 minutes or until thick and smooth, scraping sides.

6. Arrange potato slices on each of 6 lettuce-lined plates. Spoon sauce over potatoes; arrange egg wedges and olives around potatoes on each plate. Serves 6 (serving size: ⅔ cup lettuce, about ¼ cup potatoes, ¼ cup sauce, 2 egg wedges, and 2 teaspoons olives)

CALORIES 256; FAT 10.1g (sat 2.9g, mono 5.7g, poly 1.1g); PROTEIN 9.7g; CARB 33g; FIBER 2.9g; CHOL 72mg; IRON 1.2mg; SODIUM 500mg; CALC 152mg

The Spanish name *enyucado* literally means "en-yuca-ed" or "yuca-fied." Starchy yuca holds the cake together, but shredded fresh coconut adds some body and tons of flavor. The cake includes both sugar and cheese, making it sweet and savory at the same time. You can serve it as a side dish with salty soups and stews, or as dessert.

YUCA-COCONUT CAKE
(Enyucado)

HANDS-ON TIME: 25 MIN. TOTAL TIME: 2 HR. 40 MIN.

2 pounds fresh yuca (cassava), peeled and very finely grated (about 3½ cups)
4 ounces queso fresco or reduced-fat Monterey Jack cheese, shredded (about 1 cup)
1 cup grated fresh coconut
¾ cup sugar
¾ cup light coconut milk
1 tablespoon butter, melted
2 teaspoons aniseed, crushed
1 teaspoon vanilla extract
Dash of salt
Cooking spray

1. Preheat oven to 350°. Place a 10-inch cast-iron skillet in oven 10 minutes.
2. Combine first 9 ingredients in a large bowl, stirring well.
3. Coat preheated pan with cooking spray; pour yuca mixture in pan, spreading evenly. Bake at 350° for 2 hours or until cake feels a little spongy when pressed and top is crisp. Cool on a wire rack 10 minutes.
4. Run a knife around edge of skillet to loosen cake. Cut into 8 wedges. Serve warm. Store cake tightly covered in refrigerator up to 4 days. Serves 8 (serving size: 1 wedge)

CALORIES 280; FAT 7.7g (sat 4.9g, mono 1.1g, poly 0.3g); PROTEIN 3.8g; CARB 49g; FIBER 4.2g; CHOL 8.4mg; IRON 0.5mg; SODIUM 59mg; CALC 58mg

how to: GRATE YUCA

A staple of Latin American cooking, yuca is a starchy root that's also used to make tapioca. Yuca is often covered in wax to retard spoilage, but you may find a brown spot, so buy a little more than you need.

1 Cut away the peel down to the white flesh.

2 Cut crosswise into sections, then cut in half lengthwise. Remove dark, woody "string" from center of each section.

3 Grate on fine holes of box grater. As you work, keep cut pieces in cold water to prevent discoloring.

Northern Brazil's Bahia state enjoys the country's longest coastline and a tropical climate. It's no wonder seafood and coconuts show up in so many Bahian dishes. This signature stew is a shining example. Coconut milk enriches the broth, and you can add whatever seafood is freshest, such as the sea bass and shrimp called for here.

BRAZILIAN FISH STEW
(Moqueca de Peixe)

HANDS-ON TIME: 36 MIN. TOTAL TIME: 1 HR. 19 MIN.

1/3 cup fresh lime juice
1/2 teaspoon salt
1/2 teaspoon freshly ground black pepper
2 garlic cloves, minced
1 (1 1/2-pound) sea bass or halibut fillet, cut into 1/2-inch wide strips
1 1/2 pounds large shrimp, peeled and deveined
2 tablespoons olive oil
2 cups finely chopped onion
1 cup finely chopped green bell pepper
1 cup finely chopped red bell pepper
3/4 cup minced green onions (about 1 bunch)
5 garlic cloves, minced
1 bay leaf
2 cups chopped tomato (about 2 large)
1/2 cup minced fresh cilantro, divided
2 (8-ounce) bottles clam juice
1 (14 1/2-ounce) can fat-free, lower-sodium chicken broth
1 cup light coconut milk
1/4 teaspoon ground red pepper

1. Combine first 6 ingredients in a large bowl; toss to coat. Marinate in refrigerator 30 minutes.
2. Heat a large Dutch oven over medium heat. Add oil to pan; swirl to coat. Add onion and next 5 ingredients (through bay leaf); cook 6 minutes, stirring occasionally. Increase heat to medium-high; add tomato, and cook 2 minutes. Add 1/4 cup cilantro, clam juice, and broth. Bring to a boil; reduce heat, and simmer 10 minutes. Discard bay leaf.
3. Place one-third of vegetable mixture in a blender; puree until smooth. Pour pureed vegetable mixture into a large bowl. Repeat procedure with remaining vegetable mixture. Pour pureed vegetable mixture in pan. Add coconut milk and red pepper to pureed vegetable mixture. Bring to a boil over medium-high heat; cook 3 minutes. Add fish mixture; cook 3 minutes or until fish is done. Sprinkle with remaining 1/4 cup cilantro. Serves 6 (serving size: 1 1/2 cups)

CALORIES 309; FAT 8.4g (sat 2.6g, mono 2.5g, poly 1.8g); PROTEIN 41.5g; CARB 15.9g; FIBER 3g; CHOL 178mg; IRON 3.8mg; SODIUM 733mg; CALC 102mg

Although it originated in Portugal, feijoada (fay-ZWAH-da) is Brazil's most famous stew. It's made by slowly cooking black beans and a mixture of fresh and cured meats in a thick clay pot. Here, the meats include pork shoulder, bacon, a smoked ham hock, and beef short ribs, creating layers of deep, savory flavor.

BRAZILIAN PORK AND BLACK BEAN STEW
(Feijoada)

HANDS-ON TIME: 47 MIN. TOTAL TIME: 9 HR. 47 MIN.

2 cups dried black beans
4 applewood-smoked bacon slices
1 (1-pound) boneless pork shoulder (Boston butt), trimmed and cut into ½-inch cubes
¾ teaspoon salt, divided
½ teaspoon freshly ground black pepper, divided
3 bone-in beef short ribs, trimmed (about 2 pounds)
3 cups finely chopped onion (about 2 medium)
1¼ cups fat-free, lower-sodium chicken broth
4 garlic cloves, minced
1 (9-ounce) smoked ham hock
1 tablespoon white vinegar
16 orange wedges
8 fresh bay leaves (optional)

1. Place beans in a small saucepan; cover with cold water. Bring to a boil; cook 2 minutes. Remove from heat; cover and let stand 1 hour. Drain.

2. Cook bacon in a large skillet over medium heat until crisp. Remove bacon from pan; crumble. Sprinkle pork evenly with ⅛ teaspoon salt and ¼ teaspoon pepper. Increase heat to medium-high. Add pork to drippings in skillet; sauté 8 minutes, turning to brown on all sides. Transfer pork to a 6-quart electric slow cooker. Sprinkle ribs evenly with ⅛ teaspoon salt and remaining ¼ teaspoon pepper. Add ribs to skillet; cook 3 minutes on each side or until browned. Place ribs in slow cooker. Add drained beans, remaining ½ teaspoon salt, onion, and next 3 ingredients (through ham hock) to slow cooker, stirring to combine. Cover and cook on LOW 8 hours or until beans and meat are tender.

3. Remove ribs from slow cooker; let stand 15 minutes. Remove meat from bones; shred meat with 2 forks. Discard bones. Discard ham hock. Return beef to slow cooker. Stir in vinegar and crumbled bacon. Serve with orange wedges. Garnish with bay leaves, if desired. Serves 8 (serving size: about 1¼ cups bean mixture and 2 orange wedges)

CALORIES 458; FAT 17.4g (sat 6.8g, mono 6.7g, poly 1.1g); PROTEIN 39.5g; CARB 35.8g; FIBER 11.6g; CHOL 96mg; IRON 6.4mg; SODIUM 533mg; CALC 102mg

A fixture on menus in Bogotá, this Colombian stew gets most of its creamy texture from potatoes. Cubed Yukon gold potatoes impart a golden color, while grated russets release their starch to provide a velvety mouthfeel without added cream. Grate the potatoes on the small holes of a box grater to make sure they dissolve into the broth.

POTATO, CORN, AND CHICKEN STEW *(Ajiaco)*

HANDS-ON TIME: 1 HR. 12 MIN. TOTAL TIME: 1 HR. 22 MIN.

1 tablespoon olive oil, divided

12 chicken thighs (about 4 pounds), skinned

3½ cups fat-free, lower-sodium chicken broth, divided

1½ cups fresh corn kernels (about 3 ears), divided

½ cup chopped onion

½ cup thinly sliced carrot

1½ cups water

1½ teaspoons chopped fresh oregano

1 teaspoon chopped fresh thyme

2½ cups finely shredded peeled baking potato

2½ cups cubed peeled Yukon gold or red potato

¼ cup chopped fresh cilantro

1 tablespoon fresh lime juice

¼ teaspoon salt

½ teaspoon hot pepper sauce (such as Tabasco)

¼ teaspoon freshly ground black pepper

³/₄ cup cubed peeled avocado

4½ teaspoons capers

1. Heat a large Dutch oven over medium-high heat. Add 1½ teaspoons oil to pan; swirl to coat. Add half of chicken; cook 5 minutes, browning on all sides. Remove chicken from pan. Repeat procedure with remaining half of chicken. Remove from pan; discard drippings.

2. Place 1 cup broth and ½ cup corn in a food processor; process until corn is pureed.

3. Heat Dutch oven over medium-high heat. Add remaining 1½ teaspoons oil to pan; swirl to coat. Add onion and carrot; sauté 2 minutes. Stir in pureed corn mixture, remaining 2½ cups broth, remaining 1 cup corn, 1½ cups water, oregano, and thyme; bring to a simmer. Stir in baking potato. Return chicken thighs to pan; cover, reduce heat, and simmer 20 minutes, stirring frequently to keep potato from sticking to pan. Add Yukon gold potato; cover and simmer 25 minutes, stirring frequently. Remove chicken from pan; cool slightly.

4. Remove chicken from bones, discarding bones. Shred chicken into bite-sized pieces. Return shredded chicken to pan. Stir in cilantro and next 4 ingredients (through black pepper); cook, uncovered, 5 minutes, stirring frequently. Ladle soup into bowls; top with avocado and capers. Serves 9 (serving size: 1½ cups soup, 4 teaspoons avocado, and ½ teaspoon capers)

CALORIES 319; FAT 15.4g (sat 3.8g, mono 6.9g, poly 3.2g); PROTEIN 30.8g; CARB 14g; FIBER 2.3g; CHOL 102mg; IRON 1.8mg; SODIUM 535mg; CALC 24mg

North & Central America

BLUEBERRIES:
A New World food, blueberries lend sweet-tart flavor to everything from jams and sauces to pies and muffins.

MAPLE SYRUP:
It takes 40 gallons of thin, watery maple sap to produce 1 gallon of sweet, thick maple syrup.

ORANGES:
North Americans favor sweet oranges, but in the Caribbean islands, sour oranges (naranja agria) are preferred for their spicy taste and floral aroma.

TURKEY:
America's beloved bird is relatively low in moisture, but brining turkey can increase its moisture content by up to 10 percent, making it juicier even after cooking.

APPLES:
The high pectin content of apples not only thickens sauces and pies, it also helps moderate cholesterol and blood glucose levels.

SWEET CORN:
Sugars begin converting to starch the minute fresh corn is picked; keep it cold and eat it soon.

MEXICAN OREGANO:
Fragrant leaves of a plant in the verbena family; the aroma is closer to savory than to the marjoram-like scent of oregano in the mint family.

LIMES:
Most U.S. markets carry Persian limes, but Mexican or Key limes are smaller, more tart, bitter, and aromatically complex.

The Flavors of North and Central America

Some of the most popular foods in the United States originated elsewhere. Consider pizza (Italy), burritos (Mexico), and fried rice (China). Likewise, in Central America, some of the best-loved dishes, such as flan, have roots in Spain. North America is incredibly diverse both racially and ethnically—especially in its cities. That diversity extends right down to the continent's cuisines. Over the centuries, some immigrant foods have succumbed to the melting-pot effect and taken on a new identity, while others have retained some authenticity and remain distinct in the kaleidoscope of American cuisine.

Of course, not all food in North and Central America was imported from elsewhere. Just think of New England's lobster rolls and Jamaica's jerk pork. From wild rice and cranberries in Canada to avocados and allspice in Mexico and the Caribbean islands, the continent boasts a huge range of native flavors. Here's a look at some of the key foods that help define the cuisines of North and Central America.

CHILES:
Dried chiles pound out the backbeat of Mexican and Tex-Mex cuisine, and fresh ones like Scotch bonnets sing high notes in dishes from the Caribbean islands.

PUMPKIN:
Enjoyed in everything from pies and soups to snacks and sauces, both the flesh and seeds of this winter squash offer sweet, earthy, and savory flavors.

Throughout Central America, cooks fill pastries with savory picadillo, browned ground beef with onions, peppers, and garlic. This spicy Haitian picadillo features chicken instead of beef. To make these appetizers ahead for a party, refrigerate the completed pastries for up to 2 hours, then bake 20 minutes before your guests arrive.

PICADILLO PUFFS

HANDS-ON TIME: 30 MIN. TOTAL TIME: 65 MIN.

1 habanero pepper
Cooking spray
¼ cup chopped yellow onion
2 teaspoons minced fresh garlic
½ pound ground chicken breast
¼ cup shredded carrot
2 teaspoons no-salt-added tomato paste
2 teaspoons fresh lime juice
1 teaspoon cider vinegar
1 tablespoon chopped green onions
1 tablespoon chopped fresh parsley
1 teaspoon chopped fresh thyme
½ teaspoon freshly ground black pepper
¼ teaspoon salt
⅛ teaspoon ground cloves
⅛ teaspoon grated whole nutmeg
1 (14-ounce) package frozen puff pastry, thawed (such as Dufour)
1 large egg
1 tablespoon water

1. Cut habanero in half. Seed one half of pepper, and leave seeds in other half. Mince both pepper halves. Heat a large skillet over medium-high heat. Coat pan with cooking spray. Add minced habanero, onion, and garlic; sauté 3 minutes or until tender. Add chicken; cook 5 minutes or until browned, stirring to crumble. Add carrot; cook 2 minutes. Add tomato paste; cook 1 minute, stirring constantly. Add lime juice and vinegar, scraping pan to loosen browned bits. Add green onions and next 6 ingredients (through grated nutmeg); stir well. Remove from heat; cool mixture to room temperature.

2. Place cooled chicken mixture in a food processor; process until almost smooth (mixture will begin to clump).

3. Preheat oven to 400°. Roll puff pastry into a 15 x 12–inch rectangle on a lightly floured surface. Cut puff pastry into 20 (3-inch) squares. Combine egg and 1 tablespoon water, stirring with a whisk. Brush egg mixture along edges of pastry squares; spoon 1 scant tablespoon filling in center of each pastry square. Fold each pastry square in half corner to corner; press edges closed with tines of a fork. Brush tops with egg mixture; arrange 1 inch apart on a baking sheet. Bake at 400° for 20 minutes or until puffed and golden brown. Serves 20 (serving size: 1 pâté puff)

CALORIES 102; FAT 5.7g (sat 1.6g, mono 3.2g, poly 0.3g); PROTEIN 4.5g; CARB 7.7g; FIBER 0.6g; CHOL 17mg; IRON 0.7mg; SODIUM 139mg; CALC 6mg

Latin Americans have been grinding rice and nuts into milk for centuries. You just soak rice in water with spices, then buzz it all in a blender and strain. For fruit horchata, add chopped fruits along with the rice and everything else. To make a horchata cocktail, add a splash of dark rum.

SPICED ALMOND MILK

HANDS-ON TIME: 10 MIN. TOTAL TIME: 8 HR. 10 MIN.

4 cups water, divided
¾ cup uncooked long-grain rice
½ cup slivered almonds
1 (3-inch) orange rind strip
3 (3-inch) cinnamon sticks, broken in pieces
3 whole allspice
3 whole cloves
2 cups unsweetened almond milk
¼ cup sugar
1 teaspoon vanilla extract
¼ teaspoon almond extract
Dash of salt

Combine 2 cups water and next 6 ingredients (through cloves) in large bowl. Cover and chill 8 to 24 hours or until rice is soft. Strain mixture through a fine sieve, reserving solids. Discard liquid.

Place solids, remaining 2 cups water, and almond milk in a blender; process 2 minutes. Strain through fine sieve into a pitcher; discard solids. Add sugar, extracts, and salt to milk mixture, stirring until sugar dissolves. Serve over ice. Store in refrigerator up to 1 week. Serves 6 (serving size: ⅔ cup)

CALORIES 193; FAT 5.6g (sat 0.4g, mono 3.3g, poly 1.3g); PROTEIN 4.1g; CARB 33g; FIBER 3.8g; CHOL 0mg; IRON 1.8mg; SODIUM 81mg; CALC 224mg

It's tough to improve on the classic Mexican farm breakfast. I kept the salsa rustic here by blackening the tomatoes and jalapeños in a cast-iron skillet. To trim calories, only one corn tortilla accompanies each set of eggs, but you could easily serve two instead. You could also add some sliced avocado.

HUEVOS RANCHEROS

HANDS-ON TIME: 57 MIN. TOTAL TIME: 67 MIN.

2 large tomatoes (1 pound)
1 jalapeño pepper
1 tablespoon canola oil, divided
1 cup chopped onion, divided
1 garlic clove, minced
3/4 cup fat-free, lower-sodium chicken broth or organic vegetable broth
3/8 teaspoon salt, divided
4 (6-inch) corn tortillas
8 large eggs
1/4 cup chopped fresh cilantro
2 ounces queso fresco or Cotija cheese, crumbled (about 1/2 cup)
1/2 cup fat-free refried beans, warmed

Heat a large cast-iron or other heavy skillet over medium-high heat. Add whole tomatoes and jalapeño pepper; cook 13 minutes or until blackened and charred, turning occasionally. Remove from pan; cool 10 minutes. Peel and discard skins from tomatoes and pepper. Core tomatoes; remove stem and seeds from pepper.

Place pepper, tomatoes, and any juices in a blender; process 5 seconds or just until mixture is chunky.

Heat pan over medium heat. Add 1 teaspoon oil to pan; swirl to coat. Add 3/4 cup onion; sauté 6 minutes or until browned. Add garlic; sauté 1 minute. Add tomato mixture, and cook 2 to 5 minutes or until slightly thick. Stir in broth; cook 7 to 10 minutes or until thick but still easily pourable. Remove from heat; stir in 1/8 teaspoon salt. Cover and keep warm.

Heat a large nonstick skillet over medium heat. Add 2 corn tortillas and a few drops of water; cook 1 minute on each side or until thoroughly heated. Repeat procedure with remaining tortillas. Wrap in foil; keep warm.

Heat pan over medium heat. Add 1 teaspoon oil to pan; swirl to coat. Add 4 eggs; sprinkle with 1/8 teaspoon salt. Cover and cook 2 to 3 minutes or until whites are set. Carefully remove from pan; keep warm. Repeat procedure with remaining 1 teaspoon oil, 4 eggs, and 1/8 teaspoon salt.

Place 1 tortilla on each of 4 plates; top each tortilla with 2 eggs and 6 tablespoons tomato salsa. Sprinkle each serving with 1 tablespoon of remaining onion, 1 tablespoon cilantro, and about 2 tablespoons cheese. Serve each with 2 tablespoons refried beans. Serves 4 (serving size: 1 topped tortilla)

CALORIES 311; FAT 15.3g (sat 4.3g, mono 6.4g, poly 3.5g); PROTEIN 19.3g; CARB 25g; FIBER 5.1g; CHOL 377mg; IRON 3mg; SODIUM 634mg; CALC 149mg

A bolillo is like a French baguette but much shorter. It's the bread of choice for capirotada, the Mexican bread pudding traditionally served on Good Friday.

MEXICAN BREAD PUDDING

HANDS-ON TIME: 15 MIN. TOTAL TIME: 1 HR. 20 MIN.

1¼ cups packed dark brown sugar
1¼ cups water
2 (3-inch) cinnamon sticks
4½ cups (½-inch) cubed French bread (about 8 ounces)
¼ cup golden raisins
¼ cup slivered almonds, toasted
2 tablespoons butter, cut into small pieces
Cooking spray
3 ounces shredded Monterey Jack cheese (about ¾ cup)

Combine first 3 ingredients in a medium saucepan; bring to a boil. Reduce heat; simmer 10 minutes. Discard cinnamon sticks.

Combine bread, raisins, almonds, and butter in a large bowl. Drizzle with warm sugar syrup, tossing gently to coat. Spoon mixture into an 8-inch square glass or ceramic baking dish coated with cooking spray. Top with cheese. Cover with foil; chill 30 minutes or up to 4 hours.

Preheat oven to 350°.

Bake at 350° for 20 minutes. Uncover and bake an additional 15 minutes or until cheese is golden brown. Serve warm. Serves 8 (serving size: ¾ cup)

CALORIES 313; FAT 9.3g (sat 4.4g, mono 3.6g, poly 0.9g); PROTEIN 5.8g; CARB 52.6g; FIBER 1.4g; CHOL 19mg; IRON 1.6mg; SODIUM 289mg; CALC 140mg

Cinnamon Sticks

The stiff, 3-inch quills labeled cinnamon in most North American markets are actually from the bark of cassia, a tree native to southern China. True cinnamon (a.k.a. Ceylon cinnamon, shaggy cinnamon, or *canela* in Spanish) is native to Sri Lanka (Ceylon) and is softer and thinner with a more delicate yet complex aroma than cassia. It's also much easier to grind in a spice grinder. Look for Ceylon cinnamon for more authentic flavor in Latin American cooking. If you can't find it, cassia works well, too.

This wildly popular cake originated among Nicaraguans in Miami, according to Maricel Presilla, author of Gran Cocina Latina. Its moist texture comes from three milks—milk, evaporated milk, and sweetened condensed milk. The cake itself is a vanilla sponge that soaks up all the creamy milk syrup. Sweetened meringue serves as the frosting.

TRES LECHES CAKE

HANDS-ON TIME: 27 MIN. TOTAL TIME: 3 HR. 57 MIN.

Cake:
Cooking spray
1 tablespoon all-purpose flour
6 large egg yolks
2/3 cup sugar
2 teaspoons vanilla extract
9 ounces all-purpose flour (about 2 cups)
2 1/2 teaspoons baking powder
1/4 teaspoon salt
1/2 cup fat-free milk
6 large egg whites
3 tablespoons sugar
Milk Sauce:
1 (14-ounce) can fat-free sweetened condensed milk
1 (12-ounce) can evaporated fat-free milk
1/2 cup fat-free milk
2 tablespoons light rum
Meringue:
4 large egg whites
1/4 teaspoon cream of tartar
1/8 teaspoon salt
1 cup sugar
1/2 cup water
1 teaspoon vanilla extract
Fresh grated whole nutmeg (optional)

1. Preheat oven to 375°.

2. To prepare cake, coat a 13 x 9–inch baking pan with cooking spray; dust with 1 tablespoon flour. Set aside.

3. Place egg yolks, 2/3 cup sugar, and 2 teaspoons vanilla in a large bowl; beat with a mixer at high speed until mixture is thick and pale, about 2 minutes.

4. Lightly spoon 2 cups flour into dry measuring cups; level with a knife. Combine flour, baking powder, and 1/4 teaspoon salt; stir well with a whisk. Add flour mixture and 1/2 cup fat-free milk alternately to egg yolk mixture, beginning and ending with flour mixture.

5. Beat 6 egg whites in a large bowl with a mixer at high speed until foamy using clean, dry beaters. Add 3 tablespoons sugar, 1 tablespoon at a time, beating until stiff peaks form (about 2 minutes). Gently fold egg white mixture into flour mixture.

6. Spoon batter into prepared baking pan. Bake at 375° for 20 minutes or until wooden pick inserted in center comes out clean. Cool in pan 10 minutes on a wire rack. Turn cake out onto a platter with sides. Pierce entire top of cake with a fork.

7. To prepare sauce, combine condensed milk, evaporated milk, 1/2 cup fat-free milk, and rum; stir with a whisk. Slowly pour milk mixture evenly over cake. Cover with plastic wrap, and refrigerate at least 3 hours or overnight.

8. To prepare meringue, beat 4 egg whites, cream of tartar, and 1/8 teaspoon salt in a large bowl with a mixer at high speed until foamy using clean, dry beaters. Combine 1 cup sugar and 1/2 cup water in a saucepan; bring to a boil. Cook, without stirring, until candy thermometer registers 250°. Pour hot sugar syrup in a thin stream over egg whites, beating at high speed until stiff peaks form (about 3 minutes). Stir in 1 teaspoon vanilla. Spread meringue evenly over top and sides of cake. Garnish with nutmeg, if desired. Serves 16 (serving size: 1 piece)

CALORIES 277; FAT 2.1 (sat 0.6g, mono 0.8g, poly 0.7g); PROTEIN 9g; CARB 54.5g; FIBER 0.4g; CHOL 84mg; IRON 1.3mg; SODIUM 228mg; CALC 200mg

You're probably familiar with the style of American cobblers that top sweetened fruit with a cake, biscuit, or other pastry dough. This one's a little different, and I like it better. Here, a pancake-like batter goes on the bottom of the pan and the fruit is strewn over the top. In the oven, the fruit bakes into the batter, melding the two perfectly.

BLUEBERRY COBBLER

HANDS-ON TIME: 7 MIN. TOTAL TIME: 47 MIN.

¼ cup butter, cut into pieces
2.25 ounces all-purpose flour
   (about ½ cup)
½ cup sugar, divided
1½ teaspoons baking powder
¼ teaspoon salt
½ cup 1% low-fat milk
1 teaspoon grated lemon rind
½ teaspoon vanilla extract
2½ cups fresh blueberries
2 cups vanilla fat-free
   ice cream

1. Preheat oven to 350°. Place butter in an 8-inch square metal baking pan; place pan in oven 3 minutes or until butter melts.
2. While butter melts, weigh or lightly spoon flour into a dry measuring cup; level with a knife. Combine flour, 6 tablespoons sugar, baking powder, and salt in medium bowl; stir with a whisk until blended. Combine milk, lemon rind, and vanilla; add to flour mixture, stirring with a whisk just until moist.
3. Pour batter over melted butter in pan (do not stir); top with blueberries. Sprinkle with remaining 2 tablespoons sugar. Bake at 350° for 35 to 40 minutes or until bubbly and crust is lightly browned. Serve with ice cream. Serves 6 (serving size: about ½ cup cobbler and ⅓ cup ice cream)

CALORIES 217; FAT 8.2g (sat 5g, mono 2.1g, poly 0.4g); PROTEIN 2.3g; CARB 35g; FIBER 1.8g; CHOL 21mg; IRON 0.8mg; SODIUM 298mg; CALC 101mg

High in natural pectin, guavas become a thick, sweet paste when cooked long enough. Cubans love to combine guava paste with farmer's cheese or cream cheese to make pastelitos de guayaba, sweet and flaky pastries. Here's a version using soft dough made with cream cheese in addition to butter.

GUAVA AND CHEESE EMPANADAS

HANDS-ON TIME: 31 MIN. TOTAL TIME: 1 HR. 39 MIN.

Dough:

2¼ cups all-purpose flour (about 10 ounces)

⅓ cup sugar

¼ teaspoon baking powder

¼ teaspoon salt

5 tablespoons butter, cut into small pieces

6 ounces block-style fat-free cream cheese, cut into small pieces

3 tablespoons fat-free milk

Filling:

¼ cup sugar

6 ounces farmer's cheese, cut into small pieces

1 tablespoon fat-free milk

1 large egg white

6 ounces prepared guava paste, cut into 48 pieces

Cooking spray

Topping:

3 tablespoons sugar

½ teaspoon ground cinnamon

1. To prepare dough, weigh or lightly spoon flour into dry measuring cups; level with a knife. Place flour, ⅓ cup sugar, baking powder, and salt in a food processor; pulse to combine. Add butter and cream cheese; pulse 4 times or until mixture resembles coarse meal. With processor on, add 3 tablespoons milk through food chute, processing just until dough forms a ball. Press mixture gently into a 4-inch circle on plastic wrap; cover. Chill 1 hour.

2. To prepare filling, wipe food processor clean with a paper towel. Combine ¼ cup sugar and farmer's cheese in processor; process 1 minute or until well blended. Cover and chill. Combine 1 tablespoon milk and egg white in a small bowl; set aside.

3. Preheat oven to 425°.

4. Roll dough to a ⅛-inch thickness on a heavily floured surface; cut with a 3-inch biscuit cutter into 24 circles. Discard any remaining dough scraps. Spoon about 2 teaspoons cheese mixture onto half of each circle, leaving a ½-inch border; place 2 pieces guava paste on cheese. Brush egg mixture around edges of each circle. Fold dough over filling; press edges together with a fork or fingers to seal. Place empanadas on 2 baking sheets coated with cooking spray; brush tops of empanadas with remaining egg mixture.

5. To prepare topping, combine 3 tablespoons sugar and cinnamon in a small bowl; sprinkle sugar mixture evenly over empanadas. Bake at 425° for 10 minutes or until golden. Remove from oven; cool completely on a wire rack. Serves 12 (serving size: 2 empanadas)

CALORIES 285; **FAT** 9.2g (sat 6.2g, mono 1.3g, poly 0.3g); **PROTEIN** 8g; **CARB** 42.5g; **FIBER** 0.8g; **CHOL** 26mg; **IRON** 1.2mg; **SODIUM** 284mg; **CALC** 152mg

Guava Paste

Often sold in short, wide cans, guava paste is made by simmering fresh guavas, sugar, pectin, and citric acid down to a ruby-colored jam. It's so thick you can cut it with a knife. But it's also sticky. To cut guava paste cleanly, dip your knife in hot water between cuts. Spread it on toast, or cut it into cubes and serve it with cubes of fresh cheese.

Some New Englanders like lobster rolls with only warm lobster meat drenched in melted butter. Others prefer cold lobster salad made with mayonnaise, maybe something crunchy like onion or celery, and some chopped herbs. Either way, it's always served on a top-split hot dog bun.

LOBSTER ROLLS
with Shaved Fennel and Citrus
HANDS-ON TIME: 13 MIN. TOTAL TIME: 13 MIN.

3 cups coarsely chopped cooked lobster meat (about three 1¼-pound lobsters)

3 tablespoons canola mayonnaise

2 teaspoons chopped fresh tarragon

½ teaspoon kosher salt, divided

2 cups thinly sliced fennel bulb (about 1 medium)

½ teaspoon grated orange rind

1 tablespoon fresh orange juice

1 tablespoon fresh lemon juice

1 tablespoon rice wine vinegar

2 teaspoons extra-virgin olive oil

¼ teaspoon freshly ground black pepper

Cooking spray

6 (1½-ounce) hot dog buns, preferably top split

1. Combine lobster, mayonnaise, tarragon, and ¼ teaspoon salt in a large bowl.

2. Combine fennel, remaining ¼ teaspoon salt, orange rind, and next 5 ingredients (through pepper).

3. Heat a large skillet over medium heat. Coat pan with cooking spray. Add buns to pan; cook 2 minutes on each side or until lightly browned. Place ⅓ cup fennel salad in each bun. Top each serving with ½ cup lobster salad. Serves 6 (serving size: 1 lobster roll)

CALORIES 238; FAT 6.2g (sat 0.8g, mono 3g, poly 1.9g); PROTEIN 19.4.g; CARB 24.9g; FIBER 1.9g; CHOL 52mg; IRON 1.9mg; SODIUM 699mg; CALC 120mg

Maine Lobster

American (Maine) lobsters have large claws, while spiny (rock) lobsters have no claws but bigger tails. For the best flavor, choose live lobsters, and cook them yourself. The most humane way is to kill the lobster before boiling it. Flip the lobster onto its back, hold the tip of a sturdy chef's knife between the legs, and cut straight down, bringing the heel of the knife through the lobster's head.

THE HEALTHY SIDE OF MEXICAN

*M*ention Mexican food to Americans, and folks picture cheese-laden burritos, greasy beef tacos, and mounds of sour cream. But traditional Mexican and Central American cooking is light, healthy, and based on vegetables and fruits. It's actually much closer to the healthful Mediterranean diet. "If you understand the cooking of Mediterranean countries like Italy and Spain, you should be able to cook South and Central American food, as well," says Maricel Presilla, author of *Gran Cocina Latina.*

Onions, garlic, tomatoes, and peppers are central to the cuisine, along with a multitude of other healthy fruits and vegetables, and an abundance of lean fish like grouper and snapper. Thankfully, Central American and Caribbean ingredients—from mangoes and plantains to tomatillos and yuca—are now widely available in American supermarkets. For a taste of these healthy cuisines, check out Guava and Cheese Empanadas (page 276), Oaxacan-Style Grilled Corn on the Cob (page 302), French West Indian Grilled Snapper with Caper Sauce (page 284), and Sautéed Sweet Plantains (page 304).

We can thank Native Americans in the Pacific Northwest for this simple method of cooking whole sides of salmon. They would nail the salmon to cedar or alder wood planks and set the planks around a central fire, where the fish slowly absorbed smoky aromas. I like to glaze the salmon with a mixture of maple syrup and mustard.

PLANKED SALMON
with Maple-Mustard Glaze
HANDS-ON TIME: 15 MIN. TOTAL TIME: 2 HR.

1 (15 x 4 x ¼-inch) cedar grilling plank
2 tablespoons maple syrup
1 tablespoon whole-grain Dijon mustard
1 (1½-pound) center-cut salmon fillet
¼ teaspoon salt
¼ teaspoon black pepper

1. Soak plank in water 1 hour; drain.
2. Preheat grill to medium heat.
3. Combine syrup and mustard; stir well, and divide between 2 small bowls.
4. Place plank on grill rack; grill 10 minutes or until lightly charred. Turn plank over; place fish, skin side down, on charred side. Sprinkle fish with salt and pepper; brush with half of syrup mixture.
5. Cover and grill 35 minutes or until desired degree of doneness. Remove from grill; spread remaining syrup mixture over fish. Cut fillet into 4 equal portions. Serves 4

CALORIES 299; FAT 13.1g (sat 3.1g, mono 5.7g, poly 3.2g); PROTEIN 36.2g; CARB 6.8g; FIBER 0g; CHOL 87mg; IRON 0.6mg; SODIUM 277mg; CALC 31mg

how to: COOK ON WOOD PLANKS

Look for cedar or alder wood planks in well-stocked supermarkets and home centers. You can also use untreated cedar shingles, and cut the fish into pieces to fit the shingles. You'll get the most life out of your plank by soaking it in water before charring it. Charred planks can be scrubbed clean and reused.

1 Place wood plank directly over medium fire until lightly charred, about 10 minutes.

2 Turn charred side up, and place fish or other food on plank. Grill directly over fire with lid down.

"Here's how fish is served at the open-air cook shacks lining the beaches of Guadeloupe," says Steven Raichlen, author of the Barbecue! Bible cookbook series. The marinade features the four essential seasonings of the French West Indies: lime juice, garlic, fresh thyme, and Scotch bonnet chiles.

FRENCH WEST INDIAN GRILLED SNAPPER

with Caper Sauce

HANDS-ON TIME: 20 MIN. TOTAL TIME: 2 HR. 20 MIN.

¼ cup fresh lime juice
1 teaspoon salt
1 teaspoon fresh thyme or
 ¼ teaspoon dried thyme
1 teaspoon black pepper
3 garlic cloves, chopped
1 to 2 Scotch bonnet or habanero
 peppers, minced
4 (6-ounce) red snapper or other
 firm white fish fillets
2 tablespoons chopped fresh
 cilantro
2 tablespoons fresh lime juice
2 tablespoons water
2 tablespoons olive oil
1 tablespoon capers
1 tablespoon red wine vinegar
1½ teaspoons minced Scotch
 bonnet or habanero pepper
¼ teaspoon salt
¼ teaspoon black pepper
1 garlic clove, chopped
1 large shallot, chopped
Cooking spray
Lime wedges (optional)

Place first 6 ingredients in a blender; process until smooth. Combine marinade and fish in a large zip-top plastic bag; seal. Marinate in refrigerator 2 to 4 hours, turning bag occasionally.

Prepare grill to medium-high heat.

Place cilantro and next 10 ingredients (through shallot) in a blender or food processor; process until smooth.

Remove fish from marinade, discard marinade. Place fish on grill rack coated with cooking spray; grill 3 minutes on each side or until fish flakes easily when tested with a fork. Serve with caper sauce and lime wedges, if desired. Serves 4 (serving size: 1 fillet and 2 tablespoons sauce).

CALORIES 246; **FAT** 9.6g (sat 1.5g, mono 5.5g, poly 1.6g); **PROTEIN** 35.4g; **CARB** 2.8g; **FIBER** 0.2g; **CHOL** 63mg; **IRON** 0.6mg; **SODIUM** 425mg; **CALC** 63mg

The food of Québec has strong French and Irish influences. Take a look at tourtière, which resembles the meat pies of the United Kingdom such as Ireland's steak and Guinness pie. Pork is the preferred meat, spiced with cinnamon and cloves. Tourtière is usually a double-crust pie, but this version calls for individual pies to be baked in ramekins with only a top crust.

CANADIAN MEAT PIE
(Tourtière)
HANDS-ON TIME: 32 MIN. TOTAL TIME: 1 HR. 12 MIN.

Cooking spray
1 pound ground pork
1/2 teaspoon salt
1/2 teaspoon ground cinnamon
1/8 teaspoon ground red pepper
1/8 teaspoon ground cloves
1 tablespoon olive oil
1 cup finely chopped onion
1/2 cup finely chopped carrot
1/3 cup finely chopped celery
1 (1-pound) russet potato, peeled and cut into 1/4-inch cubes
3 garlic cloves, minced
2 tablespoons all-purpose flour
1 1/2 cups fat-free, lower-sodium chicken broth
3 tablespoons finely chopped fresh chives
1/2 (14.1-ounce) package refrigerated pie dough

1. Preheat oven to 400°.
2. Heat a large skillet over medium-high heat. Coat pan with cooking spray. Add pork to pan. Sprinkle pork with salt, cinnamon, red pepper, and cloves; sauté 5 minutes or until browned, stirring to crumble. Using a slotted spoon, remove pork from pan. Add oil to pan; swirl to coat. Add onion, carrot, celery, and potato; sauté 5 minutes. Add garlic, and sauté 1 minute. Return pork to pan. Stir in flour, and cook 1 minute, stirring constantly. Add broth, scraping pan to loosen browned bits; bring to a boil. Cook 2 minutes or until slightly thick. Remove from heat; stir in chives.
3. Place 1 cup pork mixture into each of 6 (8-ounce) ramekins. Roll pie dough to an 11-inch circle. Cut 4 (5-inch) dough circles. Combine and re-roll dough scraps. Cut 2 (5-inch) circles. Place 1 dough circle on each ramekin, tucking edges inside. Cut an X in the top of each circle; coat lightly with cooking spray. Place ramekins on a baking sheet. Bake at 400° for 40 minutes or until golden and bubbly. Serves 6

Note: If you don't have ramekins, spoon the filling into a 9-inch pie plate, and top with the entire pastry.

CALORIES 420; FAT 22.2g (sat 7.6g, mono 9.8g, poly 2g); PROTEIN 17.5g; CARB 36.5g; FIBER 2.4g; CHOL 54mg; IRON 1.8mg; SODIUM 489mg; CALC 45mg

The sweet-and-sour taste of bitter oranges is essential to the cuisines of Haiti, Cuba, and other Caribbean islands. For Haitian griot, cubes of pork are marinated in citrus juice, and then braised and caramelized until golden brown. This recipe comes from Bruce Weinstein and Mark Scarbrough, authors of more than 20 cookbooks.

HAITIAN PORK

with Hot and Sour Sauce (Griot with Sauce Ti-Malice)

HANDS-ON TIME: 24 MIN. TOTAL TIME: 14 HR. 32 MIN.

1 habanero pepper
¾ cup fresh orange juice (about 3 large oranges)
6 tablespoons fresh lime juice, divided
3 tablespoons minced shallots
2 tablespoons minced fresh garlic
1 tablespoon Dijon mustard
1 tablespoon honey
2 teaspoons salt
4 fresh thyme sprigs
3 pounds boneless pork shoulder, trimmed and cut into 1½-inch pieces
2 cups fat-free, lower-sodium chicken broth
½ cup thinly sliced shallots
1 teaspoon cider vinegar
1 teaspoon freshly ground black pepper
1 tablespoon canola oil

1. Cut habanero in half. Seed one half of pepper, and leave seeds in other half. Mince both pepper halves. Combine minced habanero, orange juice, ¼ cup lime juice, minced shallots, and next 5 ingredients (through thyme) in a large bowl; stir with a whisk. Add pork; toss to coat. Cover and marinate in refrigerator 12 to 24 hours.
2. Place pork and marinade in a Dutch oven over medium-high heat. Add broth; bring to a boil. Cover, reduce heat, and simmer 1½ hours or until meat is tender. Remove pork from pan with a slotted spoon, reserving cooking liquid. Strain cooking liquid through a sieve into a bowl; discard solids. Place a large zip-top plastic bag in a bowl. Pour reserved cooking liquid into bag; let stand 5 minutes. Snip off 1 bottom corner of bag; drain liquid into a medium saucepan, stopping before the fat layer reaches the opening. Discard fat. Set ½ cup cooking liquid aside.
3. Place saucepan with cooking liquid over medium-high heat; bring to a boil. Cook 20 minutes or until reduced to about 1 cup. Add sliced shallots, vinegar, black pepper, and 1 tablespoon lime juice. Cover and keep warm.
4. Heat a large nonstick skillet over medium heat. Add oil to pan; swirl to coat. Add pork; cook 10 minutes, turning to brown well on all sides. Add reserved ½ cup cooking liquid and remaining 1 tablespoon lime juice. Increase heat to medium-high; cook 4 minutes or until liquid nearly evaporates, stirring occasionally. Place pork in a bowl; pour sauce over pork. Serves 10 (serving size: about 3 ounces pork and 2 tablespoons sauce)

CALORIES 223; FAT 8.8g (sat 2.6g, mono 4.2g, poly 1.2g); PROTEIN 27.3g; CARB 7.3g; FIBER 0.3g; CHOL 75mg; IRON 1.4mg; SODIUM 668mg; CALC 33mg

Ever wonder where the name "jerk" comes from? According to grilling expert Steven Raichlen, it stems from the cook's habit of giving the pork or chicken a poke or "jook" with a sharp implement to force the spices deeper into the meat.

JAMAICAN JERK PORK TENDERLOIN

HANDS-ON TIME: 25 MIN. TOTAL TIME: 3 HR. 25 MIN.

2 cups coarsely chopped green onions
½ cup coarsely chopped onion
2 tablespoons white vinegar
1 tablespoon lower-sodium soy sauce
1 tablespoon canola oil
2 teaspoons kosher salt
2 teaspoons chopped fresh thyme
2 teaspoons brown sugar
2 teaspoons chopped peeled fresh ginger
1 teaspoon ground allspice
¼ teaspoon ground nutmeg
¼ teaspoon freshly ground black pepper
⅛ teaspoon ground cinnamon
2 garlic cloves, minced
1 to 4 Scotch bonnet or habanero peppers, seeded and chopped
2 (1-pound) pork tenderloins, trimmed
Cooking spray

1. Place first 15 ingredients in a blender or food processor; process until smooth.
2. Combine pork and green onion mixture in a dish or large zip-top plastic bag. Cover or seal; marinate in refrigerator 3 to 24 hours. Remove pork from dish or bag; discard remaining marinade.
3. Prepare grill to medium-high heat.
4. Place pork on grill rack coated with cooking spray; grill 8 minutes on each side or until meat thermometer registers 160° (slightly pink). Serves 6

CALORIES 162; FAT 4.2g (sat 1.3g, mono 1.6g, poly 0.6g); PROTEIN 28.6g; CARB 0.7g; FIBER 0.2g; CHOL 79mg; IRON 1.3mg; SODIUM 136mg; CALC 10mg

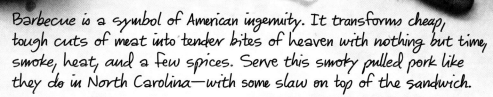

Barbecue is a symbol of American ingenuity. It transforms cheap, tough cuts of meat into tender bites of heaven with nothing but time, smoke, heat, and a few spices. Serve this smoky pulled pork like they do in North Carolina—with some slaw on top of the sandwich.

PULLED PORK BARBECUE SANDWICHES

HANDS-ON TIME: 45 MIN. TOTAL TIME: 20 HR. 15 MIN.

1 tablespoon Hungarian sweet paprika
1 tablespoon Spanish smoked paprika
1 tablespoon light brown sugar
1 teaspoon salt
1 teaspoon onion powder
1 teaspoon dry mustard
1 teaspoon black pepper
1 teaspoon ground red pepper
1 (4½-pound) bone-in pork shoulder (Boston butt)
7½ cups hickory wood chips
Cooking spray
2 cups cider vinegar
¾ cup low-sodium ketchup
½ cup water
2 tablespoons granulated sugar
1 tablespoon hot pepper sauce
1 teaspoon salt
1 teaspoon crushed red pepper
½ teaspoon black pepper
1 (16-ounce) package cabbage-and-carrot coleslaw
15 (1½-ounce) whole-wheat hamburger buns

1. Combine first 8 ingredients in a large bowl. Rub spice mixture onto pork; place pork in bowl. Cover and chill at least 8 hours or overnight. Soak hickory wood chips in water 1 to 24 hours.

2. Remove pork from refrigerator; let stand at room temperature 20 minutes. To prepare grill for indirect grilling, remove right grill rack. Preheat grill to low using both burners. After preheating, turn the left burner off (leave the right burner on). Maintain temperature at 225° to 250°. Drain wood chips. Place 1½ cups wood chips on a 12-inch square of aluminum foil. Fold edges of foil to form a packet, and seal; pierce foil packet with a fork. Repeat procedure with remaining wood chips. Place 1 packet of wood chips on right side. Coat grill rack with cooking spray; place pork, fatty side up, on grill rack covering left burner. Cover and grill 8 to 10 hours or until a thermometer registers 190°. Replace packet of wood chips every 2 hours.

3. While pork cooks, combine cider vinegar and next 7 ingredients (through ½ teaspoon black pepper) in a medium microwave-safe bowl. Microwave at HIGH 2 to 3 minutes or until sugar dissolves, stirring every 1 minute. Cool to room temperature.

4. Combine coleslaw and ½ cup sauce in a large bowl; toss well. Cover and chill 1 hour.

5. Remove meat from grill; let stand 20 minutes. Shred meat with 2 forks; discard bone and fat. Combine shredded pork and 2 cups sauce in a large bowl; toss to coat. Spoon 3 ounces pork and ⅓ cup coleslaw on bottom half of each hamburger bun. Cover with top halves of buns. Serve with additional sauce for dipping. Serves 15 (serving size: 1 sandwich and 2 tablespoons additional sauce)

CALORIES 388; FAT 13.8g (sat 4.3g, mono 5.7g, poly 2.3g); PROTEIN 28.5g; CARB 37.8g; FIBER 5.6g; CHOL 80mg; IRON 3.3mg; SODIUM 705mg; CALC 111mg

This Dutch West Indian version of Indonesian satay is known as *boka dushi*. *Boka* means "mouth" and *dushi* means "sweet" in Papamiento, the local Caribbean dialect that blends Dutch, Portuguese, Spanish, and West African. *Kejap manis*, the ancestor of ketchup, is a thick, sweet soy sauce. If you can't find it, substitute equal parts soy sauce and molasses.

DUTCH WEST INDIAN CHICKEN KEBABS

HANDS-ON TIME: 15 MIN. TOTAL TIME: 45 MIN.

¼ cup kejap manis or 2 tablespoons soy sauce plus 2 tablespoons molasses
1 tablespoon fresh lime juice
1 teaspoon ground cumin
2 teaspoons grated peeled fresh ginger
1 teaspoon sambal oelek or Thai chile paste
½ teaspoon ground turmeric
1½ pounds skinless, boneless chicken breast, cut into ½-inch-wide strips
⅓ cup fat-free, lower-sodium chicken broth
3 tablespoons creamy peanut butter
½ cup chopped seeded tomato
2 tablespoons minced green onions
2 tablespoons chopped fresh cilantro
1 tablespoon fish sauce
1 tablespoon fresh lime juice
1 teaspoon grated peeled fresh ginger
1 teaspoon minced seeded Thai chile
1 teaspoon honey
1 garlic clove, crushed
Cooking spray

1. Combine first 7 ingredients in a large zip-top plastic bag; seal and marinate in refrigerator 30 minutes.
2. Combine broth and peanut butter in a small saucepan; cook over low heat 5 minutes or until smooth, stirring with a whisk. Pour peanut butter mixture into a bowl; stir in tomato and next 8 ingredients (through garlic).
3. Prepare grill to medium-high heat.
4. Remove chicken from bag, and discard marinade. Thread chicken strips onto 18 (8-inch) skewers.
5. Place kebabs on grill rack coated with cooking spray; grill 2 minutes on each side or until done. Serve with peanut butter sauce. Serves 6 (serving size: 3 kebabs and 2 tablespoons peanut sauce)

CALORIES 212; FAT 6.1g (sat 1.1g, mono 2.5g, poly 1.8g); PROTEIN 29.5g; CARB 9.5g; FIBER 0.9g; CHOL 66mg; IRON 1.9mg; SODIUM 676mg; CALC 40mg

Fresh chorizo—spicy pork sausage flavored with cumin and garlic—is like the bacon of Mexico. It goes with just about everything. Street vendors often chop it up with a hash of potatoes to make quick tacos. These speedy snacks also include mild poblano chiles and fresh corn kernels for a spicy-sweet flavor.

POTATO, POBLANO, AND CHORIZO TACOS

HANDS-ON TIME: 30 MIN. TOTAL TIME: 30 MIN.

2 poblano chiles
1 tablespoon canola oil
2 cups diced white potato
1 cup chopped onion
1 cup fresh corn kernels
1/8 teaspoon ground red
    pepper
5 garlic cloves, minced
3 ounces Mexican raw
    chorizo, casings removed
3/4 cup unsalted chicken stock
3/8 teaspoon kosher salt
8 (6-inch) corn tortillas
1/4 cup sliced green onions
1 ounce Manchego cheese,
    shredded (about 1/4 cup)
8 lime wedges

1. Preheat broiler.
2. Cut poblanos in half lengthwise; discard seeds and membranes. Place poblano halves, skin sides up, on a foil-lined baking sheet; flatten with hand. Broil 8 minutes or until blackened. Place in a paper bag; fold to close tightly. Let stand 5 minutes. Peel; coarsely chop.
3. Heat a large nonstick skillet over medium-high heat. Add oil to pan; swirl to coat. Add potato; cook 5 minutes, stirring occasionally. Remove potato; place in a large bowl. Add onion to pan; cook 3 minutes. Add poblano, corn, red pepper, and garlic; cook 2 minutes, stirring frequently. Add onion mixture to potato. Add chorizo to pan; cook 1½ minutes, stirring to crumble. Return potato mixture to pan. Stir in stock and salt; bring to a boil. Partially cover, reduce heat, and simmer 6 minutes or until potato is tender, chorizo is done, and liquid almost evaporates.
4. Working with 1 tortilla at a time, heat tortillas over medium-high heat directly on the eye of a burner for about 15 seconds on each side or until lightly charred. Arrange about ⅓ cup potato mixture in center of each tortilla; top with 1½ teaspoons onions and 1½ teaspoons cheese. Serve with lime wedges. Serves 4 (serving size: 2 tacos and 2 lime wedges)

CALORIES 348; FAT 14.9g (sat 5.8g, mono 6.5g, poly 2.6g); PROTEIN 11.4g; CARB 46.6g; FIBER 6.1g; CHOL 38mg; IRON 1mg; SODIUM 447mg; CALC 146mg

Tortillas

"A freshly made corn tortilla is the most delicious thing on the planet," according to Rick Bayless, television host of *Mexico—One Plate at a Time.* A tortilla "becomes the canvas on which all of the other flavors are painted." Fresh tortillas are made from fresh masa, a paste made from nixtamalized field corn (see page 249). You can also make corn tortillas from masa harina (dehydrated masa), a convenience product that Bayless likens to dehydrated potatoes. And, of course, you can buy pre-made corn tortillas, also made from masa harina. Flour tortillas are the modern version of tortillas, developed after the Spanish brought wheat to the New World in the 1500s.

Similar to Colombian arepas and Mexican gorditas, Salvadoran pupusas are thick corn tortillas stuffed with cheese, meat, or beans (or all three). Filling the fresh dough, and then shaping and cooking each pupusa takes time. This recipe streamlines the process by making one big pupusa in a baking dish with a top and bottom crust.

PUPUSA CASSEROLE

HANDS-ON TIME: 33 MIN. TOTAL TIME: 68 MIN.

Filling:

- 2 cups nopalitos (about 6 chopped nopales, cactus paddles)
- 2 (4-ounce) skinless, boneless chicken breast halves
- ½ teaspoon salt
- ½ teaspoon ground cumin
- ¼ teaspoon freshly ground black pepper
- Cooking spray
- ¾ cup finely chopped onion
- 2 garlic cloves, minced
- 4 ounces shredded Monterey Jack cheese with jalapeño peppers (about 1 cup), divided

Dough:

- 7:7 ounces masa harina (about 2¼ cups)
- 1 cup water
- 1 teaspoon salt

1. Preheat oven to 375°.
2. To prepare filling, cook nopalitos in boiling water 10 minutes. Drain.
3. Sprinkle chicken with ½ teaspoon salt, cumin, and pepper. Heat a medium skillet over medium heat. Coat pan with cooking spray. Add chicken; cook 4 minutes on each side or until done. Remove chicken from pan; cool slightly, and shred with 2 forks.
4. Heat pan over medium heat. Add onion and garlic; sauté 4 minutes or until tender. Stir in nopalitos, chicken, and ⅔ cup cheese. Cook 5 minutes or until thoroughly heated.
5. To prepare dough, weigh or lightly spoon masa harina in dry measuring cups; level with a knife. Combine masa harina, 1 cup water, and 1 teaspoon salt in a medium bowl. Turn dough out onto a lightly floured surface; knead lightly. Press one-third of dough into an 11 x 7–inch baking dish coated with cooking spray. Spread filling over dough. Gently press remaining dough into a 4-inch square on heavy-duty plastic wrap. Cover with additional plastic wrap. Roll, still covered, into an 11 x 7–inch rectangle. Remove bottom sheet of plastic wrap; fit dough over filling. Remove top sheet of plastic wrap. Bake at 375° for 20 minutes. Sprinkle with ⅓ cup cheese. Bake an additional 5 minutes or until cheese melts. Serves 8 (serving size: ⅛ of casserole)

CALORIES 234; FAT 7g (sat 3.2g, mono 1.9g, poly 1g); PROTEIN 16g; CARB 26.8g; FIBER 1.6g; CHOL 35mg; IRON 3.3mg; SODIUM 474mg; CALC 244mg

With origins in African fufu, Puerto Rican mofongo is a starchy dish of boiled and mashed plantains mixed with garlic and pork cracklings. Chunky stewed chicken gets ladled over the top.

MASHED PLANTAINS
with Stewed Chicken
(Mofongo de Pollo Guisado)
HANDS-ON TIME: 55 MIN. TOTAL TIME: 2 HR.

Chicken:
1 tablespoon olive oil, divided
5 pounds skinless, boneless chicken breast, cut into bite-sized pieces
1 cup chopped onion
¼ cup minced fresh cilantro
¼ cup minced fresh culantro
1 teaspoon salt
3 garlic cloves, minced
1 (15-ounce) can tomato sauce
Mofongo:
6 green plantains (about 3 pounds), peeled and cut into 1-inch pieces
2 teaspoons salt, divided
6 bacon slices, cooked and crumbled (drained)
3 garlic cloves, minced
¾ cup fat-free, lower-sodium chicken broth
6 tablespoons olive oil, divided

1. To prepare chicken, heat a large Dutch oven over medium-high heat. Add 1½ teaspoons oil to pan; swirl to coat. Add half of chicken; sauté 8 minutes or until browned. Remove chicken from pan. Repeat procedure with 1½ teaspoons oil and remaining chicken. Return chicken to pan; stir in onion and next 5 ingredients (through tomato sauce). Bring to a boil; cover, reduce heat, and simmer 20 minutes or until chicken is done. Keep warm.
2. To prepare mofongo, place plantains and ½ teaspoon salt in a large Dutch oven. Cover with water to 1 inch above plantains; stir to dissolve salt. Let stand 20 minutes. Drain plantains, and return to pan. Cover plantains with water to 1 inch above plantains. Bring to a boil over high heat. Reduce heat, and simmer 20 minutes or until tender. Drain plantains; return to pan. Mash plantains with a potato masher. Stir in 1½ teaspoons salt, bacon, garlic, and broth. Shape plantain mixture into 24 (½-inch-thick) patties.
3. Heat a large nonstick skillet over medium-high heat. Add 2 tablespoons oil to pan; swirl to coat. Add 8 patties; cook 3 minutes on each side or until browned. Remove from pan. Repeat procedure twice with remaining patties and oil. Serve chicken mixture over patties. Serves 12 (serving size: ⅔ cup chicken mixture and 2 patties)

CALORIES 426; **FAT** 12.2g (sat 2.4g, mono 7.2g, poly 1.5g); **PROTEIN** 46.9g; **CARB** 32.9g; **FIBER** 2.8g; **CHOL** 112mg; **IRON** 2.3mg; **SODIUM** 864mg; **CALC** 35mg

GILDING THE CHILE

*n*ative to the Americas, chile peppers made their way around the world. Most countries use them sparingly as a spice or seasoning. But in Mexico, chiles are turned into sauces or flavor bases. "Mexican cuisine is based on dried chile sauces," says Rick Bayless, award-winning chef and television host of *Mexico—One Plate at a Time.*

The basic technique for making a Mexican chile sauce or flavor base is to toast the dried chiles, soak them in hot liquid until rehydrated, and then puree the mixture until it's smooth. "But the step that sets Mexican cuisine apart— and even many chefs skip this part because they don't understand how essential it is," explains Bayless, "is to heat a pan with oil, and then add the puree of red chiles and cook it until it becomes the consistency of tomato paste. This step completely changes the character of the sauce. It brings out the natural sweetness by caramelizing the ingredients and concentrating the flavors."

To taste some of the other delicious ways that dried chiles are used in Mexican cooking, check out the recipes for Chipotle Pork Tamales (page 300) and Toasted Guajillo and Pork Posole (page 308).

Tamales take time to assemble. Make them ahead, seal the cooked tamales—corn husks and all—in airtight containers, and freeze for up to 3 months. To reheat, simply steam the frozen tamales over simmering water.

CHIPOTLE PORK TAMALES

HANDS-ON TIME: 47 MIN. TOTAL TIME: 3 HR. 24 MIN.

3 tablespoons chopped fresh cilantro

2 tablespoons unsalted chicken stock

1 tablespoon fresh lime juice

¼ teaspoon salt

1 (8-ounce) container light sour cream

1 large garlic clove, minced

1 tablespoon olive oil

1 (3-pound) pork shoulder roast (Boston butt), trimmed

½ teaspoon kosher salt

1 cup chopped onion

9 crushed garlic cloves

1 teaspoon cumin seeds, toasted

6 chipotle chiles, canned in adobo sauce, chopped

1 cup unsalted chicken stock

1 teaspoon grated orange rind

1 teaspoon unsweetened cocoa powder

¼ teaspoon ground coffee

2½ cups unsalted chicken stock

2 ancho chiles

1 cup corn kernels

4 cups instant masa harina

1¼ teaspoons salt

1½ teaspoons baking powder

½ cup chilled lard

18 dried corn husks

Lime wedges

1. Combine first 6 ingredients; chill.

2. Preheat oven to 300°.

3. Heat a Dutch oven over medium-high heat. Add oil to pan; swirl to coat. Sprinkle pork evenly with ½ teaspoon salt. Add pork to pan; sauté 10 minutes, turning to brown on all sides. Remove pork from pan. Add onion and garlic to pan; sauté 3 minutes. Stir in cumin and chipotle chiles; sauté 1 minute. Stir in 1 cup stock and next 3 ingredients (through coffee); bring to a boil. Return pork to pan; cover. Bake at 300° for 3 hours or until pork is fork-tender. Remove pork from pan; let stand 10 minutes. Shred pork; return to sauce.

4. Increase oven temperature to 450°.

5. Combine 2½ cups stock and ancho chiles in a microwave-safe bowl. Microwave at HIGH 2 minutes or until chiles are tender; cool slightly. Remove stems from chiles. Place hot stock, chiles, and corn in a blender; process until smooth. Combine masa harina, 1¼ teaspoons salt, and baking powder in a large bowl, stirring well with a whisk. Cut in lard with a pastry blender or 2 knives until mixture resembles coarse meal. Add ancho mixture to masa mixture; stir until a soft dough forms. Turn dough out onto a lightly floured surface; knead dough until smooth and pliable. (If dough is crumbly, add water, 1 tablespoon at a time, until moist.)

6. Immerse corn husks in water; weight with a plate. Soak 30 minutes; drain.

7. Working with 1 husk at a time (or overlap 2 small husks), place about 3 tablespoons masa mixture in the center of husk, about 1 inch from top of husk; press dough into a 4 x 3–inch-wide rectangle. Spoon 1 heaping tablespoon pork mixture down 1 side of dough. Using husk as your guide, fold husk over tamale, being sure to cover filling with dough. Use husk to seal dough around filling. Tear 3 or 4 husks lengthwise into strips; tie ends of tamale with strips. Place tamale, seam side down, on rack of a broiler pan lined with a damp towel. Repeat procedure with remaining husks, masa mixture, and pork mixture. Cover tamales with a damp towel. Pour 2 cups hot water in bottom of a broiler pan; top with rack.

8. Steam tamales at 450° for 25 minutes. Remove and rewet top towel, and add 1 cup water to pan. Turn tamales over; top with cloth. Bake 20 minutes or until set. Let tamales stand 10 minutes. Serve tamales with crema and lime wedges. Serves 14 (serving size: 2 tamales and about 2½ teaspoons crema)

CALORIES 374; FAT 17.3g (sat 6g, mono 6.9g, poly 1.8g); PROTEIN 23.6g; CARB 32.5g; FIBER 4g; CHOL 72mg; IRON 3.8mg; SODIUM 516mg; CALC 120mg

Known as elotes, these fresh cobs are usually cooked in the husk, and then shucked to create a husk handle. Here, the shucked corn is grilled directly over a flame for extra smoky flavor.

OAXACAN-STYLE GRILLED CORN ON THE COB

HANDS-ON TIME: 25 MIN. TOTAL TIME: 25 MIN.

1½ tablespoons queso fresco
1¼ teaspoons chili powder
3 tablespoons Mexican crema
   or sour cream
½ teaspoon kosher salt
⅛ teaspoon ground red
   pepper
4 ears corn, shucked
4 lime wedges

1. Preheat grill to medium heat.
2. Combine cheese and next 4 ingredients (through pepper) in a small bowl.
3. Place corn on grill rack. Cover and grill 8 minutes or until lightly charred, turning occasionally. Place corn on a serving plate; drizzle with crema mixture. Serve with lime wedges. Serves 4 (serving size: 1 corn cob and 1 lime wedge)

CALORIES 112; FAT 3.4g (sat 0.5g, mono 0.5g, poly 0.5g); PROTEIN 4g; CARB 20g; FIBER 3g; CHOL 8mg; IRON 0.5mg; SODIUM 336mg; CALC 18mg

Maduros are like the French fries of Central America and the Spanish-speaking Caribbean. They're served alongside dozens of dishes at all hours of the day. Add a bit more sugar, and they can easily be dessert.

SAUTÉED SWEET PLANTAINS
(Maduros)
HANDS-ON TIME: 10 MIN. TOTAL TIME: 10 MIN.

4 cups (1/2-inch-thick) slices
  black plantains (about 6)
3 tablespoons sugar
1/4 teaspoon salt
1 1/2 tablespoons butter

1. Combine first 3 ingredients in a large bowl; toss well.
2. Melt butter in a large nonstick skillet over medium-high heat. Add plantains; sauté 5 minutes or until deeply browned. Serves 12 (serving size: about 1/3 cup)

CALORIES 134; FAT 1.8g (sat 1g, mono 0.4g, poly 0.1g); PROTEIN 1.2g; CARB 31.7g; FIBER 2.1g; CHOL 4mg; IRON 0.5mg; SODIUM 62mg; CALC 3mg

Plantains

Unlike bananas, plantains (*plátanos*) can be enjoyed at every stage of ripeness. Green plantains are starchy and mild like potatoes and can be boiled to make dishes like Puerto Rican *mofongo* (page 297). They can also be thinly sliced and fried like potato chips, known as *tostones*. Yellow plantains are a little softer and sweeter. And ripe black plantains taste the sweetest. Known as *maduros*, they're best for grilling or frying. Like bananas, plantains are high in potassium. Look for longer rather than shorter cultivars, and ripen them to the stage of ripeness called for in your recipe, as green and black plantains are not interchangeable.

Boiled yuca with mojo (MO-ho) is a Cuban staple. But the starchy tuber tastes even better when crisped up like French fries. I like to brown the yuca fries in a hot oven to shave calories and skip the hassle of deep-frying. Parboiling and chilling the yuca helps it brown better in the oven, as does preheating the baking sheet.

YUCA FRIES *with Mojo*

HANDS-ON TIME: 59 MIN. TOTAL TIME: 9 HR. 29 MIN.

1½ pounds fresh or frozen yuca (cassava), thawed
1 teaspoon salt, divided
Cooking spray
3 tablespoons extra-virgin olive oil
2 tablespoons finely chopped onion
¾ teaspoon ground cumin
6 garlic cloves, pressed
2 tablespoons fat-free, lower-sodium chicken broth or organic vegetable broth
3 tablespoons fresh lime juice
1 teaspoon fresh orange juice
¼ teaspoon black pepper
2 tablespoons chopped fresh parsley or cilantro

1. Peel yuca, and cut into 48 (3 x ½–inch) sticks; discard any tough fibers from yuca. Place yuca and ½ teaspoon salt in a large saucepan; cover with water. Bring to boil over high heat. Cover, reduce heat to medium, and cook 25 minutes. Drain; cool completely. Cover and chill 8 hours or up to 3 days.
2. Preheat oven to 450°.
3. Place a large baking sheet in oven. Remove yuca sticks from refrigerator; let stand at room temperature 20 minutes. Pat dry with paper towels. Coat yuca sticks with cooking spray, and arrange in a single layer on preheated pan.
4. Bake at 450° for 12 to 15 minutes or until golden brown on bottom. Turn sticks over, and bake an additional 12 to 15 minutes or until golden brown on bottom.
5. While yuca sticks cook, heat a small saucepan over medium heat. Add oil to pan; swirl to coat. Add onion, cumin, and garlic; sauté 2 minutes or until golden. Add broth and juices; bring to boil, and cook 2 minutes. Remove from heat; stir in ¼ teaspoon salt and pepper.
6. Remove yuca sticks from oven; toss with remaining ¼ teaspoon salt and parsley. Serve with mojo sauce for dipping. Serves 6 (serving size: 8 fries and 1 tablespoon mojo sauce)

CALORIES 173; FAT 7.4g (sat 1.1g, mono 5.2g, poly 0.8g); PROTEIN 1.3g; CARB 26g; FIBER 1.4g; CHOL 0.1mg; IRON 0.4mg; SODIUM 250mg; CALC 22mg

Like a Puerto Rican gumbo, asopao lies somewhere between soup and paella with many variations. It's an easy, filling, one-pot meal. Two key flavor elements are annatto oil (see page 223) and sofrito, a sauté of onions, garlic, and peppers similar to the French mirepoix.

CHICKEN ASOPAO

HANDS-ON TIME: 47 MIN. TOTAL TIME: 47 MIN.

tablespoon annatto oil (page 223) or olive oil
½ cups finely chopped onion
½ cups finely chopped red and green bell peppers
2 garlic cloves, minced
¼ cup chopped fresh cilantro
½ tablespoon tomato paste
⅛ teaspoon salt
⅛ teaspoon freshly ground black pepper
teaspoon dried oregano
¼ teaspoon salt
¼ teaspoon freshly ground black pepper
2 garlic cloves, minced
0 chicken thighs (about 3 pounds), skinned
2 tablespoons annatto oil (page 223) or olive oil
¼ cup diced plum tomato
½ cups uncooked medium-grain rice
⅓ cup dry white wine
½ cup diced lean ham (about 2 ounces)
(4.4-ounce) bottle alcaparrado (such as Goya), drained, or ¾ cup pitted green olives and ¼ cup capers
cups water
(15.75-ounce) can fat-free, lower-sodium chicken broth
cup frozen green peas, thawed

Heat a large nonstick skillet over medium-high heat. Add 1 tablespoon oil to pan; swirl to coat. Add onion; sauté 1 minute. Add bell peppers and garlic. Cook 10 minutes; stir frequently. Stir in cilantro and next 3 ingredients (through black pepper). Set aside.

Combine oregano and next 3 ingredients (through garlic cloves) in a small bowl. Sprinkle chicken with oregano mixture.

Heat a large nonstick skillet over medium-high heat. Add oil to pan; swirl to coat. Add chicken; cook 8 minutes, turning once. Reduce heat to medium. Add onion mixture and tomato; cook 3 minutes, stirring frequently. Add rice, wine, ham, and alcaparrado; cook 1 minute, stirring constantly. Add 4 cups water and broth; bring to a boil. Cover, reduce heat, and simmer 20 minutes. Stir in peas, and cook 5 minutes or until rice is tender. Serves 5 (serving size: 2 thighs and 1¾ cups rice mixture)

CALORIES 561; FAT 17g (sat 3.2g, mono 9.7g, poly 2.8g); PROTEIN 37.3g; CARB 63.2g; FIBER 5.1g; CHOL 118mg; IRON 6.5mg; SODIUM 999mg; CALC 72mg

Alcaparrado

Many Latin American dishes—especially empanadas—get a jolt of flavor from *alcaparrado*, a mix of olives, peppers, and capers packed in vinegar brine. It's important to balance sweet, sour, salty, and savory flavors, and *alcaparrado* delivers the salty, acidic punch that takes a simple sauté of meat and vegetables from so-so to so delicious. Look for bottles of *alcaparrado* in well-stocked supermarkets from brands such as Goya.

Posole is both a type of dried corn and a stew made with it. Also known as hominy in the American South, the dried field corn is soaked in a strong alkali to remove the tough outer hull, and then cooked until soft and fluffy. Corn and meat are usually the focus of posole stew, but you can make a red posole by adding chiles like the guajillos and chipotles included here.

TOASTED GUAJILLO AND PORK POSOLE

HANDS-ON TIME: 32 MIN. TOTAL TIME: 2 HR. 32 MIN.

3 dried guajillo chiles
1½ pounds pork shoulder, trimmed and cut into 2-inch pieces
½ teaspoon kosher salt
¼ teaspoon freshly ground black pepper
1 tablespoon canola oil
3 cups fat-free, lower-sodium chicken broth
3 cups water
2 teaspoons ground cumin
¼ teaspoon ground cloves
3 garlic cloves, crushed
1 medium onion, cut into 4 wedges
1 (7-ounce) can chipotle chiles in adobo sauce
1 (29-ounce) can hominy, rinsed and drained
Lime wedges, chopped onion, cilantro leaves, sliced radish and cabbage

1. Preheat oven to 400°.
2. Place chiles on a baking sheet; bake at 400° for 4 minutes or until dark. Cool; remove stems and seeds.
3. Sprinkle pork with salt and pepper. Heat a large Dutch oven over medium-high heat. Add oil to pan; swirl to coat. Add pork to pan; cook 5 minutes or until browned. Remove pork from pan. Wipe drippings from pan; return pork to pan. Add broth and next 5 ingredients (through onion), scraping pan to loosen browned bits. Add guajillo chiles and 1 tablespoon adobo sauce; reserve remaining chipotle chiles and sauce for another use. Bring to a boil; cover, reduce heat, and simmer 2 hours or until pork is tender.
4. Remove chiles, onion, garlic, and 1 cup cooking liquid; place in a blender. Remove center piece of blender lid (to allow steam to escape); secure blender lid on blender. Place a clean towel over opening in blender lid (to avoid splatters). Blend until smooth; return to pan. Stir in hominy; cook 10 minutes. Garnish with lime wedges, chopped onion, cilantro leaves, sliced radish and cabbage, if desired. Serves 6 (serving size: 1¼ cups)

CALORIES 273; FAT 10.4g (sat 2.7g, mono 4.8g, poly 1.8g); PROTEIN 25.1g; CARB 17.7g; FIBER 3.2g; CHOL 74mg; IRON 2.5mg; SODIUM 704mg; CALC 33mg

French settlers who farmed the land in rural Québec along the St. Lawrence River were once known as habitants. This is one of their favorite soups—a creamy stew of yellow split peas and bits of pork. Serve the soup in the dead of winter when you need a warm bowl of comfort. A dollop of crème fraîche makes it even creamier.

HABITANT PEA SOUP

HANDS-ON TIME: 28 MIN. TOTAL TIME: 2 HR. 5 MIN.

2 tablespoons olive oil
2 cups finely chopped onion
1 cup finely chopped carrot
1/2 cup finely chopped celery
2 cups yellow split peas
6 cups fat-free, lower-sodium beef broth
2 cups water
6 ounces salt pork
2 bay leaves
1 (12-ounce) ham hock
2 tablespoons chopped fresh flat-leaf parsley
2 tablespoons chopped fresh thyme
3/4 teaspoon kosher salt
1/2 teaspoon freshly ground black pepper
1/4 cup crème fraîche
Fresh thyme leaves (optional)

1. Heat a large Dutch oven over medium-high heat. Add oil to pan; swirl to coat. Add onion, carrot, and celery to pan; sauté 6 minutes. Stir in peas; sauté 1 minute. Add broth and next 4 ingredients (through ham hock); bring to a boil. Reduce heat, and simmer 1½ hours or until peas are tender, skimming surface occasionally, as necessary.
2. Remove ham hock and bay leaves; discard. Remove salt pork; cool. Remove 1½ cups pea mixture; let stand 5 minutes. Puree 1½ cups pea mixture, and return to pan, stirring to thicken slightly. Stir in parsley, thyme, salt, and pepper.
3. Dice salt pork. Heat a nonstick skillet over medium-high heat. Add pork to pan; cover and cook 5 minutes or until crisp and browned, stirring frequently. Ladle soup into each of 8 bowls; top each serving with 1 tablespoon pork and 1½ teaspoons crème fraîche. Sprinkle with fresh thyme leaves, if desired. Serves 8 (serving size: 1½ cups soup, 1 tablespoon pork, and 1½ teaspoons crème fraîche)

CALORIES 426; FAT 25.2g (sat 8.7g, mono 11g, poly 2.5g); PROTEIN 14.7g; CARB 34.8g; FIBER 15.4g; CHOL 30mg; IRON 1.6mg; SODIUM 839mg; CALC 34mg

NUTRITIONAL INFORMATION

How to Use It and Why

Glance at the end of any *Cooking Light* recipe, and you'll see how committed we are to helping you make the best of today's light cooking. With chefs, registered dietitians, home economists, and a computer system that analyzes every ingredient we use, *Cooking Light* gives you authoritative dietary detail like no other magazine. We go to such lengths so you can see how our recipes fit into your healthful eating plan. If you're trying to lose weight, the calorie and fat figures will probably help most. But if you're keeping a close eye on the sodium, cholesterol, and saturated fat in your diet, we provide those numbers, too. And because many women don't get enough iron or calcium, we can help there, as well. Finally, there's a fiber analysis for those of us who don't get enough roughage.

Here's a helpful guide to put our nutritional analysis numbers into perspective. Remember, one size doesn't fit all, so take your lifestyle, age, and circumstances into consideration when determining your nutrition needs. For example, pregnant or breast-feeding women need more protein, calories, and calcium. And women older than 50 need 1,200mg of calcium daily, 200mg more than the amount recommended for younger women.

In Our Nutritional Analysis, We Use These Abbreviations

sat saturated fat	CARB carbohydrates	g gram
mono monounsaturated fat	CHOL cholesterol	mg milligram
poly polyunsaturated fat	CALC calcium	

Daily Nutrition Guide

	Women ages 25 to 50	Women over 50	Men ages 24 to 50	Men over 50
Calories	2,000	2,000 or less	2,700	2,500
Protein	50g	50g or less	63g	60g
Fat	65g or less	65g or less	88g or less	83g or less
Saturated Fat	20g or less	20g or less	27g or less	25g or less
Carbohydrates	304g	304g	410g	375g
Fiber	25g to 35g	25g to 35g	25g to 35g	25g to 35g
Cholesterol	300mg or less	300mg or less	300mg or less	300mg or less
Iron	18mg	8mg	8mg	8mg
Sodium	2,300mg or less	1,500mg or less	2,300mg or less	1,500mg or less
Calcium	1,000mg	1,200mg	1,000mg	1,000mg

The nutritional values used in our calculations either come from The Food Processor, Version 10.4 (ESHA Research), or are provided by food manufacturers.

METRIC EQUIVALENTS

The information in the following charts is provided to help cooks outside the United States successfully use the recipes in this book. All equivalents are approximate.

Cooking/Oven Temperatures

	Fahrenheit	Celsius	Gas Mark
Freeze Water	32° F	0° C	
Room Temp.	68° F	20° C	
Boil Water	212° F	100° C	
Bake	325° F	160° C	3
	350° F	180° C	4
	375° F	190° C	5
	400° F	200° C	6
	425° F	220° C	7
	450° F	230° C	8
Broil			Grill

Liquid Ingredients by Volume

¼ tsp	=					1 ml		
½ tsp	=					2 ml		
1 tsp	=					5 ml		
3 tsp	=	1 Tbsp	=	½ fl oz	=	15 ml		
2 Tbsp	=	⅛ cup	=	1 fl oz	=	30 ml		
4 Tbsp	=	¼ cup	=	2 fl oz	=	60 ml		
5⅓ Tbsp	=	⅓ cup	=	3 fl oz	=	80 ml		
8 Tbsp	=	½ cup	=	4 fl oz	=	120 ml		
10⅔ Tbsp	=	⅔ cup	=	5 fl oz	=	160 ml		
12 Tbsp	=	¾ cup	=	6 fl oz	=	180 ml		
16 Tbsp	=	1 cup	=	8 fl oz	=	240 ml		
1 pt	=	2 cups	=	16 fl oz	=	480 ml		
1 qt	=	4 cups	=	32 fl oz	=	960 ml		
				33 fl oz	=	1000 ml	=	1 l

Dry Ingredients by Weight

(To convert ounces to grams, multiply the number of ounces by 30.)

1 oz	=	¹⁄₁₆ lb	=	30 g
4 oz	=	¼ lb	=	120 g
8 oz	=	½ lb	=	240 g
12 oz	=	¾ lb	=	360 g
16 oz	=	1 lb	=	480 g

Length

(To convert inches to centimeters, multiply the number of inches by 2.5.)

1 in	=				2.5 cm		
6 in	=	½ ft		=	15 cm		
12 in	=	1 ft		=	30 cm		
36 in	=	3 ft	=	1 yd	=	90 cm	
40 in	=				100 cm	=	1 m

Equivalents for Different Types of Ingredients

Standard Cup	Fine Powder (ex. flour)	Grain (ex. rice)	Granular (ex. sugar)	Liquid Solids (ex. butter)	Liquid (ex. milk)
1	140 g	150 g	190 g	200 g	240 ml
¾	105 g	113 g	143 g	150 g	180 ml
⅔	93 g	100 g	125 g	133 g	160 ml
½	70 g	75 g	95 g	100 g	120 ml
⅓	47 g	50 g	63 g	67 g	80 ml
¼	35 g	38 g	48 g	50 g	60 ml
⅛	18 g	19 g	24 g	25 g	30 ml

INDEX

ISBN-13: 978-0-8487-3998-0
ISBN-10: 0-8487-3998-1
Library of Congress Control Number: 2013956992
Printed in the United States of America
First printing 2014

Be sure to check with your health-care provider before making any changes in your diet.

Oxmoor House
Vice President, Brand Publishing: Laura Sappington
Editorial Director: Leah McLaughlin
Creative Director: Felicity Keane
Brand Manager: Michelle Turner Aycock
Senior Editor: Andrea Kirkland, MS, RD
Managing Editor: Elizabeth Tyler Austin
Assistant Managing Editor: Jeanne de Lathouder

Cooking Light® Global Kitchen
Editor: Rachel Quinlivan West, RD
Art Director: Christopher Rhoads
Project Editor: Emily Chappell Connolly
Junior Designer: Maribeth Jones
Assistant Test Kitchen Manager: Alyson Moreland Haynes
Recipe Developers and Testers: Wendy Ball, RD; Tamara Goldis; Stefanie Maloney; Callie Nash; Karen Rankin; Leah Van Deren
Food Stylists: Victoria E. Cox, Margaret Monroe Dickey, Catherine Crowell Steele
Photography Director: Jim Bathie
Senior Photographer: Hélène Dujardin
Senior Photo Stylist: Kay E. Clarke
Photo Stylist: Mindi Shapiro Levine
Assistant Photo Stylist: Mary Louise Menendez
Production Managers: Theresa Beste-Farley, Tamara Nall Wilder

Contributors
Author: David Joachim
Editor: Elizabeth Taliaferro
Copy Editors: Deri Reed, *Marra*thon Production Services
Proofreader: Jacqueline Giovanelli
Indexer: Mary Ann Laurens
Nutrition Analysis: Carolyn Land Williams, PhD, RD
Photographer: Iain Bagwell
Photo Stylists: Mary Clayton Carl, Lydia Degaris-Purcell, Leslie Simpson
Recipe Developer and Tester: Jan Smith
Fellows: Ali Carruba, Elizabeth Laseter, April Smitherman, Frances Gunnells, Amy Pinney, Madison Taylor Pozzo, Deanna Sakal, Megan Thompson, Tonya West

Time Home Entertainment Inc.
Publisher: Jim Childs
Vice President, Brand & Digital Strategy: Steven Sandonato
Executive Director, Marketing Services: Carol Pittard
Executive Director, Retail & Special Sales: Tom Mifsud
Director, Bookazine Development & Marketing: Laura Adam
Executive Publishing Director: Joy Butts
Publishing Director: Megan Pearlman
Finance Director: Glenn Buonocore
Associate General Counsel: Helen Wan

Cooking Light®
Editor: Scott Mowbray
Acting Creative Director: Dimity Jones
Executive Managing Editor: Phillip Rhodes
Executive Editor, Food: Ann Taylor Pittman
Executive Editor, Digital: Allison Long Lowery
Special Publications Editor: Mary Simpson Creel, MS, RD
Senior Food Editor: Timothy Q. Cebula
Senior Editor: Cindy Hatcher
Assistant Editor, Nutrition: Sidney Fry, MS, RD
Assistant Editors: Kimberly Holland, Phoebe Wu
Assistant Test Kitchen Director: Tiffany Vickers Davis
Recipe Testers and Developers: Robin Bashinsky, Adam Hickman, Deb Wise
Art Directors: Fernande Bondarenko, Shawna Kalish
Senior Deputy Art Director: Rachel Cardina Lasserre
Senior Designer: Anna Bird
Designer: Hagen Stegall
Assistant Designer: Nicole Gerrity
Photo Director: Kristen Schaefer
Assistant Photo Editor: Amy Delaune
Senior Photographer: Randy Mayor
Senior Prop Stylist: Cindy Barr
Chief Food Stylist: Kellie Gerber Kelley
Food Styling Assistant: Blakeslee Wright
Production Director: Liz Rhoades
Production Editor: Hazel R. Eddins
Assistant Production Editor: Josh Rutledge
Assistant Copy Chief: Susan Roberts
Research Editor: Michelle Gibson Daniels
Administrative Coordinator: Carol D. Johnson
Associate Editor/Producer: Mallory Daugherty Brasseale